To Lez.

from

Ann — enjoy it
I hope!

T H E
HORSE
IN THE ANCIENT
WORLD

ANN HYLAND

SUTTON PUBLISHING

First published in the United Kingdom in 2003 by
Sutton Publishing Limited · Phoenix Mill
Thrupp · Stroud · Gloucestershire · GL5 2BU

British Library Cataloguing in Publication Data
A catalogue record for this book is available from the British Library.

ISBN 0-7509-2160-9

Dedicated to the Memory of my
Arabian Stallion Nizzolan, 1967–2001

Typeset in 10/12pt New Baskerville.
Typesetting and origination by
Sutton Publishing Limited.
Printed and bound in England by
J.H. Haynes & Co. Ltd, Sparkford.

Contents

List of Maps and Illustrations

Maps

Plates between pages 38 and 39

Plates between pages 70 and 71

Scythian twisted, single-jointed snaffle bit.
Twisted jointed snaffle from Ashur.
Assyrian three-jointed snaffle from Nimrud.
Luristani zoomorphic straight bar square section snaffle.
Bronze Persian jointed snaffle with burrs.
Greek straight bar snaffle from Olympia.
Greek jointed snaffle with rings dependent from centre.
Greek muzzle.

Plates between pages 102 and 103

Rock painting, Ferghana.
Scythian horses and horsemen.
Nisaean horse with heavy-bodied conformation.
Horse with groom, Greek marble frieze.
Cavalryman, Aramean stone relief from north-east Syria.
Terracotta mould of rider showing donkey seat.
The Armento Rider, southern Italy.
Greek horsemen from west frieze of the Parthenon, Athens.
Ostrich fan from the tomb of Tutankhamun.
Ramses II rides down Hittite chariots at the Battle of Kadesh.
Yoke saddle from the tomb of Tutankhamun.
Double hitch yoke with yoke saddles, from the Pazyruk burials.
Saddle and fittings, from the Pazyruk burials.
Bow arch and saddle spacer.

List of Rulers

List of rulers appearing in the text. In general the regnal years appear once, when the ruler is first mentioned. The dates for Egyptian pharaohs often have alternative dates which are given in brackets.

Hattusas
Anittas	*c.* 1750
Hattusilis I	1650–1620
Suppiluliumas I	1380–1346
Muwatallis II	1306–1282

Mari
Iasmah-Adad	1796–1780
Zimri-Lim	1779–1761

Babylon
Hammurabi	1792–1750
Burna Burias II (Kassite Dynasty)	1380–1350
Kurigalzu II (Kassite Dynasty)	1345–1324
Nebuchannezzar	605–561

Mitanni
Tushratta	1385–1360

Assyria
Shamsi-Adad	1813–1781
Ashur-Uballit I	1365–1330
Adad Nirari I	1307–1275
Shalmaneser I	1274–1245
Tukulti Ninurta I	1244–1208
Tiglath-Pileser I	1115–1077
Ashur Dan II	934–912
Adad Nirari II	911–891
Tukulti Ninurta II	890–884
Ashurnasirpal II	883–859
Shalmaneser III	858–824
Tiglath-Pileser III	745–727

Sargon II	721–705
Sennacherib	705–681
Esarhaddon	680–669
Ashurbanipal	668–627

Egypt (with alternative dates)

Kamose	*c.* 1570
Ahmose I	1570–1545
Thutmose I	1525–1495 (A. 1528–1510)
Thutmose III	1479–1425 (A. 1490–1436)
Thutmose IV	1411–1403 (A. 1411–1397)
Amenophis (Amenhotep) III	1386–1349
Amenophis (Amenhotep) IV	1350–1334 (A. 1367–1350)
Akhenaten	
Horemheb	1335–1308
Seti I	1308–1291 (A. 1303–1290)
Ramses II	1290–1224 (A. 1279–1213)
Merenptah (Merneptah)	1223–1211/13/14 (A. 1224–1214)
Ramses III	1182–1151
Piahkhi	751–730
Shabako of Nubia	730–703
of Nubia and Egypt	715–703
Osorkon (of Tanis)	730–715
Ptolemy Soter	323–283

Israel

David	*c.* 1004–965
Solomon	*c.* 965–926

Urartu

Menua	810–785
Argishti I	785–753
Sarduri II	753–735
Rusa I	735–714

Medes

Kyaxares	625–585
Astyages	585–550

Lydia

Croesus	560–546

Persia

Cyrus the Great	560/59–530
Cambyses	530–522

Darius I	522–486
Xerxes I	486–465
Artaxerxes II	405/04–359/58
Darius III	336–330

Macedon

Alexander I	498–454
Pausanias	390–389
Philip II	359–336
Alexander III	336–323

Thrace

Kotys I	383–359

India

Porus	Contemporary with Alexander III
Chandragupta	*c.* 324

Seleucid

Seleucus Nicator	305–281

China

Wu-Ti	140–87

Various AD

El Nacer Kalouan (Egypt)	1290–1340
Henry VIII (England)	1509–47
Babur (India)	1526–30
Charles II (England)	(1649) 1660–85

Foreword

Professor F. W. Walbank, CBE, FBA

For at least five thousand years – down to the beginnning of the twentieth century – man and horse have lived together in a close, if unequal, *symbiosis*. This alliance has shaped cultures, determined the way men have lived and, to a large extent defined wealth and power. From the time of the ancient Greeks with their centaurs and the winged steed Pegasus down to Jonathan Swift's Houyhnhnms and Yahoos writers have spun fantasies on the relationship between horse and man. What has been much less common is for historians to try to analyse in detail the decisive role played by the horse in some of the main episodes of human history.

Sadly, in most of these the horse has been valued primarily for its contribution to warfare; and much of the present volume is necessarily concerned with the war-horse and its role, first harnessed to chariots and then as cavalry, down to the years immediately after the death of Alexander the Great. Nor is the humble baggage-animal – often a mule or a donkey – neglected.

It is a fascinating story and one which Ann Hyland, the author of many earlier books on the horse in history, is preeminently qualified to tell. The liveliness and authority of what she writes derives in particular from two circumstances. First, she has always borne in mind that reliable history must go back to original sources. Her account accordingly draws on evidence taken from Babylonia, Assyria, Palestine, Egypt and Greece, using both tablets and other documents, together with the works of contemporary writers. By way of this material she introduces us to detailed records of studs, stables and statistics and to information about how horses were bred and trained and whence and how the finest breeds were acquired (often as war booty). But what is no less important is the fact that in dealing with all this original evidence she writes as an experienced breeder and trainer of horses, skilled in the practice of endurance riding, and so fully conversant in every situation with what a horse can do or be made to do – and what it cannot do.

This is a specialised kind of knowledge not shared by all who write on the role of chariots or cavalry in ancient warfare. At every stage in her narrative, whether she is recounting campaigns and battles or discussing the infrastructure of horse management in Assyria or Egypt, Ann Hyland uses her profesional skills as a basis for the assessment and the informed criticism of sometimes rashly formulated or accepted theories. She clearly loves horses – but always in a rational fashion, free from all maudlin sentiment. Her book is full of original material, critically assessed and often illuminated by relevant anecdotes drawing on her own experience as a horsewoman. Her book should change the way we think about both the military and the cultural history of these early empires and is to be warmly welcomed.

F. W. W.

Acknowledgements

In the preparation of any book based mostly on a multitude of primary sources, I owe a debt to many generous people who have helped me in various ways. In particular I would like to thank my friends the two Franks: Professor Frank Walbank, CBE, for his help and hospitality which has extended over many years and several books, and for agreeing to write a foreword to the present work; to Frank Brudenell who, as ever, let me raid his extensive library and borrow vital texts on a long-term basis. Russell Lyon, MRCVS, who discussed practical veterinary matters with me; Lt Col Roffey of the Royal Army Veterinary Corps for his gift of two volumes of the RAVC's history, one of which I found very useful when discussing equine health conditions in areas where the ancient horses and their modern counterparts operated in the Near East; Dr Marsha Levine for her common-sense monograph on the 'Origins of Horse Husbandry on the Eurasian Steppe'; Professor J. Nicholas Postgate for his advice on the Assyrian aspect of equestrianism; Professor David Bivar for pointing me in the direction of Persian texts; Peter Connolly for allowing me to quote from his research on the Macedonian Sarissa prior to its publication and to John Duckham who discussed its functional use on horseback; Steve Weingartner for providing me with several translations of the Kikkuli Text; Caroline Dobson for the loan of biblical texts and maps. On a very practical and personal level I must also thank Mill Lane Aviaries for looking after my cockatoo Pliny II when I disappeared on research days, and above all, appreciation to my horses past and present who have shown me how horses think, react, and what they are and are not capable of under many stressful conditions. In evolutionary terms the timespan between today and the ancient world is only a blink of the eye, so that animal reactions of today can be a guide to their ancient counterparts.

Abbreviations

AA	Artibus Asiae
ABSA	*Annual of the British School at Athens*
AFO	*Archiv fur Orientforschung Int. Zeitschrift*
AHR	*American Historical Review*
AIO	*Archaeologia Iranica et Orientalis*
AJA	*American Journal of Archaeology*
ANET	*Ancient Near Eastern Texts Relating to the Old Testament*
AN. OR.	Analecta Orientalia
AN. ST.	Anatolian Studies
ARAB	*Ancient Records of Assyria and Babylonia*
ARE	*Ancient Records of Egypt*
ARRIAN. AN.	Arrian's *Anabasis of Alexander*
BEALE, HITT.	Beale, Richard H., *The Organization of the Hittite Military*
BEH	Behistun Inscriptions
CEA	*Cambridge Encyclopedia of Archaeology*
EAC	*Encyclopedia of Ancient Civilizations*
HDT	Herodotus
HIPP. HETH.	Hippologia Hethethica, Kammenhuber, A.
HJAS	*Harvard Journal of the Asiatic Society*
IAES	Institute for Ancient Equestrian Studies
IRAQ	*British School of Archaeology in Iraq*
JAOS	*Journal of the American Oriental Society*
JARCE	*Journal of the American Research Center in Egypt*
JAS	*Journal of Archaeological Science*
JCS	*Journal of Cuneiform Studies*
JEA	*Journal of Egyptian Archaeology*
JHS	*Journal of Hellenic Studies*
JNES	*Journal of Near Eastern Studies*
JSS	*Journal of Semitic Studies*
JSSEA	*Journal of the Society for the Study of Egyptian Antiquities*
KADESH	Kadesh Inscriptions of Rameses II
KAUTILYA	Kautilya's *Arthasastra*

L & C	Littauer, M.A. and Crouwel, J.H., *Ridden Animals and Wheeled Vehicles in the Ancient Near East*
MARI/SASSON	*The Military Establishments at Mari*
M & U	*Equids in the Ancient World*, Meadow, Richard H. and Uerpmann, Hans-Peter
NUZI/KENDALL	*Warfare and Military Matters in the Nuzi Tablets*
PERSEPOLIS	*Persepolis Fortification Tablets*
RCAE	*Royal Correspondence of the Assyrian Empire*
THUC.	Thucydides, *The Peloponnesian War*
WAW	*Warfare in the Ancient World*
X.Age	Xenophon, *Agesilaus*
X.Anab.	Xenophon, *Anabasis – Persian Expedition*
X.C.C.	Xenophon, *Cavalry Commander*
X.Cyr.	Xenophon, *Cyropaedia*
X.Hell.	Xenophon, *Hellenica*
X.Horse	Xenophon, *Art of Horsemanship*
X.Lac.	Xenophon, *Lacedaemonians*
Yadin, War Bible,	*The Art of Warfare in Biblical Lands*
ZA	*The Sacred Books of the East. The Zend Avesta*

MAPS AND ATLASES USED

Cassell's New Atlas, ed. George Philip, no date but published just after the Conference of Powers held in London in March 1921.

The Westminster Historical Atlas to the Bible, ed. George Ernest Wright, London, SCM Press Ltd, 1945.

National Geographic maps of: the Caspian Region, May 1999; the Historic Mediterranean, 800 BC to AD 1500, December 1982; the Holy Land, December 1989.

Alexander's Route – map from Alexander the Great, W.W. Tarn, Cambridge University Press, 1948. This map has also appeared in numerous books about Alexander.

The maps in George Roux's *Ancient Iraq*, Penguin, 1976 (1966).

Introduction

When thinking of the horse in war, usually the first images are those of the medieval destrier with knights and horses fully armoured; the Napoleonic Wars when horses were mustered in their tens of thousands; the equine debacle of the Crimean War, and the First World War, when cavalry and artillery horses suffered tremendous privations, not least from what the elements threw at them. But further back, very much further back, in the eighteenth century BC, the ancestors of these later warhorses were beginning to appear on the battlefield. Even earlier, in the third millennium BC, related equids made their appearance as battlesteeds pulling the heavy, cumbersome battlewagons over the hot plains of Mesopotamia, watered by the Euphrates and Tigris rivers.

Innumerable texts on clay tablets, incised stelae and wall and rock faces, have given us an insight into the social and military life of diverse populations from the ancient world. Among these documents many refer to antiquity's equids. As the second millennium BC unravels, more of these refer only to horses. They show how, from small beginnings, with a few chariots in the arsenal, numbers increased into the several thousand. For example, in Anatolia in the early Hittite Empire a city rebelling against King Anittas, *c.* 1750 BC, was able to field forty chariots; Hattusilis I (1650–1620) fielded eighty chariots at the siege of Urshu;[1] and by the Battle of Kadesh, *c.* 1285 BC, Hattusas fielded 2,500 chariots under Muwatallis II (1306–1282).[2]

The horse was important in a ruler's life. It was a costly and prestigious animal. It featured in gifts from one sovereign to another; it took its place in the religious and state pomp of festivals, and was the mark of a nobleman. The *maryannu*, or chariot warrior, like the medieval knight, belonged to the premier military class. The horse was high on the tribute and spoils list. The records of acquisitions are windows onto the provenance of superior stock and show how large were the herds available. Equestrian artifacts, sculptures and carvings show how the horse was equipped and controlled. Equid remains point to structural conformation. A few texts survive about training regimens, the earliest from the Hittite Empire used, and some of it dictated, by the Mitannian Kikkuli who was in Hittite employ. Other texts give small snatches of advice on horse training, but it is not until the early fourth century BC that the best sources on horse training become available. These are Xenophon's books on the *Art of Horsemanship* and its companion volume, the *Cavalry Commander*. Whether they were so intended we do not know, but for military use they complement each other. *The Arthasastra*, a detailed political and military text, includes a large section on the training of warhorses. It was written in India by Kautilya, chief minister to Chandragupta, who came to the Mauryan throne *c.* 324 BC.[3] Chandragupta came to blows with Seleucus Nicator after Alexander the Great's death.

In the following pages I endeavour to follow the hoofprints of *equus caballus* from its early domestication on the Eurasian Steppes and its appearance in the Land of the Two Rivers, and the subsequent use among successive Near Eastern empires. In its early years as a warhorse it was yoked to a chariot. By the final chapters it emerges as a weapon honed to military precision in the renowned Macedonian cavalry of Alexander the Great.

There is a wealth of information on antiquity's horses, but it is scattered in a multitude of contemporary references. Many of these are obscure, and not the texts one would at first consider to have an equine content. However, in one moderate-sized volume it is not possible to do justice to all sectors of the world's map which bore the hoofprints of the first warhorses. Some areas are only touched on, but the core countries are explored in greater detail. In general they are the civilisations which made significant use of the horse in the interminable wars that flared across the regions of the Near East, Anatolia, Armenia, Persia, Greece and India, until the whole region was brought into one Macedonian Empire.

A few introductory points may be necessary here, particularly with regard to dating and nomenclature. Unless otherwise stated, all dates are BC. In the periods covered by this book, place names changed according to which nation held supreme power and who was trading with whom, which in turn reflected fluctuating territorial boundaries of ancient times. Readers will thus find references scattered throughout the book to Togarmah in Tabal, Melid (Malatya/Melitene) in Tabal, and Melid in Kummuhu: these names refer to the same places; since although the Romans called the area Cappadocia, in earlier cultures (of Israel, Assyria, Urartu and Persia) both the land and its major towns went by a variety of names.

Perhaps attention should also be drawn to the angle adopted in this book. Most studies of social and military happenings cover the actions of man, with animals getting but a brief mention; here the roles are reversed – although of course the text can be read in conjunction with works on ancient warfare that highlight man's achievements. Finally, an explanation as to why there is some repetition of facts in what follows. For example, in the section on practical horsemastership and horsemanship, matters concerning Hittite, Egyptian, Assyrian, or Greek equestrianism are parts of the puzzle on how horses were utilised. They appear again in the relevant cultural context, as I consider it would be annoying for the reader to have to constantly refer back to a previous chapter.

The Near East in the Second Millennium BC

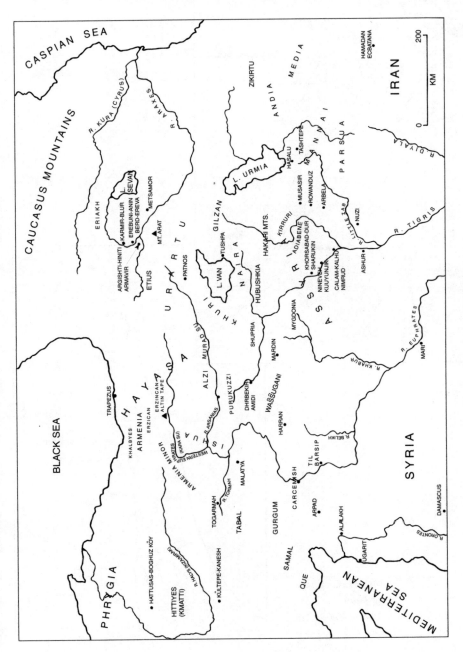

Urartu Armenia c. 2000–600 BC

xix

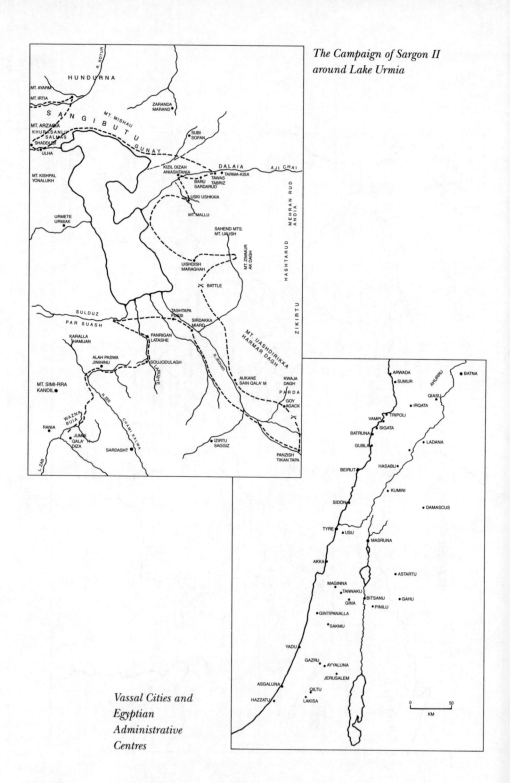

The Campaign of Sargon II around Lake Urmia

Vassal Cities and Egyptian Administrative Centres

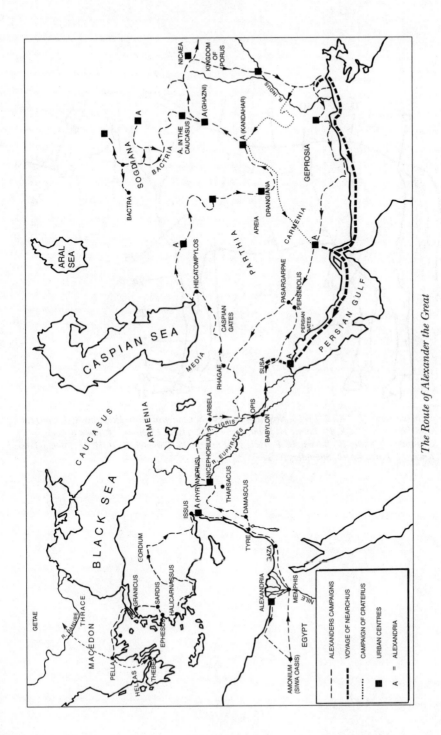

The Route of Alexander the Great

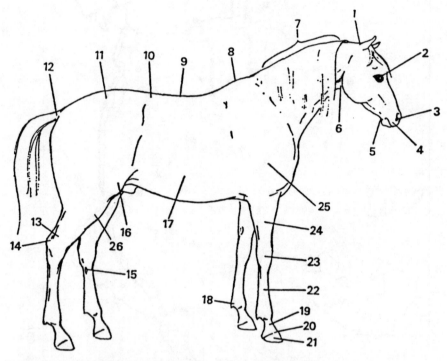

Points of the horse: 1. Poll; 2. Eye; 3. Nostril; 4. Muzzle; 5. Chin groove; 6. Throatlatch; 7. Crest (of neck); 8. Withers; 9. Back; 10. Loins; 11. Point of croup; 12. Dock; 13. Hock; 14. Point of hock; 15. Chestnut; 16. Stifle; 17. Barrel; 18. Fetlock; 19. Pastern; 20. Coronet; 21. Hoof; 22. Cannon bone; 23. Knee; 24. Forearm; 25. Shoulder; 26.Gaskin

CHAPTER 1

Horse Trace Through Time and Locale

Many of the areas that became known in the early medieval period for producing prime warhorses had been so doing by at least 1000 BC, and some for many centuries before. Movements of equestrian peoples supplied some of the equid mix that formed later breeds, as did war, tribute, and spoils, often by retaliatory raids, where livestock of horses, cattle and sheep changed hands and locations. This happened at least in the case of equids, cattle and sheep being eaten. This interchange led to a melting-pot of genetic attributes for those equids desired as breeding stock, and thus saved them from the dangers of death or injury in battle, or from the many hazards en route to war. These included starvation, dehydration (which can cause total physical seizure), and wild swings in temperatures which can be extremely detrimental to a horse's condition, rendering it unusable at best, and therefore a liability, or prone to death at worst.

The constant refreshment of different blood must in some cases have led to improvements in stock reared, often with hybrid vigour imparting size increases when allied to judicious selection.[1] On the downside much of the breeding stock must have produced real 'mongrels'. However, it is to be expected that knowledgeable horsemasters selected the best for their royal masters' breeding herds. We know there were such men: Sama from Samaria was horse trainer/breeder to Nergal-zeru-ibni, who was possibly a son of Sennacherib (705–681).[2] The Assyrians in particular have left texts concerning the stocking of herds, such as those of Tiglath-Pileser I (1114–1076).[3]

ARTISTIC DEPICTION OF HORSES IN THE ANCIENT WORLD

For representations of horses that meet believable criteria acceptable to knowledgeable horsemen we need to look at Egypt's magnificent tomb paintings and sculptured reliefs, which, although stylised – almost in the way that the modern Arabian is frequently portrayed, with a fiery look, arched neck, dished head, huge eyes, flaring nostrils, and a very pronounced high-set, plumelike tail – yet withal indicate correct conformation. So, too, we can appreciate how the basic, quality royal horses in pharaonic stables must have appeared. Other Egyptian renderings of animals and birds are so accurately depicted that we can, for example, recognise an Egyptian goose, a lanner falcon, and various herons, egrets, and ibises, from ancient wall paintings.[4] On the same basis, Egyptian renderings of horses can be trusted to be close to reality, allowing for royal steeds being the best of their type. This is borne out by the Buhen horse remains, *c.* 1675, which show an affinity to the typical modern Arab conformation in regard to height of 150 cm (*c.* 15 hands high (hh), a 'hand' being 4 in), fine limbs, and, especially, concave skull.[5] For comparably accurate equine portrayal we have to wait until after the eighth century, when Assyrian expansion was at its greatest, and the horse, and other military assets were recorded in minute detail on city gates and palace audience halls, doubtless impressing foreign notables with Assyria's power and emphasising what happened to those who challenged her. For similar early, and almost contemporary, European portrayals Etruria has yielded painted and sculpted horses, both types on view at Museo Etrusco di Tarquinia. A painting on a sarcophagus, the colours still fresh, shows a dark chestnut horse. The horse's conformation is that of a well-bred light horse with some hot blood; the size indicated is about 14 hh judging by the men handling it. As the equine proportions are so accurate I see no reason to doubt the human to horse ratio. The sculpture is the exquisite winged chariot pair, again with accurate conformation. The 'wings' need comment. Although allegorical, they may stem from real Phoenician armour, as an exact 'wing' replica is seen on a statuette of a Phoenician horseman found at Byblos, dating to the eighth to sixth centuries, and now in the Musées Royaux d'Art et d'Histoire, in Brussels. The horse wears a breastplate which continues in wings swept back to protect the rider's vital mid-section and upper thighs.[6] As Phoenician cavalry mostly consisted of Numidian and Celtic mercenaries, the connection is quite possible, as Etruria had links with Carthage, and modern DNA tests have linked Phoenicians and Etruscans.[7] There is also the possibility of an armorial link with Persian equestrian equipment from Daskyleion in Phrygia (see chapter 10).

The suggestion that the (apparently) long back was a weakness that precluded riding is inaccurate. This aspect is only shown in the stylised gallop common to most depictions, where sweeping curves convey animation. The fourteenth-century relief from Tell Amarna has a horse walking; its back is of normal length.[8] However, an excessively long back is considered weak whether for riding or driving. The senior arm, the chariotry, would not have been stocked with a race of weak animals.

DOMESTICATION

Early equid usage falls into several categories. The horse was hunted for its meat on the vast plains that cover much of Russia and the Eurasian Steppes. Once the first stages of domestication of the horse took place the animal was still used as food, though it was now easier to cull for the pot in managed herds.

A thought-provoking work by archaeologist Marsha Levine has challenged the theories held by eminent scholars working on the origins of equine domestication, suggesting that it was at Dereivka in the Ukraine, *c.* 4000–3500 that man first tamed and rode the horse.[9] She asserts there is no *reliable* textual or artistic evidence for horseriding earlier than the end of the second millennium. There are earlier depictions of people riding equids in the Near East, but it is difficult to determine which equid is being ridden.[10] This may be so for much of the Near East, where representations are crude and to distinguish between horse, donkey, onager or mule is not easy, but certain aspects are useful: only horses have full tails with long hairs from the top of the dock downwards; other equids have either skimpy-haired docks and/or fullness of hair at the lower extremity; the donkey has extremely long ears; onagers were considered never to have been tamed,[11] and horse obviously preceded mule. However, there are small representations of ridden horses on clay plaques dating to the first quarter of the second millennium which are the earliest *certain* depictions of ridden horses from Iraq. Among these is an exceptionally fine example shown in a photograph taken for the Ashmolean Museum, Oxford, from a plaque now in private possession. This is most certainly a horse. It has a full tail and a very full mane, which other equids lack, and a horse's ears pricked forward.[12] A rider perches insecurely on the horse's loins, and he controls the horse using a nose-ring. From Egypt come accurately delineated horses with riders. Examples include a plaque from the reign of Tuthmose III (1479–1425) showing an Egyptian mounted warrior armed with mace and bow, his horse trampling a fallen foe;[13] the relief on the chariot of Tuthmose IV (1411–1397) which clearly shows an arrowshot Asiatic brandishing an axe and falling from his horse, who is wounded in mid-belly.[14] A statuette of a black and white horse with a rider from the Amarna period, *c.* 1350, is now in the British Museum;[15] and a relief from Karnak (*c.* 1303–1290) shows a fleeing Canaanite warrior on a horse which appears to be jumping over a fallen compatriot.[16] A very fine relief from the tomb of Horemheb (1320–1292) shows a rider using the 'donkey seat' on the horse's loins.[17] At Abu Simbel a wall painting of the Battle of Kadesh, opposite a painting of

Pharaoh Rameses II (1290–1224), shows mounted military personnel.[18] At Thebes a relief illustrating an attack on 'the city which his Majesty desolated in the land of Amurru [Syria]' has a mounted Egyptian archer.[19]

However, despite proof positive of earlier horseriding, Levine's paper has convincing arguments in equine and common-sense contexts as to why previous thinking that evidence from Dereivka in the Ukraine, Botai in Kazakhstan, and other Eurasian Steppe sites with equid remains from the late neolithic, eneolithic, and early Bronze Age, do not *necessarily* represent domesticated horses. For the reasons stated for domestication, Levine gives a common-sense reason for non-domestication. She consulted horsemen and herders from Mongolia and Kazakhstan where horses are a way of life and nearly all families (outside the main cities) own horses. The numbers of horses per household ranged from under ten, to an average of twenty to forty, and a maximum running into thousands.[20] This recalls the many Turkic herds seen by Ibn Battuta in the fourteenth century AD when one man often owned a single herd of many thousands.[21] This suggests that in the steppe culture horse-owning and rearing has an extremely long history. Levine established the 'herd cycle' of breeding, ratio of mares to stallions, geldings, and the kill rate, as horses not required for breeding or work are still used for food. In Mongolia slaughter generally occurs with youngsters of two to four years old and mares past breeding, usually fourteen to sixteen years old. In Kazakhstan where foals are usually raised for meat the ages for killing are one to four years old for youngstock, and fifteen to thirty years old for mares and geldings. Some mares continue to foal up to the age of thirty-five.[22] The quality of such a mare and her offspring would be questionable. A 35-year-old mare with foal at foot and bred back that I saw at a Gujerat State Stud in India in 1996 was in an emaciated condition due not to a lack of food, but simply worn out from sheer old age and continual foal-bearing.

The Dereivka remains showed just over half the animals had died between five and eight years old. If domesticated these would have been prime work and/or breeding animals. Also, nine out of ten sexable tooth rows were from males. This suggests that the Dereivka horses were from wild stock hunted for meat. Of the Botai remains 99.9 per cent were of horses, indicating that hunting by herd drive was used. This did not preclude hunting from horseback: Levine pointed out the look of amazement her Mongol and Kazakhstan informants registered when asked if horses could be herded and hunted on foot.[23] From among the mass of horse bones at Dereivka, counted at 2,412, and at Botai with 10 tons, it is unlikely that a possible few tamed/domesticated horses can be filtered out. That is until the new research project at Cambridge

University Veterinary College into pathologies, especially of the back, shoulder, lower limbs, and hooves yield results, determining traction and/or ridden/pack use. Modern skeletons and archaeological deposits from several periods are being analysed to such use in the past.[24]

It now appears there are still huge unanswered questions over the origins of domestication, and still no *firm* evidence for exactly when or where man first rode the horse. Nor is it precisely known which came first in the usage sequence, apart from eating the meat and utilising the hide; milking presupposes domestication or hooves would fly! Was the horse used as a baggage or people carrier? Logically, pack use preceded riding. Even with less volatile equids such as steppe ponies/horses it must have made sense to first load them with expendable baggage and note their reactions. It was a small step, albeit a brave one, for man to mount a horse. It is one thing to load a horse, and then lead it, quite another to bestride it. Two things can alarm a horse at a first mounting: 1. the height of the human above the horse who, with his lateral vision can be frightened by the rider's sudden appearance well above him; 2. the feel of moving forward and manoeuvring with such a burden, and being directed by the rider's hands, legs and body movements.[25] Initially there was a lack of the learning curve from pack, to mounting a docile animal, and from that to mounting an animal that had never carried *any* weight.

Once domesticated, the horse had an immense influence on human life, the most significant being when used in war. Of course the horse could have been used in war earlier than records show, but in the 'grey steppe area' no early trace was left.

USES OTHER THAN WAR

In addition to war other uses were found for the horse, all pertaining to society's highest classes, mostly monarchs, nobility, warriors and priests. Only the wealthiest could afford horses, and it is mostly from royal annals that the early history of the horse is revealed. It was a partner in the hunt. In antiquity this was equally dangerous for man and horse, as the quarry hunted from a speeding chariot was often a horse's feared and sometimes predatory enemy, such as a lion, or a wild bull which could deliver a sharp-pronged charge and overturn horse and chariot. A horse will sense the presence, or even the recent presence, of a lion. This is not exaggeration. When riding in India where the Asiatic lion and the leopard take regular toll of livestock in the 'outback' of Gujerat, the horse I was riding, a very forward-going mare, suddenly proceeded with the utmost caution, then just as suddenly reverted to a brisk pace. My host, Raghuraj Sinh Jhala, a retired police inspector, horseman and game hunter, said this was normal in lion territory.[26] In many societies, ancient to nearly modern, hunting was a training for war. Courage was needed. It prepared horse and man for working over rough country, and improved coordination of mind, eye and limb in both. Above all it formed a bond between horse and man, enabling the hunter to recognise any quirks in his horse's performance, and to block undesired characteristics. For example, many horses jink to left or right at what is seen as a threat. Such a move could be disastrous in battle with a chariot overturned, wrecked, and/or weapon delivery disrupted and going wide of the mark in both chariot and cavalry warfare. In the latter, the saddleless, stirrupless rider could well 'go out of the side door'.

Religion also took its cut of the horse herds. Horses, usually white, were associated with cultic donations/demands/punishments. In ancient times religion and war were inextricably linked. Throughout history white horses have featured in religious and ceremonial use. The Assyrians, Persians and Germans used white horses, and today their use still prevails, with England's Royal Windsor Greys, and the white (grey) horses pulling the gun carriage at US President John F. Kennedy's funeral.

A horse was one of the highest value gifts from one monarch to another. An early example was the *Sulmanu* gift of a chariot and a pair of horses sent by Ashur-Uballit I (1365–1330) to Egypt's pharaoh as a trade and diplomatic opener once Assyria had gained her independence from Mitanni. Of course, it was expected that the 'gift' be reciprocated by gold from Egypt; Assyria complained when insufficient was sent.[27]

As a more versatile means of transport, able to go where a chariot could not, and less likely to break down, the horse was preferable for fast long-distance travel; the Persepolis Fortification Tablets show its use in the courier service to advantage (see chapter 10).

GENERAL OUTLINE FOR EARLY STAGES OF THE RECORDED USE OF THE HORSE AMONG WARRIOR PEOPLES

Egypt, Syria, the Bible lands, Asia Minor, the Near Eastern Mesopotamian tracts, Armenia (Urartu), and the territory beyond the Zagros Mountains all made military use of the horse. Initially, equestrian warfare was conducted by rival chariot corps, which gave to their armies the vital mobility that could put a corps in place at a speed denied to massed infantry, and sometimes put it in place before the enemy knew it was there. The thorny question of whether chariots charged head-on is dealt with below.

The chariot mode of warfare dominated the second half of the second millennium and the early centuries of the first millennium, until the Assyrian Empire expanded and formed *some* of the earliest-known true cavalry divisions under Tukulti Ninurta II (890–884).[28] However, Assyria was not the first to use the mounted warrior. In addition to Egypt and Canaan noted above there are others. The Nuzi Tablets have several references to mounted military. Two texts from the end of the fifteenth or early fourteenth century note animals described as 'complete' or 'fully equipped' and refer to men of units of mounted armed horsemen. Mycenae and Syria have representations of mounted warriors, mostly few in number, or individual depictions, but from Ugarit in Syria comes a plaque, dating to the end of the twelfth century, showing a line of horsemen, one of whom clearly is armed. This has been identified as a file of cavalry.[29]

The question is open as to whether, with the exception of the Ugarit and Nuzi horsemen, these representations were just individuals or members of a mounted corps not recorded as such. Taken collectively these early representations indicate that mounted warfare was becoming common over a wide territorial span. They also indicate a definite improvement in horsemanship.

In almost all the above-named territories from 1600 to 600 there were diplomatic ties, wars, followed by subjection of provinces, signing and subsequent breaking of treaties or alliances, and more wars as dynast fought dynast to expand his lands. Rarely was there quiet on all fronts.

From the emergent warrior nations several stand out for either expertise in horsemanship, or the sheer numbers of equids amassed as tribute, from trade or by breeding. Most records are from antiquity's successful monarchs, and are accordingly biased, boasting of their military prowess. The records from Egypt and Assyria are the most revealing. In later antiquity the horse was an important weapon for the cavalry of the Medes, Persians, Greeks, Macedonians and Seleucids.

CHAPTER 2

Introduction of the Horse into Mesopotamia and Neighbouring Lands

Dr O. Antonius, a respected hippologist of the early twentieth century and director of the Schönbrunn Zoo, Austria, was convinced that domesticated horses had a multiple origin, a possibility most authors do not exclude. A recent publication in the *Proceedings of the National Academy of Sciences*, noted in the *Daily Telegraph* of 14 August 2002 (appearing too late for me to research and make substantial alterations to this chapter) has recorded the findings of Dr P. Forster, Dr M. Levine, Dr T. Jansen et al. Mitochondrial DNA tests conducted on over 600 horses from 25 breeds worldwide prove that at least 17 genetic groups are involved; that horses originally came from diverse locations; and that there were at least 6 locations in which horses were domesticated. This does not preclude the Eurasian Steppes as being the first locale for domestication, but as Dr Levine said, at present there is no 'direct glimpse of how the first horse was domesticated'.[1] Nor, as shown on pages 3 and 4 above, is there firm evidence of *when* or *where* it was first ridden. Here it is the Near East that is relevant.

Opinion among experts varies as to the introduction date of *domesticated* horses into Mesopotamia. Once they were introduced, however, they were prized, high-status animals. Zarins maintains the domesticated horse was present from about the mid-third millennium at the latest. He also notes horse remains found in Syria dating to 2400–2100, at Arad in Palestine, dating to the early Bronze Age, and at several sites in Anatolia from the fourth to early third millennium, and the early Bronze Age – at Norsun-Tepe, Tepe Cik and Tulintepe. They have also been found at Demircihuyuk. The earliest find in Mesopotamia so far dates to the Isin/Larsa period (2000–1600).[2]

The most likely route for the introduction of the horse (*equus caballus*), into Anatolia and Mesopotamia was via the Caucasus in the late fourth millennium. The horse was preceded by the domesticated donkey (*equus asinus*) which came from either Egypt/North Africa or south-west Asia.[3] The other early equid present was the onager (*equus hemionus*), hunted for its meat and hide and also captured and managed in herds. Crossed with donkeys the onager gave a larger and stronger animal than either parent, the offspring being destined for draught work.[4] Hybrid vigour would account for size greater than either parent, and the desired characteristics of onager strength and donkey malleability were better suited to traction.

By the first half of the third millennium equids hitched to two or four solid-wheeled cumbersome battlewagons – too heavy to be termed chariots – were in use throughout Mesopotamia.[5] Artifacts illustrating these, dating to *c.* 2800–2500, include several two-wheeled, four-equid abreast hitches; most famously, the 'Standard of Ur' depicts five four-wheeled wagons with four equids apiece. There is also a harness terret surmounted by an equid, and many other representations held in Baghdad, the University of Pennsylvania, and the British Museum.[6]

Equid bones and teeth from numerous early sites excavated throughout Mesopotamia and neighbouring lands have been analysed, and although horse remains feature in some deposits, they are greatly outnumbered by those of donkey, onager, and the resulting hybrids.[7]

Postgate cites Sumerian texts noting the horse, in small numbers, as present from at least the Ur III period (*c.* 2100), and maybe even earlier.[8] The horse appears in a Sumerian text, *The Curse of Agade* (*c.* 2000), where the Goddess Inanna of Agade, capital of Sumer, sought to bring harmony to men and animals, among them the 'ass of the mountains', *Anše Kur Ra* – the horse.[9]

One example from a selection of Sumerian animal proverbs and fables, remarks, 'you sweat like a horse [it is] what you have drunk'; more humorously, from Ur, the horse, after he had thrown his rider, said, 'If my burden is always to be this, I shall become weak.' These proverbs already formed part of a standard collection used for school purposes.[10] The Ur III text shows that horseriding was known in Mesopotamia, even if rarely, at a very early date, though specific instances were not recorded until more than two centuries later.

There is a divergence of opinion as to the identities of some equids attested in cuneiform literature, namely *anše-LIBIR* and *anše-BAR×AN*. Zarins translates the first as horse, the second as mule,[11] a cross between donkey stallion and horse mare. Postgate tabulates the equids noted in cuneiform sources:

Anše	generic term for *equid* or *e. asinus*
Anše-DUN.GI or *anše-LIBIR*	*e. asinus*
Anše-eden-na	*e. hemionus*
Anše-BAR × *An*	*e. asinus* × *e. hemionus*
Anše-zi-zi or *Anšekur-ra*	*e. caballus*[12]

An account covering a three-year period lists 37 horses, 360 onagers, 727 hybrids, and 2,204 donkeys.[13] From this it is logical that most crosses were donkey/onager. A few hybrids could have been mules, or onager/horse, or the horse/onager crosses (that is, onager stallion on horse mare, or horse stallion on onager mare). There must have been a trial period to determine which hybrid cross using horses produced the superior animal in size, strength and tractability. With the horse highly valued, some horses surely would have been kept for producing their own kind. Even with the shorter lifespan in ancient times of ten to fourteen years, as opposed to fifteen to twenty-five years today,[14] increases would rapidly make a sizeable pool available for chariot duty. That some horses were aged is shown by the Buhen horse, which died at nineteen years.[15]

Stud records dating to 2300 from Girsu and Diyala list mares and hybrid offspring of foals and youngstock. The Girsu document on the obverse lists 80 mares which have foaled, 2 stallions, 33 hybrid youngstock; the reverse side shows 72 mares and 18 hybrid youngstock. The Diyala records show 1. on the obverse: 8 mature broodmares, 1 stallion, 12 hybrid offspring, 2 male onagers, for a total of 23 equids; 2. On the obverse 37 onagers, 10(+) two-year-old mules, 1(+) yearling mule(s), 3(+) yearling onagers, 6 donkey stallions, for a total of 62 equids. A fourth text shows 32 mature broodmares, 7 mule foals, 2 filly foals, 6 onager mares, 2 onager fillies, 2 onager colts, and 4 horses.[16]

In the Girsu document 152 broodmares are shown, a not inconsiderable number from one stud (if these are horses at this early date) but not at all surprising if, as is more likely, they are onager mares. From among the total of 345 animals from these four documents only four are classified as horses, which points to an early shortage. If, on the other hand, *Anše-LIBIR* denotes horse, the totals from the text, counting the 'foal-bearing mares' as horse mares, come to 184 mares, 7 fillies, 5 colts, 9 stallions and 4 horses, with horses far outnumbering mules and onagers. Such a huge number of mares indicates a similar number of males destined for war, since although some stallions have a tendency to sire more fillies, on the whole the sexes are fairly evenly balanced. Even if the presence of horses in Mesopotamia is extended back to 2300, their scarcity would preclude individual studs being stocked with huge numbers of horse mares. Therefore the hybrids were not mules, but donkey/onager crosses.

Malyan in Fars Province in the highlands of south-west Iran has yielded a few domestic horse remains from the Kaftari era (2100–1800) and a greater amount from the middle Elamite era (1600–1000).[17] The size of the horses from Malyan is shown to be similar to contemporary Egyptian horses from Thebes and Buhen. These were, from Thebes, a horse of 143 cm at the withers (*c.* 14.1 hh), and from Buhen 150 cm, or about 15 hh.[18] A mummified horse from Saqqara stood at approximately 14.1½ hh.[19] Three of five horse bones analysed from the Elamite level are said possibly to be from the same animal. These are a metacarpal, and a first and third phalanx,[20] but as the metacarpal compares well to that of the Buhen horse, the first phalanx is almost identical to that of the Theban horse, and the third phalanx is smaller than the Egyptian horse bones, but larger than the Bastam, Urartean, horses of the 2200–700 era[21] – it is hard to see how this could be so unless the animal had very peculiar conformation! One probable use for horses from Malyan was in the long-distance trade,[22] but as Elam was frequently embattled, more horses would have been required for war purposes.

From a Hittite burial site near Hattusas in Anatolia, remains have been found of a horse of about 1.5 m at the withers (roughly 15 hh).[23] Although some people may consider the range 14.1 hh to 15 hh to be small, bearing in mind that most people of that time were not as tall as people are today, these sizes were adequate for the work necessary in draught, and later for cavalry use, even when the horse was carrying an armoured rider and also armour itself. This could range from chamfron, breastplate and housings that covered the body from wither to just beyond the hip; later, of course, the Persians developed full armour for their warhorses. Height alone does not have much bearing on weight-carrying ability. What the finds do indicate is that horses of these and other regions were of a size comparable to a great mass of modern saddle horses in the range of 14.1–15 hh.[24] Too diminutive a horse (pony) would not have been of much use in war, especially in the later cavalry phase. A 12–13 hh animal gives a decidedly more unstable platform for a warrior, than a longer, smoother-striding 14–15 hh horse. Ponies with short stature often have trappy, up and down action, short stride and, unless in gross condition, a back that would not have been conducive to maintaining a seat for a fully grown adult, particularly as adequate saddles were centuries in the future.

Once present the horse's rapid increase was important for producing the larger, stronger mules to replace donkey/onager crosses which, even if bigger than both parents, must still have been small. Donkeys stand around 12 hh or less; onagers are 10 hh or less for the Syrian, and 11–12½ hh (1 m 110–27 cm) for the Persian and Turkmenian varieties.[25]

After the horse had been introduced into Near Eastern warfare, the mule made its appearance. With it came ancient superstitions regarding the dire results if the impossible happened and this supposedly sterile beast foaled. Passages from Herodotus, Pliny the Elder and others illustrate these fears. Herodotus' tale records the siege of Babylon early in the reign of Darius I (522–486). The Babylonians, thinking to be secure behind their walls, jeered that the city would fall when mules foaled. In the twentieth month of the siege a baggage mule foaled and Babylon fell.[26] A mule foaling is not impossible; it depends on the chromosome count. If the count of both parents when divided by two comes to an odd number the animal is sterile. In the rare instances in which the division results in an equal number, the animal can be fertile.[27] In the USA there are fourteen documented cases of mules foaling up to 1984, and it is even on record that one pregnancy resulted in twins, one of which was a horse, the other a mule (presumably from one jackass and one horse sire, and the mare having two fertile eggs).[28]

The most important step was the harnessing of horses to the new, better-designed spoke-wheeled chariot. This was a major military advance of the second millennium, and was used by all the warrior cultures of the ancient Near East and Mediterranean. Subsequently, cavalry superseded the chariot, and the horse as cavalry charger was to have a future encompassing almost three millennia.

CHAPTER 3

The Horse in the
Early Second Millennium

THE HYKSOS AND THE STATE OF MARI

The Hyksos

Egypt came relatively late to using *equus caballus*, although *equus asinus* had long been indispensable for carrying burdens for merchants, farmers and the army. From a position of unified strength and material wealth in the nineteenth century, Egypt's situation declined in the eighteenth century as power was fragmented among a plethora of monarchs. This left Egypt weakened and ripe for takeover by the Asiatic Hyksos, who first seized control in the Nile Delta *c.* 1750–1730, siting their capital at Avaris; by the end of the century they ruled all Egypt, Lower Nubia, and controlled the Egyptian trade with Kerma in the Sudan.[1] The Hyksos have often been represented as sweeping in in a chariot-borne invasion, and thus introducing the horse into Egypt:

> . . . warriors in chariots drove into the country like arrows shot from a bow, endless columns of them . . . day and night horses' hooves thundered past the frontier posts. . . .[2]

However, a literary accounting by Manetho – although some 1,500 years after the event, but drawing on early sources – suggests there was no major military invasion, but rather a takeover made possible by political chaos in Egypt.[3] The Hyksos had contacts with Asia and introduced Asiatic military elements into their army.[4] It is unlikely that it will ever be conclusively proven that they introduced the horse to the Egyptians. What is known is that remains of horses have been found dating to the period of the Hyksos sojourn in Egypt. The horse remains at Gaza have been radiocarbon-dated and calibrated to fall into the Hyksos period.[5] The famous discovery at Buhen in the Sudan, one of the Egyptian fortresses and trade centres, yielded an almost complete skeleton dating to 1675 in which the teeth showed bit wear.[6] This demonstrated use of the horse in an *Egyptian* context during the first half of the Hyksos period of occupation, but whether the horse was Egyptian- or Hyksos-owned is not known, nor is the specific use to which it was put. These early specimens may now be joined by the most recent discovery, at Tel al Kibir in the Nile Delta, of skeletal horse remains dating to 1750, which pre-dates Hyksos arrival in the area.[7]

There is an intriguing biblical passage, Genesis 47:16f, that concerns Joseph. His family was present in Egypt c. 1700. It had long (from as early as 1900) been an Egyptian custom to allow people from Palestine and Syria to settle in the Delta in hard times. Joseph rose to high office under Egypt's pharaoh. According to the biblical story a famine had hit Canaan and Egypt. Egypt was prone to famine (presumably when the Nile failed to rise and inundate the land sufficiently for a good crop), but stockpiled food in good years. Canaanites had come requesting food from Egypt; this was granted 'in exchange for their horses, their sheep and goats, their cattle and donkeys'.[8]

As dates this far back are only approximate (unless of rulers whose exact regnal years are known), this suggests that horses were known in Egypt sufficiently well to be a desirable commodity. If the pharaoh (or his official) could demand them in the Delta it also implies that the Hyksos had not yet taken full control of the area. This in turn indicates the gradual entry of horses into Egypt prior to the Hyksos' gradual arrival.[9]

During the 17th Dynasty, Kamose, c. 1570, reigned at Thebes over an area from the first cataract to near Cusae.[10] He determined to break the treaty which existed between Egypt at Thebes and the Hyksos at Avaris and expel the invaders, even though the Kamose stela shows conditions were hardly harsh, as the Thebans were permitted to breed and graze their cattle in the Delta, and grain from there was provided for the Thebans' pigs.[11] Kamose sailed down the Nile: '. . . the region of Pershaq [unknown] was missing [that is, deserted] when I reached it. Their horses were fled inside. The patrol . . .'. Kamose relates how he imprisoned Hyksos women in his ships, and boasted that he would capture the Hyksos chariotry and much spoil from the land of Retenu (Syria) which was also under Hyksos control.[12] The expulsion was not immediate, as Kamose's brother Ahmose I (c. 1570–1545) continued the task. This incident was related by one of his troops, a sailor and soldier, also named Ahmose, son of Eben. He describes Ahmose, the Pharaoh, in his chariot – the first mention of horse and chariot use by the Egyptians.[13] The same Ahmose, son of Eben, then served Thutmose I (1525–1495) in his Syrian campaigns as an infantryman. He described Thutmose's arrival in Naharin (Mitanni), the great slaughter that followed, and his own part in the action:

... I brought off a chariot, its horses, and him who was upon it as a living prisoner and took them to his majesty. One (his majesty) presented me with gold in double measure.[14]

Syrian campaigns continued during subsequent pharaohs' reigns. There was loot to be gained, and, very importantly, control of the regions beyond Egypt's natural boundaries enforced a buffer zone against any further incursions.

Although from these few references it appears that Egypt was not using chariotry in any great measure, it would be strange to conclude – with the horse known in Egypt at least a century before the Hyksos' final expulsion, and maybe earlier – that the Egyptians had not implemented at least some force of chariotry, especially as immediately after their expulsion, and the opening of the 18th Dynasty, mentions of horses gain momentum in the royal annals.

From the reign of Thutmose III (1479–1425) there is a considerable amount of information. He was a great military leader, and campaigned incessantly throughout his very long reign, mostly in Syria, and as far as the Euphrates. He warred against the Mitanni, and from his reign we are introduced to the Hittites.[15]

Mari

Although there is the earlier evidence of the horse from Sumer, it is from the city state of Mari that military equestrian data begins to unfold from the hoard of tablets known as *The Royal Archives of Mari*. They were recovered by the French just after the First World War. They have yielded information from the time of the usurping Shamsi-Adad I (*c.* 1813–1781) of Assyria who included Mari in his annexations, and set one of his sons, Iasmah-Adad (1796–1780), in control. Assyrian territory shrank soon after Shamsi-Adad's death, and King Zimri-Lim of Mari (*c.* 1779–1761), with help from Syrian allies from Halab (Aleppo), regained his inheritance. Iasmah-Adad then ruled a much diminished appanage from Chagar Bazar, some 150 or so miles north-east of Mari.[16]

Mari used chariotry in war, and also donkey-mounted couriers, although it is possible that horses could have been used on occasion.[17] From Mari comes the earliest personal record of horseriding. King Zimri-Lim was advised to take the safer option of riding a mule, or in a chariot, rather than risk riding horses.[18]

The scarcity of horses at this time is shown by the value of a single animal: it was worth thirty times that of a slave, or 500 sheep, or 5 minas of silver (2,400 grams, or about 5 lb 3½ oz). One-fifth of this was the cost of the high army and administrative post of *Suqaqum* in the Mari military establishment.[19] Mari was known for its expertise in crafting chariots to which donkeys, mules, and horses were hitched.[20]

Zimri-Lim maintained cordial relations with his Syrian allies and visited Halab.[21] He had probably been requesting temple horses when he asked Aplahanda of Carcemish for white horses, but was informed that only bays were available.[22] This request introduces Syria as a very early exporter of horses. Cordial ties and reciprocal military assistance existed between Babylon and Mari, but when the time was ripe this friendship did not prevent Hammurabi of Babylon (1792–1750) attacking Mari and incorporating it into his kingdom. Zimri-Lim became a vassal of Babylonia, and Mari ceased to exist as a sovereign power.[23]

TABLETS FROM CHAGAR BAZAR

From Iasmah-Adad's appanage comes evidence of early feeding regimens for equids. Tablets from Chagar Bazar show that Iasmah-Adad kept teams of horses, donkeys and bovids. Their rations were outlined. Wages for grooms and a trainer are also recorded.[24] Several types of donkey are noted: riding, common, those in the royal establishment, and one other, not specified, but from its rations of greater significance. Rations are in *sila* or *qa* (*c.* 6⅔ oz each).

Riding asses got 5 spd (sila per day), youngstock 2 spd, foals 1 spd.[25]
Common asses received 2 spd.[26]
Asses in the royal establishment got 3 spd, and some 5 spd.[27]
The *Anše Nu Na* category received 7½ spd.[28]
Mature working-horse rations varied. Some received 5 spd, others 10 spd.[29]

Apart from rations for single animals, foals and youngstock, rations were also given for numbers of 'yokes', the amounts indicating a three-horse team, and in one case a team of two which received 10 spd per horse.[30] Some other horses not represented as 'yokes' or teams received 10 spd each.[31] Donkey rations were on the sparse side, the common donkey at about 14 oz per day must have been burro-sized, but the 7½ spd animals a more hefty ass. (Poitou in France raises a horse-sized ass.) The horse rations could indicate several categories: prestigious, larger than average horses, and/or horses doing heavier work such as pulling a heavy state or temple vehicle. Fodder rations are also noted.[32]

EQUESTRIAN SIGNPOSTS

After the disappearance of Mari as a kingdom, and the expulsion of the Hyksos from Egypt, the equestrian scene becomes more intricate. During the middle of the second millennium, from about 1600 to 1200, a considerable intermeshing among horse and chariot peoples of the Near East took place. During this period Mesopotamia and Syria were constantly embattled, as was Egypt, although her campaigns took place outside her homeland.

Hurrian communities from the mountainous north-east and Indo-European Hittites from their Anatolian heartland with its capital at Hattusas (modern Boghasköy) spread into Mesopotamia, Syria and Cilicia. Mitanni, the strongest of the Hurrian kingdoms was established east of the Euphrates. She warred with both the Hittites and Egypt, and as she expanded gradually absorbed Assyria until war between the Hittites and Mitanni enabled the Assyrians to seize Mitannian territory and establish Assyrian independence.[33]

Much is owed to Egyptian and Assyrian documentation for the unravelling of these wars, and the place of the horse within them. In nearly all instances the horse is highly prized, and from these documents we learn who was allied to or warring against whom, the political coalitions formed, the cost in human and material wealth to enemies, and the huge material gains to be had; and although the texts are nationally biased, when it comes to the horse – when there is no political axe to grind – the information gives us an indication of the equestrian infrastructure far beyond the squeal of chariot wheels and thunder of hooves on the battlefield. Indeed, without this infrastructure, which is common to all equestrian peoples other than the strictly nomadic, there would have been no chariot corps or cavalry divisions.

CHAPTER 4

The General Acquisition
of Horses

Some understanding of the general infrastructure of horse management is necessary before we can appreciate how the military equestrian divisions could have operated. We have seen the early evidence for the place the horse held with early nomadic equestrians and its gradual appearance in the military of Near Eastern cultures. From the second half of the second millennium the horse plays a much greater role in the wars, and equestrian sports such as hunting, for all the major players in their continual struggles for supremacy. At some period in the next 1,200 years, stretching from the sixteenth to the fourth centuries the horse was a constant factor in the successive armies which ranged from Egypt to India.

The equestrian infrastructure had several major aspects. The most important are:

1. The general acquisition of horses.
2. Choosing and training the warhorse: its physiological and psychological aspects.
3. Control mechanisms.
4. Hazards and health.

Sections 2–4 are covered separately in the following chapters. The points can largely be dealt with in a way that is applicable generally to horses serving in any of the warrior cultures. Naturally other points occur in the specific chapters on individual nations' use of the horse in the military.

Modern experience of management, training and veterinary techniques allow us to better understand the practicalities of ancient equestrianism. With the modern approach to animal welfare we may abhor some of the past, crude methods, but we can understand why they were used. The modern as opposed to the historical approach to horses needs to be considered. In today's affluent societies horses are, for the most part, kept for pleasure. Strong emotional bonds exist between horses and their owners and carers. In the ancient world, while undoubtedly some emotional bonds existed between a portion of drivers and/or riders and their horses, for the most part horses were seen as articles to be used, mostly in hazardous employment that went against the animals' natural inclinations. These inclinations were often subverted by methods that are unacceptable today.

There are a few treatises on horse training, care, and veterinary practice on which we can draw for the earlier period, mostly from the last half of the second millennium. These include the Hittite work of the Mitannian horsemaster Kikkuli, fragments of an Assyrian text on horse training and very fragmentary Ugaritic veterinary tablets, and reference to training chariot horses from Egypt in the time of Tuthmose III. From Greece there is the fourth-century horsemanship manual of Xenophon. many of whose other works contain equestrian elements, notably his *Cavalry Commander* and his *Anabasis*. Much of Xenophon's equestrian wisdom is still relevant. From India there is the late fourth-/early third-century *Arthasastra of Kautilya,* which mostly concerns military matters. Several sections deal with horses and their care and training. Indeed, there is far more on training than in the repetitive Kikkuli text.

Greek veterinarians were renowned for their skill with equines, and most veterinary texts belong to the first few centuries AD. However, much of their lore was recorded at least four centuries earlier in the works of Varro, *c.* 37 BC, who wrote on farming, and those of the first-century AD writer Columella. The poet Virgil (70–19 BC) commented on breeding and training in his *Georgics.* Many of the basic tenets of horsebreeding and management remained constant over the centuries. Some ancient practices lasted well into the twentieth century AD, especially that of firing for leg ailments. Therefore, it can be expected that much of the Graeco-Roman literature was reiterating a much earlier body of equine management data.

The first section to be considered is the caballine map.

THE CABALLINE CANVAS

The desire to expand territory and acquire wealth were the main catalysts that sparked the wars in which the horse was a significant part of the wealth accrued. Military canvasses unroll, illustrating the interrelation of one group, culture, or dynasty with its close neighbours and, for the ambitious dynasts, with countries well beyond their immediate boundaries. From the sixteenth century the horse was in the forefront of the military events that involved almost all the Near East for the next 1,200 years, and even beyond that, on a more extensive range as other cultures came into focus. Insurgents from outside the Near East, some of whom utilised chariot warfare, occupied and imposed new rule on some settled peoples; other conflicts were contained within Near Eastern confines. Nations flourished, declined and some resurged.

The most powerful military peoples, the Mitannians, Hittites, Egyptians, Assyrians, Urarteans (Armenians), Persians and Macedonians took their acquisitive wars well outside their boundaries. Such peoples stand out for their high-profile use of the horse, and for the equestrian information that can be garnered from their cultures. Frequent wars were fought in Syria, a land occupied and fought over by most of the nations mentioned, and a country that had an equestrian impact from as early as the eighteenth century BC (see chapter 2) right down to the eighteenth century AD, when Aleppo was the mart where people from both East and West sought their blood horses. The first Seleucid monarch, Seleucus Nicator (c. 305–281) sited his huge military stud at Apameia on the Orontes. But Syria continued in importance throughout many eras, and Charles II (AD 1660–85) imported bloodstock from Aleppo, chosen for him by Lord Winchelsea, his ambassador to Constantinople. Around AD 1700 one of the three famous Arabian ancestors of the modern thoroughbred, the Darley Arabian, was purchased at Aleppo. He was of the Muniqi or Managhi strain, which in all probability goes back to the Arabian stock raised by the Munqidh family of Shaizar, near Aleppo, about the twelfth century AD.[1]

Before looking at the place of the warhorse in these cultures it is useful to map as comprehensively as possible caballine locations relevant to the period, so that the equid content can be seen as a continuing thread, rather than as individual markers in each culture. This overview of locations known for horsebreeding, and/or as areas repeatedly tapped by the military for horses, shows that many endured as such for centuries, and some for millennia. Documentation from the second and first millennia attests to many locations.

THE INDO-EUROPEAN AND OTHER MIGRATIONS

Around the second millennium a movement of Indo-European-speaking peoples from the steppes of south Russia began a multi-track emigration to western Asia, the Near East, India and Europe. In Asia the migrations split into several groups, one of which crossed the Caucasus into Armenia and the Taurus region, mixing with the Hurrian population.[2] The migrations had earlier come via the Caucasus into Anatolia and into areas east of the Tigris and to the Zagros Mountains.[3] Another group of Indo-

Europeans seized control of the Kassites of the Zagros and the Iranian Plateau; others known as Aryans[4] descended on Sind and the Punjab in India. These migrations extended over several centuries, down to the mid-second millennium. In Europe their trail reached Poland, Germany, Denmark and the Rhine Valley, mingling with the Beaker culture by 1600.[5] Remains of wild equid stock have been attested at many European sites.[6] The Beaker culture is credited with the diffusion of the domesticated horse in Europe.[7] The horse was a partner in these migrations. By 2000 it had long been domesticated on the Eurasian Steppes.[8]

Even though the domesticated horse was already present in the Near East, these migrations boosted its dispersal. Peoples who established military supremacies based largely on the use of the horse included the Mitannians in Upper Mesopotamia and Syria,[9] the Hittites of Anatolia and Syria,[10] and the Kassites who overthrew the Babylonians in about 1600.[11] In Persia, Turkestan, India and Baluchistan the horse was known from very early times, but it was the Aryans who pushed its use forward in India as chariot warhorse;[12] this occurred around 1500 when they overran the Indus civilisation.[13]

THE LINGUISTIC AND PRACTICAL ASPECTS

Evidence from the Indo-Europeans highlights their affinity to, and dispersal of, the horse. From Mitanni comes the link with Indo-Aryan names: Biridašwa – possessing great horses; and *Sattawaza* – he who has won seven prizes (at the horse races).[14] Other Indo-Aryan names from the *Zend Avesta*, the holy book of the Zoroastrians, are equally revealing: *Drvaspa* (a goddess) – she who keeps horses in health; *Vistaspa* (a king of Bactria), son of *Aurvat-Aspa*; *Pourus-Aspa*, father of Zarathustra – he who possesses many horses;[15] *Arbataspa* – master of warlike horses; *Huaspa* – having good horses.[16] These, coupled with numerous references throughout the *Zend Avesta* to warhorses, show that the whole of the Iranian/Median/Persian cultures revolved around horses. In the horse training manual of Kikkuli of Mitanni are terms which are akin to Sanskrit.[17]

Kikkuli	Sanskrit	Meaning
wartanna	*Vartana*	a turn
aika	*eka*	one turn
tera	*tri*	three turns
Panza	*panca*	five turns
Satta	*sapta*	seven turns
Nav(artanna)	*nava*	nine turns

From Sanskrit comes the term *marya*, while from the Kikkuli manuscript, and other documents from Hattusas, *maryannu*. This was borrowed by the Egyptians – *m(a)-ar-ya-na* – by 1470, and appears in *Papyrus Anastasi I* where *maryan* clearly means chariot warrior.[18] The Persian word for horse is *aspa*, the Sanskrit *asva*. Alexander the Great's wars with Persia show other areas that had a strong equestrian link and Persian influence. Bactria's capital was then known as *Zariaspa* – (of the) Golden Horses; the *Arimaspai* – (of the) well-schooled horses.[19] The *Zariaspans* and the *Arimaspains* (*Arimaspians*) featured in the tribal conquests of Alexander's campaigns. In time Zariaspa became Balkh, famous for warhorses, trainers, and horse trade. The Golden Horse link can quite clearly be shown to refer to one of the many strains of Turcoman horse, one known for its bronze-gold coat. This is the Akhal Teke, bred by the Tekke Turks. However, the links for this come from a host of clues dating to the early and mid-medieval eras.[20] At Aravan, near Ferghana, are excellent rock drawings dating to about the first century. They show a stallion just prior to mounting a mare.[21] Both horses are definitely not of common steppe type, but of very oriental appearance, that is, hot blood type. Ferghana lies within the Turanian area said by Hancar to have had superb horses from at least the first millennium. Ferghana continued to supply quality horses well into the medieval period. For instance, to procure the horses of Tayüan (Ferghana) the Chinese mounted massive military campaigns in the reign of Han Wu Ti (140–87), and in the early Mughal era the Jigrak of Andijan, capital of Ferghana, provided the first Mughal emperor, Babur (AD 1526–30) with many horses.[22]

Xenophon (born *c.* 430) noted horses of very good conformation in Armenia on his march back to Greece after serving in Cyrus the Younger's army.[23] They were finer but smaller than those of the Persians, to whom they were to be surrendered as tribute, thus giving that empire an added strain on which to draw. Clearly, finely structured horses were being bred over a very wide range of the ancient world.

THE PRACTICAL LINK

A strong link in the equestrian migrations comes from the Russian Steppes and India's epic, the *Rig Veda*, which frequently features the warhorse. Excavations of 1985–8 of a kurgan burial, *c.* 2200–2000, at Potapovka near Samara on the River Sok revealed that placed over the grave shaft of kurgan no. 3 was a decapitated man with a horse's skull replacing his head. In one of the *Rig Veda*'s myths a man named Dadhyanc Atharvah, incurring the wrath of the Asvins – twin gods represented as horses – was decapitated, his head replaced by a horse's skull; the dead man thereafter became an oracle.[24]

Strengthening the steppe-Aryan Indian link is the *Asvamedha* horse sacrifice. It is the territorial/military thread, not the religious aspect, that is important here. On the steppes land claims were to areas of grazing for tribal herds which were guarded by a chief's mounted and armed herdsmen. A powerful chief wishing to claim territorial supremacy would turn loose a horse and allow him to graze at will. The horse was guarded by armed warriors who repulsed any who tried to drive away or harm the animal. After a year the horse was sacrificed and its owner, the chief, then proclaimed his overlordship over all the land comprising its grazing area. In Aryan India this sacrifice continued well into the time of the Guptas in the fourth century AD. At Jaggayyapeta is a relief where the horse is depicted as a symbol of the world ruler Cakravartin.[25] The horse sacrifice also appears regularly in the *Zend Avesta*, albeit in religious fiction, when 100 male horses, 1,000 oxen and 10,000 lambs are offered up to Ardvi Sura Anahita on the Hara, the Alborz Mountains south of the Caspian Sea.[26] This location suggests a tribal breeding ground. It is in the path of the early Aryan migrations, and the whole area continued down to modern times to be a major supplier of horses for war.[27] These links prove how important was the horse to all the cultures with an Indo-European/Aryan heritage.

FURTHER NOMADIC MOVEMENTS

Around 700, by which time cavalry had largely superseded traction in war, other nomadic waves were on the move, with the Cimmerians and the Scythians coming into Anatolia, the Near East and Iraq, the Sakae into India and Persia, and the Parthian (Parnii), a Scythian group, into the territory that became known as Parthia, where they ruled from 247 BC to AD 226. The Scythians were followed by the kindred Sarmatians, well known from the Roman era. The Wu Sun moved into the Tien Shan. Their horses were acclaimed by Ssu Ma Chien of China who also catalogued the attacks on them by the Hsiung Nu in the second century. The Turkic/Mongol Hsiung Nu of the Gobi Desert had risen to power in the last centuries of the first millennium and spread into the Altai, Mongolia, the Tien Shan, and most notably onto the borders and eventually into the northern sector of China. Beginning with the third century, the predominantly Turkic Huns, related to the Hsiung Nu, moved across Asia and into Europe, their predations continuing until well into the first half of the first millennium AD. All these nomadic peoples were noted for their horses and horsemanship. Many blended into their eventual homelands and left a rich equestrian heritage.[28]

THE LITERARY MAP

Between the first and second waves of horsepowered migrations, one can begin to fill out a map using written evidence from Near Eastern, Egyptian, biblical and Anatolian cultures, and from people whose ancestors were involved in the migrations. Specifics of concentrations of horses are rare for the second millennium, but shortly after the expulsion of the Hyksos from Egypt there is evidence of the thriving breeding status of Syria. Indirectly this points to a source of horses that the Hyksos may have tapped. It is known that the chariot and equestrian terms reached Egypt from Canaan.[29]

A comprehensive animal booty list comes from the aftermath of Thutmose III's victory at the Battle of Megiddo, c. 1468, in Syria (Retenu).[30] The caballine haul amounted to 2,041 mares, 191 foals and 6 stallions. There were also 924 chariots, to which must be added a proportion of the pairs that drew them, allowing for equine deaths and injuries. Huge numbers of small cattle (sheep and goats) and large cattle (bovines) were also taken.[31] Such huge herds take considerable time to become established, and this figure represented only part of the available stock. To have denuded Syria of all stock would have meant that annual tribute demands could not have been met. With the accent on mares the pharaoh obviously was looking to establish studs in Egypt on a grand scale. Fearfully impressed by the Egyptian victory, Assur, Babylon and the Hittites sent placatory gifts.[32]

Thutmose III usually campaigned in Syria, but as revolts flared, where necessary, on an almost yearly schedule. Sometimes tribute was paid to ward off imminent attacks, sometimes as battle spoils. Many sources provided tribute and/or booty in horses: Assur;[33] Naharin (Mitanni) – a considerable number running into many hundreds;[34] Lebanon;[35] and Cyprus.[36] Syrian forfeits were the heaviest. Annual levies raised 328 and 229 from individual Syrian towns.[37] From unknown and/or unidentified places numbers ranged from the 20s to just over 100. Occasionally unspecified tribute was levied, as for the ambitious eighth campaign when Thutmose crossed the Euphrates and set up a stela to mark his territory. He captured huge booty from the Mitannians, and levied tribute on the Hittites and Babylonians.[38] We can be sure the horse haul was huge.

Where time has partly erased inscriptions I suggest that some blanks following a number were intended for horses, as they usually appeared after prisoners/slaves. Some horse numbers tie in with the numbers of chariots won or demanded, but the larger, irregular numbers clearly indicated herds and studs, as more certainly outlined in the Megiddo haul where chariots were divorced from breeding stock. The peoples and places providing horses are informative. The Mitannians and the Hittites were firmly established in the locales which had been infused with equestrian increments from the migration period noted above. Incoming horses would have given numerical and genetic boosts to stock already available throughout their territory. The reference to Cypriot horses proves it was already normal to ship horses by sea.

Assyrian sources up to the reign of Tiglath-Pileser I (1115–1077) give only general information on horses. Tiglath-Pileser was not only an aggressive ruler, but he was concerned to improve Assyria's agriculture and stockbreeding. Horses were regular gains from battle spoils. In his first five years of campaigning he claimed to lay tribute on forty-two lands from the further side of the Lower Zab to the east of the Euphrates, as well as on the Land of Hatti.[39] Nairi, a confederation of small states south of Lake Van stands out. From these he 'led away great herds of horses', and '1,200 horses and 2,000 cattle I imposed as tribute'.[40] Nairi was attacked repeatedly. On his third expedition its horses were seized and tribute *reimposed*,[41] which suggests his 'conquest' was not exactly solid. This area, later part of Urartu (Armenia) was a major target of Sargon II (721–705). Urartu and adjacent countries were home to some of the finest horses of the ancient world. In Assyria the relocated herds were productive. Tiglath-Pileser claimed he 'stocked the land with horses, asses . . . planted parks and gardens . . . and increased the output of chariots and their teams more than any previous king of Assyria'.[42]

HORSES AND THE BIBLE

After the initial mention of importing horses from Canaan, *c.* 1700, in the Book of Genesis,[43] we have to wait until *c.* 1000 for more precise information on tribute and trade: 'and all the earth sought Solomon . . . and they brought every man his present . . . horses and mules, a rate year by year'.[44] Solomon's merchants bought horses from Kue (Coa/Cilicia/Que), and from Egypt came chariots at 600 shekels and horses at 150 shekels each. The same merchants exported 'them to all the kings of the Hittites and of the Arameans'.[45] A similar text is quoted in II Chronicles,[46] the difference being that the merchants are termed royal merchants. It is strange that such a warlike king permitted sales to foreigners, unless his merchants were traders on their own account and received commissions from Solomon. If they traded in horses to foreigners on Solomon's behalf, the king had a nice sideline in the bloodstock trade. The passage suggests Solomon was not powerful enough to prevent sales to the foreigners, who could be potential enemies. On the other hand, maybe peace was bought at a price. Throughout history there have been embargoes on selling horses outside one's own country, as horses were considered part of the war arsenal. Thus, Medieval Spain, France, England and Russia had banned exports, and under the Tudors exports to Scotland were forbidden in England, although the bans were flouted frequently. Embargoes by the Spanish Netherlands on shipments to England were defied by Henry VIII (AD 1509–47).[47]

However, the Bible is extremely confusing and contradictory in that Solomon's equestrian establishment(s) are variously given. To add to the confusion, translators do not always agree over whether there were only chariot horses, or a large number of cavalry horses. This latter needs to be discounted, since regular large cavalry divisions belonged to the future.

Solomon's Numbers

4,000 stalls and 12,000 horses.[48]
1,400 chariots and 12,000 horses.[49]
1,400 chariots and 12,000 horses.[50]   same number different books.
4,000 stalls and 12,000 horses, and horses imported from Egypt and all other countries (unspecified).[51]

In some of the quotes for *horses* there is an alternative translation of *charioteers*, or *horsemen*. We also learn there were '*other horses*' in addition to the chariot horses.[52] To confuse the issue even further one translation of I Kings 26 has 40,000 chariot horses and 12,000 cavalry horses.[53]

In an article in the *Journal of Semitic Studies* the exact meaning of words concerning Solomon's equestrian establishments are considered, in particular the word for *stall* or *stable*, and the word *pārāšîm*, which could mean either *horses* or *horsemen*. The article takes the 4,000 chariots or stalls and the 12,000 horses as the most probable strength of Solomon's establishment. This gave three horses per unit, or, if *pārāšîm* is taken to mean horsemen, three men per unit. In ninth-century Assyria three-horse teams were used, and the practice of three men per unit was also growing, although not universal.[54]

The prophet Ezekiel, living at the turn of the seventh and sixth centuries, noted Tyre as the entrepôt for Syria. There all manner of luxury goods were to be found from Syria, Africa, Greece, Anatolia, Arabia and Assyria. Togarmah, capital of Tabal in Cappadocia, sent horses, mules and horsemen (that is, mercenaries and cavalrymen).[55] The biblical references illustrate the continuity of international trading.

NEO ASSYRIAN HORSE SUPPLIES

After Tiglath-Pileser I's reign Assyria suffered a decline until its steady climb back to prosperity under Ashur Dan II (934–912).[56] Ashur Dan's son, Adad Nirari II (911–891), claimed he increased horsebreeding of 'horses broken to the yoke throughout my country over those of former days'.[57] Tukulti Ninurta II (890–884) is the first to record 'horsemen who go at my side'[58] (that is, a cavalry bodyguard), who were provided with horses as tribute from Ami-Ba'li of Nairi[59] in a campaign which yielded a total of 2,700 horses from Gilzani, Nairi and the Shubari.[60] Nairi, later subsumed into Urartu, became a major provider of cavalry horses trained in the adjacent province of Mannai. This province regularly changed overlords from the King of Urartu to the King of Assyria. Assurnasirpal (883–859) campaigned incessantly during his reign of terror, and without real provocation, conducting *razzias* on neighbouring lands. He acquired loot, horses in particular, from Urartu in the east to Syria to the west of Assur, plundering Gilzani and Hubushkia, Bit Halupe, Tush in Nairi, Shupre, Nirdun, Hanigalbat (Mitanni), Hatti, Zamua (neighbourhood of Suleimaniyah), and again fleecing Ami-Ba'li of Nairi, Karduniash (Babylon), Carcemish and Amurru (the Levant).[61]

Under Shalmaneser III (858–824) great gains were made in lands and spoils, especially in plundering Urartu, which now replaced Nairi as a key source of horses.[62] Syria endured repeated Assyrian invasions and depletion of stock.[63] In Shalmaneser's thirtieth year he sent his *Turtan* (Commander-in-Chief), Daian-Assur, with an army on a tribute-collecting tour, and Parsua (Persia) made its appearance, surrendering horses to him.[64]

From the reign of Tiglath-Pileser III (745–727) to that of Ashurbanipal (668–626) the records show an immense span of territory from which Assyria drew her warhorses. All but one major source continued in subsequent centuries and cultures to provide a wealth of military horseflesh. Although represented by different names, some areas can, I suggest, be shown to have had continuous breeding practices rather than being new-found sources. Around this period there is also a demand for more substantial horses, and certain locales produced such stock. This surely indicates that selective breeding and more knowledge of maintenance was improving not only height but body mass. Missi in Mannea produced 'large' draught (chariot) horses;[65] Susa and Elam yielded 'great' horses;[66] the Medes were renowned for 'mighty' steeds.[67] From Tabal in the Taurus Mountains of Anatolia a quota of 'large' horses was levied as yearly tribute.[68]

Both Sargon II and Ashurbanipal received tribute of horses from Egypt which were described as 'great' and 'large'.[69] One consignment from Pharaoh Osorkon IV (c. 750, one of the Delta dynasts and the Silkanni of the Assyrians) consisted of '12 big horses from Musri [Egypt] which have not their equals in this country [Assyria]'.[70] Apart from Egypt, these areas continued to be recorded as producing excellent stock. The horses of the Medes were famous. Syrian stock was renowned. Asia Minor in general was, and continued to be, a great producer and exporter by trade and tribute, horses coming in via Syria on the trade routes. Coa (Cilicia) exported to Israel (see above) and to Persia.[71] Melid (Malatya/Melitene) in Cappadocia (part of Anatolia) supplied tribute horses to Assyria,[72] and continued to render tribute in horses to the Persians.[73]

A group of letters called the 'Horse Reports', from the archives at Kouyunjik (Nineveh), record a three-month tally of horses, and a few mules, coming into Nineveh, most likely during the reign of Esarhaddon (680–669). This was prior to the start of the annual campaigning season in the fourth month.[74] The total number of horses for draught was 1,840, and for cavalry 787.[75] The two main breeds, or rather types, are Kusaean and Mesaean. The Kusaean derived initially from Kush in Nubia, and the Mesaean from Iran. They were intended solely for draught.[76] The Mesaean all came from the eastern sector of Assyria and her provinces. The Kusaean were more widely spread over the empire. Several entries have each a few Kusaeans described as *sibte* – of the increase (of the lands/breed of Kush), indicating Kusaean studs throughout the empire. Some Kusaeans came from as far away as Parsua, and Lahiru (near Elam).[77] No Mesaeans are described as *sibte*, but this does not preclude the existence of Mesaean studs. The riding horses, which appear under the cavalry column (*pēthallu*), are not breed designated.[78]

THE EXPANDING HORSE WORLD

The last half of the first millennium affords a much clearer picture of horse concentrations. To numbers and locations descriptions are now frequently added. Persian cylinder seals, the Apadana frieze at Persepolis, Greek sculpture, and Scythian goldsmiths' work, often influenced by Greece, allow us to see correct conformational points of a variety of horses: the finer but robust Greek animal; the stockier steppe horses of many of the nomadic tribes; Persia's tiny Caspian horse, long thought extinct, but in the last quarter of a century found and rescued from extinction. Also shown from Persia's Apadana frieze are the smaller Lydian tribute horses, and Persia's own massive, muscular, ram-headed Nisaean. From Han China somewhat stylised depictions nevertheless indicate horses of good breeding. Certainly many of the ancient world's equids deserve to be labelled 'quality horses'.

Proof of this quality comes from the Scythian kurgans at Pazyryk of the fifth to third centuries, and from many other deposits of horses in the Russian Steppes. At Pazyryk several types of animal are represented. They range from 12.2½ to 14.3 hh.[79] Several of the taller specimens had a fine golden coat.[80] This brings to mind the Akhal-Teke Turcoman noted above. Littauer records Vitt's idea that, in addition to gelding, good feeding and selective breeding can change the short stocky animals into the larger, finer specimens.[81] While selective breeding and good nutrition allow an animal to reach its genetic potential, with gelded males having certain structural changes in the length of certain bones in the limbs and neck, it will not change the stocky horse into a totally different animal. For example, no matter how many generations pass a Fell pony will not turn into a Thoroughbred horse!

While on the matter of size it is relevant to comment on the height of horses in this period. A Chinese court official of the first century AD wrote that Ferghana horses were 'all of 7 chi in height [63.66 in (161cm) = 15.3½ hh]'. A Chinese document of the tenth century AD said 'official horses were still of the stock of Ferghana which was extremely large'.[82] Couple this with the Ferghana rock drawings mentioned earlier, and it suggests that this region – and spilling outwards to what used to be called Turkestan, but now comprises many of the old Soviet, and independent states of Uzbekistan, in which lies Ferghana and its old capital of Andijan, Tajikistan, Kyrgyzstan and Turkmenistan – had long bred a superior blood horse whose dispersal was augmented by the migrations of the steppe peoples who availed themselves of these horses, in addition to their stockier steppe ponies.[83]

THE NISAEAN HORSE

In modern texts concerning ancient Persia's cavalry the Nisaean horse is nearly always mentioned. So far, to the best of my knowledge, specifics about the breed have not been ascertained. There are many references to it in ancient works: Herodotus, Strabo, Oppian, Nemesian, Diodorus Siculus, Arrian, and Ammianus Marcellinus mention it specifically, Xenophon obliquely. Notes on the breed occupy a timespan from the fifth century BC to the fourth century AD at least.

When describing the army of Xerxes I (486–465) on its way to Greece, Herodotus comments on the 'sacred horses known as Nisayan in magnificent harness, so called because they come from the great Nesaean Plain in Media where horses of unusual size are bred'.[84] On the question of this unusual size, corroboration comes from Sándor Bökönyi, distinguished historian and writer on equestrian archaeology, that he saw remains of about 16 hh in an Achaemenid context.[85] The second-century AD poet Oppian rated the Nisaean 'the most beautiful, gentle to ride, and obedient to the bit and [unusually] with a small head'.[86] However, the Nisaean horses on the Apadana frieze have fairly large ram (convex) heads, but this could be a difference of appreciation of certain equine traits from the ancient to the modern world. Arrian terms them the 'royal breed of Nisaea'.[87]

Although the exact location of Nisaya in the Nisayan Plain, where these horses were raised, is not delineated, it is approximately five to six days' journey south of Ecbatana (Hamadan) for infantry, less for mounted men. It is possible that the breeding grounds were in the Vale of Borigerd, about 90 miles from Ecbatana. The species of clover known as Median grass can be found in that locality.[88] Median grass is today known as alfafa/lucerne, a highly nutritious legume fodder and hay. The protein level of other hays, even those of premium quality, struggle to reach 7 to 10 per cent, with poor hays much less. Alfafa can almost double the level to nearer 20 per cent.[89] The nutritional aspect is significant. Over considerable time superior growth was established, the animals reaching their genetic potential so long as nutrition remained excellent and selective matings were used. (Through improved feeding in England between AD 1710 and 1795 the average weight of sheep and cattle sold at Smithfield Market in London doubled.[90])

To explain this in reverse a look at the Spanish Andalucian and the American Mustang is pertinent. The horses landed in the Americas by the Spaniards in the late fifteenth, sixteenth and seventeenth centuries AD were initially quality stock. By royal *cedula* (decree), especially after cavalrymen had been found guilty of substituting *casta distinguida* horses for low-cost inferior mounts, no low-grade animals were allowed out of Spain. With escapees going feral in America, over the following centuries the size and good qualities of the original stock diminished to the 14 hh or so stature of the average mustang. They reverted in type to one of the Andalucian's primitive ancestors, the Sorraia, from the area in Spain bounded by the Rivers Sor and Raia.[91]

This process could have happened to the Nisaean breed raised out of its pasture-rich Median homeland, if the finer-bred Armenian horses Xenophon encountered on his 'Persian Expedition' were Nisaean or part

Nisaean.[92] However, the geographer Strabo (*c.* first century BC) tells us that Armenia *also* bred Nisaean horses, which were not inferior to those of Media.[93] Xenophon, an astute horseman, would have been far more perspicacious over breed differences than Strabo, who wrote largely from information acquired at second hand. There is the strong possibility that both men were accurate as Nisaean horses were the prerogative of Persia's royalty and nobility, and Armenia, when known as Urartu, had long been famous for its horses. Armenia was no doubt home to several breeds, the Nisaean being introduced there, if not initially at least with greater concentrations during the Median and Persian eras. By the time the Medes sacked Nineveh in 612 they must have brought the Manneans and the Urarteans in Armenia under their control.[94] From the Assyrian records we know that both these countries had a wealth of equestrian expertise. The Nisaean is shown on the Apadana frieze as massive bodied, ram-headed, muscular and somewhat stocky. With the mixing of the different strains available from all these equestrian cultures – Luristan, Media, Armenia (Urartu) and Mannea – backed by centuries of expertise in selecting stock and improving offspring, the fertile Median Plain was able to produce a very superior horse. It was also able to maintain the huge numbers reportedly grazing on the plains, although the numbers given could be highly suspect. Strabo gives us 50,000 mares.[95] Herodotus, according to Arrian said 150,000, but Alexander the Great saw 'no more than 50,000 as most of them had been stolen'.[96]

NORTH AFRICA

The first written record of horses from Libya comes from the inscriptions of Pharaoh Merenptah (variously ascribed to 1223–1213, 1235–1227).[97] Horses are also mentioned being driven by the Garamantes of Libya, in Herodotus' *Histories*.[98] Work by French and Italian archaeologists, especially that of Henri Lhote who conducted investigations in the 1930s and again in the 1950s, discovered a wealth of animal pictures and carvings in the Sahara, the Fezzan, and the Tassili, including over 200 of horses and chariots, and many of riders.[99] The equestrian pictures are dated no earlier than between 1500 and 1000.[100] The chariot depictions show distinct affinities with Mycenaean art, and tie in with the arrival in Cyrenaica in the late thirteenth century of immigrants from Crete, and Achaeans and Dorians from the Balkans, with their horses and chariots. These mingled with the Libyans, and together they advanced against the Delta, where they were defeated by Merenptah at the Battle of Perire. The spoils included horses and chariots of the Libyan chief, Mereyey.[101]

Lhote considers that the Mycenaean immigrants were the first importers of horses into the Sahara.[102] This may be so for the Sahara, but there is strong evidence that horses were already present in Africa, albeit still probably in the wild state. Research conducted by Spanish hippologist Dr d'Andrade almost conclusively proves that Spain's Sorraia was also the primitive ancestor of the North African Berber horse (the Barb). The Sorraia entered North Africa from Spain as early as 10,000 BC, or even earlier, settling into the area that now constitutes Morocco, Algeria and Tunisia.[103] It may be that the new immigrants were the ones to teach the indigenous peoples the art of equestrianism.

ARABIA

Many theories have been offered about the ancestors of the Arabian horse, but there is no firm agreement on this. However, there are references to horses in Arabia, if not necessarily horses of Arabian breed. Some people quote Strabo when maintaining that Arabia lacked horses in the ancient period under discussion. The quote used, though, is only a partial one as he did say that Nabatea had no horses, but it did have mules! He then goes on to give a confused tale of horses having been driven out of Arabia and eventually ending up in Persia.[104] At one time Arabia did have horses, as fossilised remains of them have been found in eastern Arabia, and further research was conducted by the Palaeontology Department of the British Museum.[105] The tantalising, possibly unanswerable question arising from this find, is, did these prehistoric specimens have any evolutionary impact on the horses of the ancient world?

FURTHER EQUINE DIVERSITY

The above by no means covers every area which fielded *equus caballus* in antiquity. Other examples will be met with as the wars and changing political scenes unfold down the centuries; but this chapter does open up the huge territory over which antiquity's horses ranged.

CHAPTER 5

Choosing and Training the Warhorse

The prime requisite when choosing a horse was, and is, soundness in wind and limb. The only detailed 'ideal horse' description from our period is that of Xenophon. From the Roman era there is a clutch of descriptions, many of which are so similar that plagiarism is likely. However, although written in Roman times many of these stemmed from works of Greek veterinarians and other authors; there are certainly echoes from Xenophon's works to be seen.

The basic correct conformation of a horse has changed little throughout history, as it is only a question of good proportions and symmetry that enable a horse to function adequately. The better the conformation the better the ability to perform. To this must be added a temperament that is amenable enough to be directed by handler, driver or rider. Of course there are differences, but these are type and/or breed orientated. The *basic* proportions remain constant. For instance, weak hocks or pasterns are to be avoided whatever the type, as are long backs, poor shoulders, and so on.

With few exceptions, Xenophon's criteria for a good warhorse are still relevant for any good modern saddle horse. It is also significant that the Assyrian reliefs, many of which are in the British Museum, dating from as early as the ninth century, show many of Xenophon's ideals. This suggests that although he wrote down his advice, knowledgeable breeders had long known what went into producing an animal that functioned best under physical and mental stress. Greek sculpture also shows many representations of good equine conformation.

Because it is clear which is Xenophon's advice, and which is the modern explanation, constant distinction has not been made between the two when describing equine anatomy and some of its faults.

XENOPHON'S IDEAL HORSE

Xenophon mention the salient points, from the ground up. The hooves should have thick horn and be high and hollow to keep the frog off the ground, and on impact they should sound like 'cymbals'. Low hooves were to be avoided. Pasterns should slope and be springy. 'Upright pasterns jar the rider' and are 'apt to get inflamed'. Too sloping a pastern allowed damaging contact on rough ground. The shank (cannon bone) should be strong and clean. If fleshy, 'over hard ground the "shanks" veins would become varicose, the legs swell, and the flesh recede, and often the back sinew gives way and the horse becomes lame'. Xenophon is describing a bowed or ruptured tendon which is the result of a severe wrench. It renders the horse useless for many months, and often leaves the horse permanently impaired and unfit for further strenuous work. Too sloping a pastern often predisposes a horse to this rupture. The knees should be supple, the forearms substantial, the chest deep and broad to allow the limbs to be free of interference. A base-narrow horse can 'interfere', that is, one hoof can clip the other, and in some extreme cases 'scalp' the lower limbs.

The neck should have no thick muscle underneath, and should have a clean throatlatch. These faults would have made the horse a 'stargazer' and harder to control, and because his gaze was directed upwards more prone to tripping or stumbling. Xenophon notes that a good neck position 'helps guard the rider, and allows the horse to see properly in front of him'. A high neck carriage may have guarded the rider in close contact manoeuvres, but for missile weapon usage a lower head carriage would have been better as it gave a clearer sighting.

The head should be small, dry (that is, bony), with small ears and small equal jaws. It should flex at the poll which should be wide. A wide poll, raised crest and wider neck are marks of an entire. The polls of geldings and mares are noticeably narrower, and necks usually have a less marked crest. The nostrils should be thin, wide and flaring. Xenophon appreciated enhanced respiration and a semblance of fierceness. The clean throatlatch also aided good respiration, vital for both warhorses and racehorses.

The description of the body is what we would recognise as a short-coupled horse with wide, strong loins, a well-sprung ribcage, and without a gross belly. 'All these parts, if firm [that is, fit] would ensure speed in the horse.' The hindquarters should be broad, the hind legs set well apart: 'this will enable him to "gather himself in"'. Xenophon is describing the levade, which was the favoured way of showing the enemy being trampled. From the levade a warhorse could spring, turn in a confined space, spin so he always faced the enemy, and also launch an aggressive lunge and/or strike with forefeet and teeth. Xenophon said the hindlegs and hocks should be similar to the forearms: sinewy, strong, and with sloping pasterns. The stones (testicles) should be small. Xenophon states the cannon bone which grows least is an indicator of size in the mature horse. It can still be used as a rough guide to mature height.

Two points relevant to saddleless cavalry are that a high wither and a 'double back' were highly desirable. The high wither helped a rider keep in the proper 'sitting place' and the 'double back' meant a broad back with pads of muscle either side of the spine. A narrow, bony back would have been very uncomfortable, even painful, and would have given a very insecure seat, further exacerbated if it was also combined with a low wither.

Xenophon is correct in warning against a 'low hoof', that is, a shallow hoof, as this is more prone to stone bruising. Most of the terrain that the ancient world's horses manoeuvred over would have been stony, dry, sandy or mountainous – all abrasive conditions. Thick horn abrades more slowly. As a hoof grows between ¼ in and ½ in per month a shelly-hooved horse would have been useless. However, Xenophon is wrong about keeping the frog off the ground. The frog is designed to cushion impact.

A small, light head and refined neck allowed the horse to better balance himself. A coarse, heavy head puts a horse on the forehand which in turn makes him a bad mover.[1]

SEX OF WARHORSES

Most warhorses were entires, but there were exceptions. All the Egyptian and Near Eastern depictions show stallions. Among nomadic peoples it was common throughout history to geld colts. The Pazyryk tomb horses were all gelded.[2] Strabo, among others, comments on Scythians and Sarmatians who had 'the peculiarity' of gelding their horses to make them easier to manage.[3] There is evidence across a wide timespan that some peoples used mares. A soldier in the army of Tuthmose III captured and dispatched a mare that the Prince of Kadesh had sent out to disrupt the chariot stallions of the Egyptian army. During the political and military upheavals of the Amarna period, many of the vassal rulers of Syria and Palestine wrote to Amenhotep III (*c.* 1386–1349) and Akhenaton (1350–1334) for military assistance. Biridiya of Megiddo appealed for help to Egypt in his quarrels against Lab'ayu, Prince of Shechem, a bandit raider. Biridiya's 'mare' was shot from under him in an engagement against Lab'ayu, forcing him to alight and ride in a chariot with Yahdata, who was killed in the fight. This also suggests that possibly riding, even if not common, was used by the military as mare is in the singular. Or maybe only one part of the chariot team was crippled?[4]

The Assyrians denigrated the use of mares in war. Two references from the Assyrian annals concern Urartu. Tiglath-Pileser III crushed an

Urartean revolt and Sarduri of Urartu (753–735) fled on a mare. In the eighth year of Sargon II's reign he captured 260 of the Urartean elite royal cavalry, and Ursa (Rusa II, 735–714) fled on a mare, much to the Assyrian's derision.[5]

CHARIOT TRAINING

Hunting

Kikkuli of Mitanni outlines the training of chariot horses, and although he did not specify this was a training for war, sport, other than hunting, was then – and continued to be, until horses ceased being used in cavalry regiments – one of the ways of getting horses mentally and physically fit for war.

The main psychological factor in the ancient hunting field was fear of attack from an enraged hunted animal. If the team of horses did not panic and bolt in proximity to a bull, lion, leopard or boar, but stood up to a charge, it would have been suitable for the chariot corps. A golden patera of the fifteenth or fourteenth century depicts the King of Ugarit hunting. While he shoots antelope, a bull is charging his chariot, its head lowered and horns too close for comfort.[6]

The Assyrian kings delighted in proving their own and their horses' courage out hunting. Tiglath-Pileser I boasted of killing 800 lions from his chariot. Adad Nirari II hunted on foot and in his chariot, outdoing his predecessor and overcoming a multitude of ferocious animals, 'lions, charging bulls, elephants on the rush, wild oxen, boars and crocodiles'.[7]

KIKKULI'S DISTANCES, SPEEDS AND ENDURANCE

There are strong similarities between the *Manual of Kikkuli* and his *Training Texts*. Both illustrated daily regimes for getting chariot warhorses fit. The regimes can be likened to modern endurance horse training, and some sections resemble interval training. Some of the practices are reprehensible.

Kammenhuber has translated one section[8] as a stint of about 44 miles trotted in one night, and both she and her reviewer Guterbock regard the distance covered in one section to be impossible. However, Guterbock, disagreeing with her translation, considered it should be that distance spread over seven nights. He also thought it impossible for a horse to gallop (canter) continuously for 12½ miles.[9] Both distances at the noted gaits and speeds are possible. Winning speeds for recent 100-mile endurance rides in one day are in excess of 10 mph. The minimum permitted average speed is 5 mph. Admittedly there are veterinary inspection halts every 25 miles. The trot is the main gait used, with considerable cantering, and very little walking.[10] In the depths of the winter of AD 1241 Mongol armies moved through the Carpathian Mountains in the invasion of Europe covering 60 miles per day, and Russian records show that a Kazakh horse covered 66 miles in 4½ hours travelling over desert terrain. Another Kazakh horse covered 33 miles in 1 hour 58 minutes.[11]

Chariot horses performed mostly on level plains. When pursuing the rebelling Urzana of Musasir, Sargon II used a single chariot and 1,000 cavalry. He transferred to horseback when the way became steep and too narrow; his chariot was hauled up on ropes.[12]

Kammenhuber refers to Kikkuli's slow speed as trot, the fast speed as gallop. Guterbock also refers to trot and gallop, but gives other translators' variations of walk and trot for the slow speed, and gallop for the fast speed, as well as a fast speed which could be any fast trot or gallop. He states these are based on 'the three paces of horses nowadays considered normal', that is, walk, trot and gallop. There were/are four normal paces. He omits canter, a three-beat gait; gallop is four-beat. He notes the original text distinguished between slow(er) and fast(er).[13]

In early equestrianism, some horses possessed gaits in addition to, or instead of, the 'normal' gaits. These were the four-beat gaits of slow gait, faster rack, and the running walk. All have identical hoof placement sequence but differences in rhythm and/or speed, extension, or height of hoof above the ground. Hrozny suggests the gaits used by Kikkuli's horses were the gallop and the amble,[14] a four-beat gait which could have been one of the noted four-beat gaits (other than walk or gallop) according to the speed, action and hoof elevation with which it was performed. In soft going these gaits can appear to be the lateral two-beat pace. On a hard surface the difference can be seen, and more importantly, can be heard.[15] To this day the descendants of the ancient warhorse breeds of India, the Marwari and the Kathiawari, execute these smooth four-beat gaits (although going by Indian names) in addition to walk, trot, canter and gallop. The Marwari gaits equate with slow gait and rack, that of the Kathiawari with the four-beat running walk.[16] These points are important in understanding the locomotor mechanics of horses. I would suggest many chariot and ridden horses used these four-beat gaits, particularly in view of the early 'donkey seat' perched far back on the horse's loins. The transitions from walk, to canter, to gallop could have been very unseating, whereas the four-beat gaits are supremely comfortable and allow even an inexperienced rider to maintain his equilibrium on a horse's back.

DAILY TRAINING

The *Manual of Kikkuli*[17] is more comprehensive and seems closer to a training schedule than the manual specifically on training. It covers 184 days of incremental exercise. As we shall never know the precise gaits used by chariot horses I prefer to use moderate speed and fast(er) speed, as slow speed suggests walk, or maybe a 'slow gait' (Hrozny's amble).

THE IKU AND RELATED DISTANCES IN THE KIKKULI TEXT

There were two main measurements used in the Kikkuli text(s): the *danna* and the *iku*. There were 100 *iku* to the *danna*. The interpretation of the length of the *iku* is crucial to estimating the actual distances travelled by Kikkuli's horses in training. There has been wide divergence over the linear estimate for the *iku*. Kammenhuber uses the Mesopotamian mile of 10.7 km for one *danna*, and 107 m for one *iku*. Hrozny uses the Neo-Assyrian/Babylonian mile of a 6 km *danna* and 60 m for one *iku*. Potratz uses 5 km for one *danna*, and 50 m for one *iku*.[18] The first four days of introductory training taken from Kammenhuber's translation are given as:

DAY 1. Three sessions of: 3 *danna* moderate, total of 17 *iku* fast
                              1   "   "   "   7 " "
                              1   "   "   "   17 " "
DAY 2. Two sessions of   2½ "   "   "   17 " "
                       and leading back 3 *danna*
                              1   "   "
DAY 3. Two sessions of   2   "   "
                              1   "   "
DAY 4. One severe session 1   "   "   return of 1 *danna*, 20 *iku* fast.

Using any of the above measurements, the introductory phase of training unfit horses taken up from pasture would have been excessive, and beyond the comprehension of any horseman, ancient or modern, as a means of sensible training. What it would have done is rapidly weed out any horses that did not possess the toughest physical attributes. In the process of inevitably being discarded as unsuitable, horses would have run the gamut of stress injuries such as muscle strain, tendon ruptures, loss of condition, wind impairment, and hoof breakdown, to name a few. One point on stress should be emphasised: incremental stress is part of training. Undue stress is that placed on a horse not fit enough to sustain it.

Neo-Assyrian, stone reliefs from the palace of Ashurnassiripal II, Nimrud (Kalhu), northern Iraq, 883–869 BC. Above: 3-horse chariot charging into battle: note the use of the chariot as a platform for infantry (mounted foot archers) to shoot high to avoid crippling valuable booty horses. Below: the king hunting bulls, with the quarry lying under the horses' hooves. The king has turned either to speak to following cavalrymen, now riding independently, or, more likely, has just thrust a lance into the bull's withers. Note the similarities between war and hunting tactics. (© British Museum)

Stone reliefs from the palace of Sennacherib at Kouyunjik (Nineveh) depicting the siege of Lachish (Tell el-Duweir) and Sennacherib's fortified camp, chariotry and cavalry. Excellent depiction of horses' conformation, and of a 2-horse chariot. The proportions of the cavalrymen on the horses indicate sizeable horses of c. 15 hh. As the proportions of the horses' anatomy are so accurate the size relation of man to horse is believable. Note also that the draught (chariot) and cavalry horses are identical. Cavalryman's panoply includes spear, short sword, and bow; men are armoured with short tunic, greaves and helmet. (© British Museum)

Neo-Assyrian stone relief from the central palace of Tiglath-Pileser III, Nimrud (Kalhu), northern Iraq, c. 730–727 BC, showing the reversion to a 2-horse, 3-man chariot, now with much heavier wheels. (© British Museum)

Neo-Assyrian, stone relief from the palace of Ashurnasirpal II, Nimrud (Kalhu), northern Iraq, 883–859 BC. Inside Ashurnasirpal's camp: the horses are tethered at a feeding trough, and a groom uses a brush, or more likely a scraper, to clean the horse. Note the stocky conformation. (© British Museum)

Opposite: *Ashurbanipal, c. 640, from the northern palace at Nineveh. This is an exceptional carving with instructive details. The horses are of stocky, well-bred conformation with muscling and tendons clearly defined. Bridle details are excellent, showing the bit attachment, protection from the poll pad and from the strip running down the centre of the horse's face. The reins are a short loop over the neck, which prevented them falling to the ground. The tension on the reins from the pompom allowed the rider the use of both hands on weaponry, while still keeping the horse under control. The reins appear of a heavy plait, maybe metal-covered to prevent them being cut by a sword. The riders are seated well forward in an excellent position going with the horses' movement. The weaponry is comprehensive: the king has a sword and bow and arrow, but no quiver. The rider behind has quiver but no bow and appears to be holding an arrow ready to come alongside the king's horse with arrow offered to his master. The following spearman appears to be holding the rein of a a horse (following behind as a reserve mount for the king?). Note the smaller pompom on the reins of non-archers.*

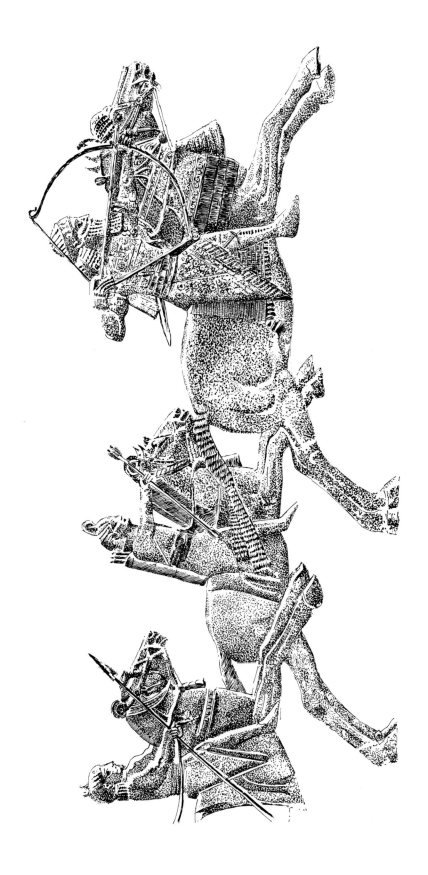

Bronze figure of a horse and rider from the Achaemenid period (5th–4th century BC, and possibly from Egypt) showing Persian heavy cavalryman. The horse has the heavy ram head typical of the Nisaean breed. His equipment shows a vestigial saddle over a fringed saddle cloth with breast and haunch retention. (© British Museum)

Gold model chariot from the Oxus Treasure, Achaemenid Persian, 5th–4th century BC from the region of Takhoi-Kuvad, Tadjikistan. Persian 4-horse hitch. Although the miniature scale of the piece makes it difficult to attempt categorising the horses, it appears to show the ancient Caspian horse (of small pony size, c. 12 hh) of Iran; but it is doubtful these were powerful enough for war; and the ram (convex) head is not typical of the Caspian, but of the Nisaean. Viewed from a certain angle a ninth spoke is visible, extending from the hub – possibly an instance of the Persian scythe chariot. (© British Museum)

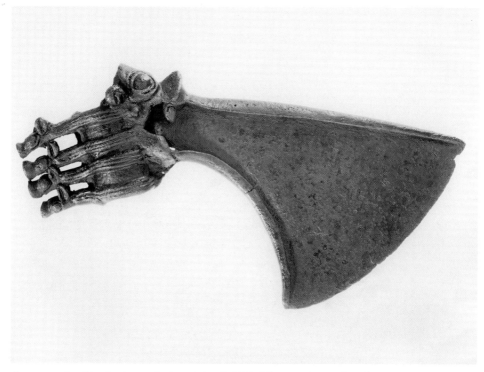

Bronze axe head in the shape of a horse's head, 10th–7th centuries BC, from Luristan, western Iran. A beautiful example of Luristani metallurgy. Luristan had a very strong equestrian culture. (© British Museum)

Comb from the Solokha Barrow, late 5th/early 4th century BC, depicting Greek cavalryman in full armour assailed by two Scythians, with, below, an equine casualty. Considering the small size of the comb, the Scythian workmanship is exquisite, the details accurate and the quality horses conformationally correct. (© The State Hermitage Museum, St Petersburg)

Only the toughest horses would have entered full training. There was then a three-week period of rest, grazing, good stable care, multiple washings down (translated as submergings, which does not make good horse sense), anointings, and careful feeding. On the fourth rest day the horse was blanketed and put in a very warm stable to sweat, and much needed salts were replaced via a drink of saltwater and crushed malt.[19] On day 24 the horse was led 10 *iku*, and the next day put out to grass. Then for each of ten days it was led for 2 *danna* at a moderate pace. On day 36 it was led 2 *danna*, and in the evening hitched up and driven moderately for 30 *iku*. Day 37 was a moderate drive for ½ *danna* with no galloping, then the horse was turned out to grass. From the 37th to the 46th day the horse was driven 2 *danna* a day at a moderate pace. Thereafter, training slowly escalated. The 120th day was demanding, with 7 moderate *danna*, finishing with a sprint of 8 *iku*. As would be expected, work then temporarily decreased before a very hard stint on nights 131, 132 and 133, of 7, 3 and 7 moderate *danna*, ending each nightly session with a sprint of 10 *iku*. By day 145 moderate work decreased, faster work increased, on some days to well over ½ *danna*, on others to almost ½ *danna*. Day 178 was the toughest with five sessions totalling 75½ km, or approximately 47½ miles, which although not the longest distance covered in twenty-four hours, was by far the most strenuous with 46.759 km done at high speed, of which one fast stint alone was 1 *danna*, 80 *iku*, that is, 19.26 km, or over 12 miles.[20]

It should be remembered that the end result was not to win an endurance race but to train horses for war and hunting, which, although requiring very fit horses is not so demanding. The cumulative stress, and the inordinate mileage covered, if using any of the above three distance equivalents, would have destroyed any horse. Or as top endurance ride winner and California veterinary surgeon Richard Barsaleau, DVM, said in his foreword to my *The Endurance Horse*, 'A horse should be used, but not used up.'[21]

One more point. Such continual distances covered without the use of horseshoes, which were 2,000 years in the future, would have abraded the hooves faster than regrowth could have repaired horn loss.

However, there is a far more rational regime if one accepts the reasoning of Melchert, who sought outside the Kikkuli texts for the length of the *iku*, and who also consulted well-known equestrians. Among these was internationally renowned veterinary surgeon and author, Dr Mathew Mackay-Smith, DVM, who was a prodigious endurance ride winner on his black mare Sorya, and also many times a judge on American endurance rides.[22] Melchert has established that the *iku* measured about 15 m, and the *danna* 1,500 m. Working out the distances travelled with these measurements we have an entirely different and more sensible training regime, and one that could have brought the horses on slowly and without undue initial stress.[23] Melchert also picks up on inconsistencies in other translations. Taking day 1 from the Kammenhuber translation of 3 *danna* out at moderate speed, and 7 *iku* fast, the return journey is ignored in the calculations, but the horse had to return the same distance which he went out,[24] plus do another 7 fast *iku*.

The Kikkuli texts must have had a widespread distribution, a fairly long 'shelf life', and an influence on equestrianism far beyond Hattusas. A Middle Assyrian text, and other minor texts dating to around the time of the reigns of Adad Nirari I (1307–1275), Shalmaneser I (1274–45), and Tukulti Ninurta I (1244–1208), are clearly patterned on those of Kikkuli. The basic structures in training and stable are in many respects similar. The most marked difference is that in the Assyrian regime the work was much less severe. The frequent training sessions were much shorter, mostly of 7 and 10 *iku*, and worked on a purpose-built track.[25] However, the surviving Assyrian text may not describe the full regime as the Kikkuli texts do, which start with an unfit horse and continue through to full fitness.

Although some of the Hittite training was also conducted on a track, it is hard to think that the extended distances were undertaken in this fashion, and the way the daily schedules were written out suggests they were conducted in rather more open territory, as circular or oblong track work is only mentioned infrequently towards the end of the training months.[26] The track work done in Kikkuli's regime varied as to facilities, since the *wasanna* (track) could be anything from 5 *iku* long by 2½ *iku* wide, that is, a total distance of 15 *iku* for the whole track, to the other dimensions of 4.3 *iku* by 5 *iku*, and 6 *iku* by 4 *iku*.[27] Modern dressage arenas come in two sizes, 40 × 20 m, and, for the higher level competitions, 60 × 20 m. Even with the smallest Hittite or Assyrian track of less than twice the size of the smaller dressage arena, there would be scant room to work at speed a constantly turning chariot team to its horses' best capabilities. Too excessive a use of track work would have put a considerable and insupportable strain on the limb joints, and on the neck as well with the crude yoke harness used at that time, especially using the short *iku* of 15 m, as the turns would have been that much tighter.

CARE THROUGHOUT TRAINING

Throughout training, feeding and watering was carefully regulated. Small amounts, measured in handfuls, were fed several times a day between workouts and last thing at night. More rarely, amounts by the bucketful were fed. Although Kikkuli knew how much by weight was fed, there is no way of accurately assessing ration weights. The main feed components, other than grass, were wheat, barley, groats, chaff, long hay and chopped straw. On some days, feed and water were denied. Frequently water was denied, especially after a heavy workout. In one way this makes sense, as free access to water immediately after very hard work can cause colic and/or founder if it is too cold. Denying water for considerable time, as is implied, was bad management and must have led to dehydration and thickening of blood plasma. Occasionally salt and malt were added to water. Most washings were with ordinary water, some with warm, some with cold. Many were at the river, to which the horse was often led. Cold-water washing can dramatically lower a horse's core temperature in excessive heat conditions, allowing a more rapid heart rate recovery after exercise; although it is to be doubted that the clinical reason was understood, it is probable that the results were seen to be advantageous and thus the practice adopted. Kikkuli advised blanketing after washings. The horse was frequently anointed with oil, a custom common to the era. If accompanied by massage this would have helped take the kinks out of sore muscles. The excessive number of washings must have removed the coat's natural oils. A stabled horse was often muzzled and tied up. This could have been to prevent straw-bed eating, or to prevent biting his equine neighbour, which would also have been his team mate. For the daily caring and washings muzzling was not indicated, so the anti-biting device was the most likely reason. Stallions in particular are given to nipping, which if unchecked can lead to very harmful biting.

Perhaps without realising the clinical reasons for some of the practices Kikkuli was on the right track, but some practices that should have occurred regularly were only randomly utilised. Maybe in dictating, or even writing himself, Kikkuli neglected to include regular items that for him and his contemporaries would have been commonplace. A practice at complete variance with modern care was keeping a fit but resting horse confined to stables for several days with no chance of exercise. In light of the very strenuous workouts this was very detrimental to the horse's well-being. It must have caused azoturia on many occasions, a condition of muscle damage that very fit horses suddenly confined and without ration reduction are prone to. Again, there is the possibility that the animals were turned out to gentle exercise in a paddock, but such was not recorded.[28]

CAVALRY – THE SOURCES

Xenophon, an early source for cavalry training, gives a lot of common-sense advice. He had a sympathetic approach to horses. Kautilya gives details of many warhorse manoeuvres.

Xenophon advised the would-be cavalryman to put his potential warhorse with a horsebreaker/trainer, with a contract as to what he expected from the breaker. Prior to entering the trainer's yard Xenophon stressed the horse should have been well handled and should associate man with kindness, food, water, relief from flies, and have been reassured in alarming situations.[29] The purchaser of a trained horse should have ensured that it would work solo and be willing to leave the group, tested, obedient (even if struck, as a disobedient horse could have jeopardised the cavalryman's safety); that it be gentle, reasonably fast, able to jump ditches and walls, climb and descend from banks and work up and downhill and on a slope; and not be hardmouthed or 'barn sour', and thus bolt for home. Once the horse's spirit and soundness had been tested, any refinements could be taught later. Timid and skittish horses, and those who were aggressive to other horses, were to be avoided.[30]

Two further tactics to elicit the best from a warhorse, indeed any horse, were never to deal with the horse in anger, and to be ready to reassure him when he was fearful.[31]

The cavalryman's general horsemanship was addressed, highlighting the areas that most concerned his and his horse's performance in order to gain the utmost usefulness in attack, and the most safety in retreat. Xenophon insisted on an upright seat to ensure efficient weapon usage. The rider's lower leg was to hang loosely down. A stiffened leg was likely to get broken if struck. The rider's upper body was to be supple to help maintain his seat if pushed or pulled.[32] This position enabled a rider to move with his horse, feel the horse's back muscle movements and be forewarned of the horse's next move.[33] At canter, leading with the left leg was recommended, but no reason is given. However, there were times when taking the right lead would have been preferable. In the rapid turns that are advocated, a left lead with a right turn could have brought the horse down. Circles and directional changes are proposed, to teach the horse to turn on either rein. The career (the gallop on the straight) is also advised. It was essential when turning from the career to collect the horse, as otherwise too rapid a turn could have brought down both horse and rider, particularly on slippery ground. Xenophon often omits to give the reasons for specific movements, and the mishaps that could have occurred if the rider did not adhere to his principles. These were no doubt understood by his readers and therefore not considered necessary to explain, but today, with engine horsepower replacing real horses, modern readers may not appreciate the equestrian implications. Immediately after the turn at the end of the career the horse was to spring away, because in war this manoeuvre was used in pursuing or retreating.[34] This manoeuvre resembles the Celtic *toloutegon* described by

Arrian,[35] as well as the modern *rollback* of American stock seat horsemanship. Other manoeuvres were to gallop the horse fast, stop suddenly, then launch straight away into a gallop. Xenophon affirms these manoeuvres would have been necessary in war.[36]

Riding in the hunt developed a firm seat on the horse as he negotiated all manner of terrain.[37] Hunting, then and now, teaches the horse to think for himself, even when the rider does not. In vigorous one-to-one confrontations Xenophon advised using button-tipped javelins. Opposing horses worked flank to flank, each rider endeavouring to unseat his adversary. At the critical moment the attacked man (or in practice the one who had the momentary advantage) spurted away, pulling his opponent with him and off his horse.[38] Such manoeuvres taught a horse to be unafraid of a cast weapon if in practice it did him no harm, and not to flinch at a rider fighting on his back. Above all, from the rider's point of view, it taught each one to control his own body, and at the same time direct and control his horse.

Regarding temperament, the advice was not to get too high mettled an animal, nor one too sluggish.[39] The subtle way of managing too high spirited a horse takes so much time that in the midst of battle, where there was no time for subtlety, such a horse would have been a liability. Tardy responses from a sluggish animal would also have endangered the rider.

INDIA

Kautilya, a famous Brahman of the late fourth/early third century, is credited with overthrowing the Nanda Dynasty and placing Maurya Chandragupta on the Indian throne. Megasthenes, ambassador to India of the Syrian King, Seleucus Nicator, incorporated some of Kautilya's work into his own.[40]

Kautilya wrote just after Alexander the Great's death, when Alexander's empire was fragmenting among his former generals, of whom Seleucus Nicator was one. Alexander and Seleucus brought much Greek influence to India, an influence reflected in some of the best horses of Kautilya's time. He lists those of Kambhoja (Tibet), Sindhu (Sind), Aratta (south of the Hydaspes/Jhelum (that is, the Punjab)) and Vanaya.[41] The links between India and the Seleucids encouraged trade. The Greek kingdom of Bactria would have continued to supply quality horses into India, as it had to Alexander's cavalry.[42]

Although Kautilya's *Arthasastra* was written right at the end of the period covered by this work, from the equestrian content it must be taken as a distillation of what was current at, and for a considerable time prior to, Alexander's era. By the mid-sixth century the Persian Empire extended to India, and it is to be expected that both Persian and Indian equestrianism interacted well before the *Arthasastra* was written. The expertise noted by Kautilya would have evolved over many generations, if not centuries, as did most equestrian disciplines. Many of the warhorse manoeuvres remained in use up to the Mughal era. Some manoeuvres that have been credited to the European Renaissance horsemasters had already had an ancient history in India.[43] Due to their conformation and capabilities, and to the uses to which a cavalry horse was put in the ancient world, it is to be expected that movements similar to those found in the *Arthasastra* were also employed by the cavalry of other nations. The difference is that India's literati took the trouble to record the details for future generations. Kautilya's work gives a comprehensive account of the complete cavalry set-up in one of history's most exciting civilisations.

The *Arthasastra* is a political work on governmental procedures and military matters. So detailed are these that every aspect of equestrianism can be extrapolated. These include breeding, feeding, training and deploying chariot and cavalry horses, and their duties en route, in camp, and in battle. Chariot horses receive the least attention. Nevertheless, their importance is obvious as their training was closely supervised by the king.[44] His safety was guarded, in that he was not to ride in a chariot or mount a horse or elephant until his hereditary driver or rider had first tested the safety of the respective animal.[45]

THE INDIAN WARHORSE

The Superintendent of Horses kept a register of all horses under government control. The state carried on a lively trade buying and selling horses, and acquiring them as booty. Government/royal stud farms raised youngstock until maturity at four or five years old, when they embarked on their preparation for war. Horses were graded according to breed, type, size and temperament. Quality was determined as best, middle and ordinary. Size was measured by *angulas* (three-quarters of an inch). Each part of the animals' anatomy was measured:

> Grade 1. stood at 15 hh, and had a barrel measurement of 100 *angulas* (75 in).
> Grade 2. stood at 14.2½ hh, and had a barrel measurement 5 per cent less than grade 1.
> Grade 3. stood at 14.1¾ hh, and had a barrel measurement 5 per cent less than grade 2.

Temperament was graded as 'furious, mild, stupid or slow'. This decided if they were suited to war or riding (non-military), the latter presumably of the slow, stupid category. Only stallions were used in war. Those rendered unfit due to age, disease, or hardship of war (that is, injury or debility), were 'allowed to cross steeds [mares] belonging to citizens'.

War training consisted of numerous movements, one of which eluded the translator. From a literal translation many dressage movements can be recognised. Others are peculiarly Indian and cannot be related to ordinary (modern) saddle horse movements. Movements such as trotting, galloping, pacing 'like a lion', and 'running and jumping simultaneously', which can only be an elevated bounding sort of progress, are easy to understand. The dressage movements had a utilitarian cavalry function. They were mostly defensive, to be used when the rider was under attack, and/or to make the cavalryman hard to come to grips with, at the same time enabling him to strike with one of the many Indian weapons.

THE MOVEMENTS

The movements and their military applications and explanations were:

1. 'Turning in a circle of a hand in diameter.' This was the canter pirouette: the horse continuously turned to face the enemy, his hind hooves describing a tiny circle, the head, neck, and body being the radius of the circle. This made it difficult for an assailant to strike. The rider's weapons would have cut a lethal swathe as the horse pirouetted.
2. 'Advancing, keeping to the circular movement previously begun.' This was an imperfect pirouette where the hind hooves did not maintain the same turning circle. Unless completely hemmed in a warrior would have moved forward to escape entrapment, at the same time continuing his defensive circular movement.
3. 'Movement of only the front portion of the body.' This was a turn on the haunches. From a military point of view it was similar to the pirouette, but done at a slower pace, with the hind legs describing a small circle, the body moving either right or left according to which rein it was executed on. This movement could be used to avoid an opponent's weapon aimed at the forepart of the horse, or at the rider. It depended for success on the horse responding immediately to the aids.
4. 'Movement of only the hind portion of the body.' This was a turn on the forehand, the opposite of no. 3, where the forelegs described a

small circle, and the body and hindquarters moved around the forehand. Useful for evading a rear or flank attack.

5. 'Movement sideways.' This was a side pass if executed in a straight line across the ground, a full pass if done at a sharp angle, and a half pass if done at a shallow angle. Militarily useful as a defensive action. As most of the instructions to the horse came from the rider's lower leg, it left the weapon hand free.

6. 'Moving with the front part of its body bent.' This was a shoulder in.

7. 'Moving with the hind part of the body bent.' This was a shoulder out.

These were used as suppling exercises. The military application would have been to avoid crippling contact, bending the horse's body out of the line of weapon fall.

In the battle situation of one-to-one fighting all reactions would have had to be very rapid to be effective, and horses needed to be responsive to the touch of the rein on the neck to move them at the rider's command. The indirect rein, not the direct rein, would have been employed.

8. 'Zigzag motion.' This movement could have been used to prevent an enemy getting a sighting or aim on a particular horse or rider.

9. and 10. These were two movements that the literal translation leaves unclear. They were 'Movement using only three legs', and 'Moving by using three legs and two legs alternately'. One can only think they were phases of canter, a three-beat gait where the three-beat motion could clearly be seen on one phase; and on the next phase, to the untutored eye, the horse appeared to be using two legs laterally, as in the pace.

11. 'Moving straight without a rider.' This would have been of use when a rider fell. If the horse swerved, or doubled back, it could have brought chaos among horses moving as a unit in a charge, or in the actual engagement. It could have started a rout.

Many forms of gallop and jumping were used, likened in each instance to a bird or other animal's movement.[46] There is one form of jumping (forward, not over obstacles) that equates with the courbette. The horse elevates his forehand and bounds on his hind legs. In Hindi this is the *Uran*, *Udaan*, or *Oran*, from the Hindi verb *urna*, to fly. It was used in medieval India only when attacking an elephant, and was laced with enormous danger. Its aim was to put the lancer in a position to attack the warriors in the howdah on the elephant's back. Great precision was needed in placing the horse, as war elephants' tusks were armed with swords. For maximum damage the lance thrust was made at the point of highest aerial extension when the speed and power of the horse's leap were harnessed to the attack.[47] In our period India used war elephants, as did the later Persians, and Alexander and Seleucus.

DEPLOYMENT

Distances were measured in *yojanas* (variously given as 4.54 and 5.4 miles). Chariot horses covered 6, 9 or 12 *yojanas* per day; cavalry horses covered 5, 8 or 10 *yojanas* per day.[48] When en route to war, distances were dictated by the size of the army and the terrain. Indian armies have always been huge, and Indian kings travelled with their households, which included the harem with all its appurtenances. Composition of the army included vast numbers of combatants, and an even greater number of servants and animal carers for the horses, bulls, oxen, elephants and camels used in war, plus meat on the hoof, and the trains of the provisioning merchants.

In battle stations each detachment's van was occupied by three groups of chariots, with a similar number on each flank, and the same on each wing, making a total of 45 chariots, to which were added 225 horses and 675 infantry. A similar number of servants (grooms) attended to the war animals. The number of elephants matched that of the chariots. Kautilya called this 'an even array of troops'. He gives nine additional permutations of battle arrays. Only horses in the van were armoured.[49] These specific numbers can only have been the traditional, or maybe the hoped for numbers, and in practice these would have depended on what was currently available.

CAVALRY DUTIES

Many cavalry duties related to reconnaissance, to spy out enemy positions. Cavalry was also used to hold strategic positions, such as river fords, to protect the baggage, and to destroy that of the enemy. They also protected the flank of the army, brought up the rear, and carried and protected the treasury and the princes.

In combat, cavalry was to launch the first attack, attempt to disperse the enemy, trample it down, attack from the rear followed by pursuit of the enemy. It was also detailed to 'containment' (of the enemy?). Chariots were also used to protect the army, and to repel attacks. In battle Kautilya says they were used to break the enemy's line, and when the army dispersed, to round it up. Ostentation and noise were used to put fear into the enemy.[50]

It must be said that cavalry and chariotry were not best suited to some of the tasks devolved upon it from the idealised framework set out. Chariots were not known for success in seizing and abandoning positions in battle, nor was cavalry tailored to seizing and holding the enemy, unless in a ring fence of cavalry horses surrounding small groups of enemy. The unique feature of both arms was mobility, not static duties.

CHAPTER 6

Control Mechanisms

The horse's basic thought processes and instinctive movements have remained the same throughout its period of domestication. Indeed, considering that the horse's evolutionary development is in the region of 50 million years, it would be strange if any drastic change in these processes had taken place in the last 5,000 years, which in the timescale is only a tiny fraction. What has changed, of course, are the uses to which the domesticated horse has been put and the skills it has learned during this time. It was and is an animal of flight, predated upon by man and by large felines. It is remarkable that such an animal's physical capabilities were able to be channelled into the complete opposite, that of attack. To achieve this man had to be able to control and direct the horse. A fact less well understood is that man had to be able to control his own body when driving and riding a horse. Driving meant in particular maintaining balance in a moving vehicle. Riding opened up a wide spectrum of skills.

Nearly all physical training of the horse is by pressures, from the very soft, subtle touch to the sharp use of hand, leg, weight, whip, or spur. Such communications can be delivered in numerous places on a horse's anatomy.

The basic physical control mechanism for all horses consists of tack designed to exert pressure on a horse's head. Another aspect of control is psychological and achieved by gradual repetitive training so that the horse is conditioned to obey with what eventually appears to be automatic responses. In the ancient world both the head controls and the training were frequently so severe that the animals learned that cooperation was the better option. Perhaps the first recorded example of forced obedience is from the time of Tuthmose III. It is inscribed on a stela near the Sphinx at Giza and concerns Crown Prince Amunhotep:

> . . . now when he was [still] a lad, he loved his horses and rejoiced in them. It was a strengthening of the heart to work them, to learn their natures, to be skilled in training them and so enter into their ways. Thutmose ordered 'Let there be given to him the very best horses in my majesty's stable which is in Memphis, and tell him "take care of them. *Instill fear into them*, make them gallop, and handle them if there be *resistance to thee*" [my italics].'[1]

49

Much of the control was induced by fear and pain. Witness to this comes from a variety of punishing bits. Conversely, these did not always achieve the desired control. At Mons Graupius in Scotland, Aulus Atticus was killed when his horse bolted into the enemy ranks.[2] The horse might have panicked and 'run straight through the bit', blindly resorting to flight; alternatively, the buccal pain, instead of restraining him, caused him to bolt. This often happens with horses who are overbitted. Because it is a complex issue, 'Head Control' is explored in detail below.

Early comments on training horses in harness are devoid of almost any understanding of the horse's mind; yet undoubtedly there must have been such an understanding. The only hint is from the Kikkuli text, in which on several occasions the handler is told to reassure his horse (*beruhigt*).[3] However, as this usually comes after work the horse-sense meaning is 'to make much of', a typical cavalry phrase for petting a horse after work. Although most horses can be bullied into cooperation, abused horses never give of their best; cooperation is always the minimum that will be tolerated by its handler, driver or rider. Some abused horses become dangerous rogues.

To some extent chariot horses were able to be pushed forward rather better than early cavalry horses, for two reasons: the coercion came from behind, and the driver was ensconced far more securely in his chariot box than was the early cavalryman on a horse's back.

RIDER POSITION

The early cavalryman had an extremely precarious position, often termed the 'donkey seat', seated towards the loins. In the early centuries of cavalry warfare he lacked a saddle; at best he used a saddlecloth which absorbed sweat and the oil with which warhorses were frequently anointed,[4] thus making the back less slippery.

The military rider's position is illustrated on reliefs and orthostats from the mid-second millennium onwards and shows the progression from 'donkey seat' to balanced seat. Egyptian mounted couriers and archers are seated almost *on* the horse's loins. One fine example is from the fourteenth-century tomb and temple of Horemheb. A tenth-century Aramaean cavalryman, from Tel Halaf in north Mesopotamia, shows a slightly better seat, but still with the weight badly distributed *towards* the loin area; the rider's thighs and lower legs are thrust forward behind the horse's movement, similar to the old hunting seat where the horse's loins area, especially over a fence, was battered.

Assyrian reliefs show this steady progression from early cavalry to the time when, largely because of better horsemanship, it became a more efficient military arm. In Ashurnasirpal II's reign cavalrymen rode in pairs, one rider leading his partner's horse, thus freeing the warrior to use his weapon. At Nimrud the archer is shown insecurely perched on the horse's back, his thighs almost parallel with the horse's topline, his lower legs drawn up, gripping the horse's barrel. The magnificent Balawat Gates, now in the British Museum, show this position remained during Shalmaneser III's reign. By Sargon II's day the rider sat further forward, each cavalryman now able to control his own horse, as shown at Khorsabad. Lancers, javelineers, and archers are shown using a position closer to the modern balanced seat. This enabled the rider to deliver his weapon more accurately. Spearmen/javelineers are depicted with left arms and shoulders drawn back while the lower body remains in a good position. Lancers and other riders not actually launching a weapon ride centrally balanced. At Nineveh Ashurbanipal's archers have their weight more on their thighs as they lean forward from the hips to loose arrows.[5]

RIDER POSITION AND A HORSE'S GAITS

A horse's weight is borne mostly by the forehand. The impulsion comes from the hindquarters. The loin area, under which are the kidneys, and whose only bone is the spine, is the weakest part of the horse's anatomy. Add to this the locomotor means of a variety of gaits and it can be appreciated that a central seat was far more efficient for cavalry, or for any rider.

As discussed in the section on training, there are and were many gaits performed by horses in addition to those considered normal in the Occident. I would suggest that these additional gaits were common to many of the ancient world's chariot and riding horses.[6] At the walk the 'donkey seat' can be adequate. At the two-beat diagonal trot it would be impossible to maintain any sort of balance. The three-beat canter is smoother, and the four-beat gallop the smoothest. The pace, unless executed very fast, rocks a rider from side to side. The slow gait, the rack and the running walk, which can be as fast as a gallop, confer considerable stability to the rider. Pliny the Elder describes Spain's Asturian horses, 'which have not the usual paces in running but a smooth trot straightening the near and offside legs alternately from which they are taught to amble'.[7] The lateral 'trot' described could be either the pace or – because the hoofbeat sequence is so rapid it gives the appearance that the legs on each side move absolutely simultaneously, whereas in fact there is a split second difference in the beat sequence – it could be the slow gait or rack. (For amble substitute rack or running walk.)

Apart from directly controlling the horse, the military rider must have been able to control his own body at any gait in a manner that ensured he was firm on the horse's back. Without such control weapon delivery would have been inefficient.

SADDLE EVOLUTION

Xenophon describes an advance in tack that would have conferred extra stability to a rider:

> Above all, the horse's belly should be protected as being the most vital and the weakest part. It may be protected with the cloth. This cloth must also be of such material and so sewed together as to give the rider a safe seat and not to gall the horse's back.[8]

This does not sound like a mere saddlecloth, but a contoured pad *into* which the rider sat, and extensive enough in length and depth to protect the horse's barrel.

A further advance was seen in saddles of the Pazyryk kurgans in the Altai Mountains. Dating from the fifth to the third centuries, these saddles are illustrated in Rudenko's *Frozen Tombs of Siberia*.[9] They were constructed of two cushions with rigid bow arches to the front and rear of each cushion. The cushions were stitched to a felt underpad, and stuffed to maximum capacity they were reasonably rigid. The addition of wooden spacers both held the cushions apart and prevented them splaying out, so forming a true saddle that stayed clear of the horse's withers. A saddle pressing on a horse's withers will cause abrasion and suppuration, resulting in fistulous withers. This renders the horse temporarily unusable. Possibly Xenophon's cloth was stiff enough to prevent wither damage, as he mentions preventing galling the horse. A felt wall hanging from mound 5 at Pazyryk clearly shows the horse's saddle in use, as well as the breast and haunch attachments used to facilitate keeping the saddle from either slipping forwards or backwards. No girth is apparent but this was possibly hidden by the rider's legs.

The evidence for the development of the true saddle is just outside the period covered by this work, but in the nature of equestrian equipment progression, definitive changes occur slowly, so that although there are examples of true saddles in several cultures from approximately the first century AD, it is more than probable that they, or their earlier prototypes, had been in existence for a considerable time prior to their depictions on carvings and metalware.

Many of the cultures that used cavalry, or were invaded by cavalry, such as the Celtic invasion of Greece in the third century, would have had contacts with or known about the Scythian nomadic horsemen. It was the Scythians whose Altaic tombs provided the saddles noted above. There are also other depictions of Scythians with horses wearing saddles, although seemingly of a pad, rather than one with a hard tree, such as one of the horses on the Chertomlyk vase dating to the fourth century BC. People in contact with these nomads would have learned much of their equestrianism and used similar functional equipment. With the advent of the armoured and heavily armed cavalryman the need for a better form of equipment for staying on a horse's back would have driven experimentation. The Persian armour from Daskyleion in Phrygia described in chapter 10 could not have been attached to a simple saddle cloth. A carpet of Achaemenid design found in mound 5 at Pazyryk[10] has several horses woven into it which are identical in conformation, movement, mane and tail style, with the ridden horse on the far left of the east front of the Apadana frieze and gateway of Xerxes at Persepolis.[11] Talbot Rice is wrong in assigning this equestrian style to Assyria. It is definitely Persian, with the horse of the ram-headed, muscular Nisaean conformation. With such trade and/or cultural exchanges it would be strange if practical aspects of equestrianism were not also disseminated. By the first century AD both Roman and Parthian military were using saddles with front and back horns.[12] During the Chin dynasty (220–207) Chinese cavalry were using saddles with retentive moulding at cantle and pommel, a haunch-breeching strap, and central girth.[13] From the Former Han dynasty (207 BC–AD 9) Sau Ma Chien records General Li Kuan (died 119 BC) ordering his men to dismount and undo their saddles.[14] A 1999 Channel 4 television documentary on Tocharian Mummies of the Tien Shan Mountains showed a well-preserved saddle *reputed* to be from the fourth century AD.

RÉSUMÉ OF SADDLE EVOLUTION

It appears that the true saddle emanated from the nomadic equestrian steppe cultures and spread into the oriental and occidental spheres over several centuries; that is, unless the idea of a true saddle occurred simultaneously to diverse cultures as heavy armoured cavalry became an important military arm. The progression was from saddlecloth to contoured pad, then to stuffed cushions, then to the reinforced front and rear horns of the Roman saddle, and finally to a hard-treed saddle. However, it is difficult to understand why the stirrup took so long to appear in the major cavalry nations of the ancient world. In India stirrup loops appear on carvings of the second century BC at Sanchi in the Deccan,[15] and China was employing this security by AD 302.[16]

HEAD CONTROL: DIRECT CONTROL

Bridling, the main means of eliciting obedience from the horse, is complex. Without control the horse would only have been useful as a meat, milk and leather provider. Other than among steppe folk, where the horse was plentiful and so used, it was too valuable to exploit as human fodder.

Some pressures on the head touch very sensitive areas, and benignly applied are pain free. Such an ideal is only reached by empathy with the animal, coupled with an understanding of its mental processes. Blending these achieves a willing partner. Xenophon appreciated this in theory, but not always in application. When discussing types of bit his 'smooth bit' inflicted what would today be considered unacceptable pain.[17] When the horse was first domesticated, understanding the mental processes would have been absent or limited. However, forceful pressures were understood, if only in man's treatment of his human adversaries.

THE NOSE RING IN THE ANCIENT EAST

Oxen, domesticated before the horse, were controlled by a ring through the nasal cartilage, as were early domesticated equids, including the horse, in the Near East.[18] Control was achieved by the principle of the twitch, which releases endorphins from the brain to mask pain. A twitch prevents adverse reactions and renders a horse tractable. Nevertheless, some horses react violently against twitching, which is used when an unpleasant but necessary veterinary practice has to be performed. Directing the horse would at best have been by a crude pulling. A direct pull would have indicated deceleration or stop. Lateral pressures indicated turns. This may have been aided by a flick of a whip on the opposite side of the neck or shoulder. There is an echo of nasal control from Assyria in the role of the *Kartappu* official whose title meant 'He who holds the nose (rein) of the horse'. The title in post Kassite Babylonia could, in addition to groom, mean an official of higher standing.[19]

CONTROL AMONG EARLY STEPPE HORSEMEN

The primitive method of using a rope or hide thong, either wound around or slotted through pierced antler tines, has been found in graves with equid remains, mostly from steppe locales. They represent a considerable timespan from the Copper Age Dereivka settlement of late fourth to early third millennium to at least the Scythian Altaic Pazyryk burials of the second half of the first millennium. Antler-type cheekpieces are also shown on some Assyrian reliefs, but at this stage they were metal cheekpieces (and bits) rendered in the antler style. Bits from sites in Mesopotamia and Iran indicate that the style was long-lived.[20]

In a ritual deposit at the Dereivka settlement a horse's skull showing (potential) bit wear was found. It has since been discovered to be an intrusion from over 1,000 years later.[21] This still puts possible bit wear earlier than that in the ancient Near East cultures. The site at Botai, Kazakhstan, has also yielded several premolar teeth showing 'bit wear',[22] but there is some doubt that the wear so described could not have another explanation. Brown and Anthony conducted experiments on thirteen horses using metal bits, but only 21 per cent of the teeth of these horses showed bit wear. From a subsequent test using four horses with, respectively, hemp rope, horsehair rope, leather and bone bits in 150 hours of riding over three months, none showed significant wear. Brown and Anthony reason that 300 hours with a bone bit would be needed for significant wear to show as such wear is episodic. They define bit wear as: 'the damage that occurs on the chewing surfaces of the second premolars when a horse chews the bit'. However, similar, if not identical, wear on the lower second premolar can result from abnormalities in the teeth.[23] From my experience *most* horses do not chew the bit. A few do seriously enough so, if of rubber or polyurethane, their bits disintegrate. With rope or leather mouthpieces such horses would quickly chew through the material.

The horseman's reasoning is that it is not necessary to bit a horse to ride it. It is far more likely that nasal control via a halter or rope preceded control via the mouth. Bit wear may indicate domestication. It does not necessarily show its initial stages.

BASIC BIT ACTION

It is generally considered that the snaffle is milder than the curb. With modern snaffles this is usually so. Nevertheless, misused snaffles can cause pain, but significantly less than a harsh curb.

The Snaffle and the Curb

Snaffles act primarily on the tongue and the bars of the mouth. If the snaffle has excessively long canons (mouthpiece), when activated in the way termed 'nutcracker' the central joint can damage the roof of the mouth. Control is by a direct pull on the rein attached to the ring at the end of the mouthpiece. Most snaffles are jointed, but there are numerous variations.

Curbs have a more complex action. The *true* curb has a mouthpiece, which in some cases can be exactly like that of a snaffle, but the external part of the curb consists of a cheekpiece above the mouthpiece, and another, usually longer, shank below the mouthpiece, to the end of which the rein is attached. However, the curb bit did not start to make its appearance until the Roman era among some of that empire's equestrian subjects. Some mouthpieces are fused with the cheekpieces and shanks. Others, termed 'loose jawed' and permitting subtler manipulation, have the cannons running through the cheekpieces. The mouthpiece exerts pressure on the lips, bars and tongue. If the canon has a port – a U-shaped rising in the middle – this increases severity according to how high it is and how narrow. Some very high ports can press, or in very rough usage punch through, the palate. Narrow ports pinch the tongue.

METAL BITTING IN THE ANCIENT WORLD

Metal bitting in the Near East is certain from the fifteenth century onwards, but specimens from Tel el Ajjul (Gaza) have been dated as early as the seventeenth century; however, their find context suggests the later date.[24] For well over a millennium metal bitting was always a snaffle. Early snaffles were simple, jointed bits. Subsequently straight, and slightly curved bar types occurred. The action of many bits was exacerbated by the accretions on the canons and cheekpieces. These included ports, burred mouthpieces, sharp rotating discs on the canons, small spikes, and prickers on the cheekpieces.

Confusion arises over some bits from ancient cultures. A snaffle gets classified as a curb because it has a metal curb strap, but the action is that of a snaffle. Severe bits are called curbs because understanding of the action is lacking. For example, a bit called *lupata* is described as 'a curb armed with sharp teeth' (like those of a wolf).[25] The bit is severe because of the wolf's teeth, that is the burrs on the mouthpiece, not because it is a curb. A further confusion is that in many texts, and in some museums, bits are shown upside down and to a non-horseman give the wrong information, and illustrate some historians' lack of equestrian knowledge.

Johannes A.H. Potratz's *Die Pferdetrensen des Altes Orient* illustrates a huge number of bits from many areas of antiquity, including Mesopotamia, Syria and Egypt, Iran, especially Luristan, south Russia and north Caucasus, Transcaucasia, Greece, and Rome (or rather the Roman sphere). There are also a few from Europe – Austria, Hungary, Italy, for example.

SNAFFLES FROM THE PERIOD UNDER DISCUSSION

All oriental and the early Greek and Italian bits are snaffles, mostly jointed. Some have disc cheekpieces, the canons running freely through the cheekpieces. Other cheekpieces are oblongs. Those from Luristan have huge zoomorphic cheekpieces that would have covered much of the soft tissue of the horse's cheeks and lower jaw. Most had spikes on the inside of the cheekpieces. Allied with free-running canons this enabled great pressure to be put, not only on the mouth, but on the cheeks, which would have been lacerated by the spikes. Great force would have been exerted in turning the horse, and the tighter the turn the harder the pressure. In a straight stop cheek pressure would have been far less. The cheek prickers also kept a horse with a tendency to pull to one side, or to shy off course, running straight. Today a similar brush device is used for the same reason, but of humane construction. A rounded mouthpiece was far less severe than the crude square section bits whose edges were capable of cutting the tongue, bars and lips, or at best delivering harsher action.

Other bits were twisted snaffles, resembling a rope twist, but with multiple sharp contact edges. Another variation was a burred mouthpiece which placed multiple pressure points on the tongue. Such bits are still used in India today, but with much modified minor burrs. The Greek bits in particular had many accretions, such as burrs, on the mouthpiece, moving spikes, and sharp discs, which could both pinch and cut the tongue. The Greeks, or rather Xenophon, preferred a horse to keep his mouth open. The accretions aided this and prevented the horse grabbing the bit with his teeth.[26] A properly fitted bit prevents the horse grasping the canon with his teeth. Examples of Egyptian bits are smooth snaffles, some with and some without spiked cheekpieces; some have twisted canons.

In the main, the bits from south Russia and the north Caucasus are much milder, being jointed snaffles, some without cheekprickers. Many do not have free-moving canons to exert the excessive pressure via the cheekpieces.

In the Roman era the *veterinarius* Pelagonius' advice for a tongue that had been mauled in chariot racing was to stitch up the tongue, wash it with wine and smear honey on the cut each day until it healed.[27] The wine and honey had antiseptic qualities. Some of the bits noted above would have caused such punishment if used brutally.

CONTROL ACCESSORIES

These act on a horse's head, although some are not fixed there.

Muzzles

These have two primary, and one other function:

1. To stop a 'mouthy' stallion biting either other horses or his handler or rider. With a vicious horse damage can be severe.[28] Their use need not be restricted to entires.
2. To keep the mouth closed so bit action is not negated.
3. A less common function may have been to prevent horses, especially entires who are at times extremely vocal, from neighing and betraying their presence to an enemy whom the opposition wishes to surprise. A quiet 'wuffle' is possible when muzzled, but not a full neigh for which a horse distends his nostrils and usually opens his mouth wide.

   Early muzzles were of the simple basket-like weave which went around a horse's nose and mouth, but did not encase the tip of the nose to which the ring was attached. Later examples were of filigree work which encased the whole area. Many muzzles also had an indentation at the side to accommodate the bit.

Psalia

The *psalion* was designed to be used in conjunction with the bit. Many examples come from the Roman era, but much earlier *psalia* came from the Assyrian site of Sultantepe, about the seventh century.[29]

   The *psalion* is often called a hackamore, but it should more correctly be called a mechanical hackamore. The true hackamore is the American bosal, a braided, flexible rawhide noseband. Hackamore is a corruption of the Spanish word *jaquima* meaning noseband, and the Arabic *hakamāh*. The *psalion*'s action is similar to today's drop noseband, but infinitely more severe as it had no give whatsoever. It kept the horse's mouth shut, as does the drop noseband, thus enabling full force of bit action. Being of rigid metal the horse's mouth was held in a vice by noseband and underjaw metal. It provided powerful underjaw pressure, as well as powerful pressure over the nasal bone. If a horse tried opening his mouth the pressure increased in proportion to how wide he did so. Degree of severity was also governed by the cheek length of each *psalion*.

The Terret

This equipment is part of the body harness on chariot horses, and is clearly shown on Egyptian wall paintings and reliefs. The control it exerts is linked to the bit. The reins passed from the bit, through the harness terret on the yoke, and then to the driver's hands, or in some cases the reins wrapped around his waist. It had two functions:

1. To stop the reins flopping down and entangling themselves around the chariot pole or around the horse's legs.
2. To increase poundage on the bit, at the same time reducing the force needed to be exerted by the driver to control his team if the horses raised their heads too high in order to evade control. The action worked much like a running martingale on a modern ridden horse, the martingale rings increasing the force only when the horse tries evasion by poking his nose and raising his head, instead of flexing at the poll.

The Assyrian Pompom

This device assisted in maintaining tension on the reins. According to its weight it would also help induce a lower head carriage via bit action and poll pressure. The fact that most Assyrian and Egyptian reliefs show horses with very high heads must, one feels, be down to convention. They are stereotyped, ignoring the functional implications of intervention to lower head carriage. Such intervention would certainly have been abandoned if it had been useless. Today, in western riding disciplines where loose rein riding with no bit contact is used, a heavy rein is a training aid to help lower a horse's head. There is a downward pull via the bit shank of the curb which is transferred to the poll. This in turn induces a more flexed head position.

The really heavy pompom was usually used on a horse ridden by an archer who needed a horse with a level head carriage. He also needed both hands free to draw his bow, nock and loose an arrow. The British Museum's Assyrian reliefs from Ninevah from the reign of Ashurbanipal show an archer, his horse with much rein pressure induced by the weight of the pompom.[30] The horse is also armoured from withers to past the hip, and to just above the lower belly line. The corners of the barding hang down, suggesting the barding was of leather, as appendages of metal would have lacerated the gaskin and forearm areas. The smoothness also indicates leather. However, metal armour was used on Assyrian horses too, as noted during Shalmaneser III's campaign in Ararat (Urartu). The Sultantepe Tablet STT I 43, line 22 mentions 'coats of iron mail for horses'.[31] Presumably any metal housing would have had a felt or cloth underlay of some kind to stop scalding the hide in hot weather, or galling it at any time during wear.

Horses from the reign of Sennacherib (704–681) are similarly equipped with pompoms; the archers also carry swords and lances. Cavalry horses shown at Khorsabad from the reign of Sargon II are shown with riders who are armed with swords. The rein pompom is vestigial, thus strengthening the reasoning that it was primarily an archer's aid to control. Another facet is the weight of the reins. Those on chariot horses are light. Those on some cavalry horses are extremely heavy. The bridle details of a horse's head from Khorsabad, exhibited in the Louvre Museum, Paris, are explicit. The rider is a spearman. No pompom depends from the rein which is wrapped with rope, or more likely metal to prevent the reins being cut. However, there is a very heavy cord and pompom depending from the horse's poll area. The poll is also protected by a crest and heavy, thick poll pad. Chariot and cavalry horses are often shown with this poll pad, which protected a horse from being poleaxed. The weighty rope and neck pompom helped to keep the horse's head lowered.[32]

The Poll

This area of the horse's anatomy is significant for two reasons:

1. Without protection it is extremely vulnerable.
2. The Assyrian pompom, and the much later and more effective combination of curb and *psalion* acted very much on the poll. A horse is under more control if he flexes at the poll, drops his nose and relaxes his jaw. The Assyrian device encouraged this.

A severe bit can be pain free with a rider who has 'good hands'. The same bit in heavy hands can be torture. In battle no rider had the time to think of such niceties as bit application. Saving his skin, not his horse's mouth, was of prime importance. Xenophon comments that bit severity is in the manner of handling: 'you can make the rough bit anything you like by holding it lightly or drawing it tight'.[33]

CHAPTER 7

Hazards and Health

A warhorse was subjected to manifold hazards, mainly those inflicted by man, such as battle wounds, psychological trauma, damage to the anatomy caused by inefficient and/or excessively severe tack, bad driving or riding, endemic diseases, territorial and climatic conditions, and common but debilitating ailments and conditions.

GENERAL HEALTH CARE

Very little veterinary literature has survived from the ancient world. There are a few fragmentary texts that give clues about ailments and treatments, but it is not until the Roman era that literature on veterinary medicine proliferates. However, many of the common ailments of horses recognised, for instance, by Varro (first century BC) and Columella (first century AD) are found in later writers such as Pelagonius from the fourth century AD onwards. He mentions Mago of Carthage, whose work on husbandry was lost but which had much of use to animal keepers.

A residue of Assyrian 'dung pharmacopoeia' remained in Roman practices, according to which the dung of various animals and birds was powdered and added to potions, unguents, and included in the moist plasters and poultices. Indeed, dung poultices remained in use among country folk right into the twentieth century AD. An eighty-year-old neighbour of mine, who termed himself 'an 'eavy 'ossman', used to put a fresh cowpat on a horse's skinned leg to save the cost of the 'vitniry'. Advice, backed by scientific rationale, was offered by Jim Kerr, MRCVS, veterinary adviser to the Endurance Horse and Pony Society of Great Britain. He recommended the addition of dried droppings from a healthy donor horse to the feed of a yearling who had a bacterial imbalance of the gut. Also recommended to correct the same problem was the administration of fresh droppings from the donor horse via rectum or naso-gastric avenue.

Much of the ancient Roman treatment followed homeopathic lines. Numerous plant extracts and some metals were used in Roman veterinary medicine, as well as the now redundant 'firings' which also persisted for some leg lamenesses into the mid-twentieth century AD.

In Pelagonius' work there are numerous references to the use of a crude form of oral vaccine containing either blood or purulent matter from a wound. In homeopathic veterinary medicine it is recommended that a nosode should be made from infected blood of a horse suffering from equine infectious anaemia. Infected matter is also used in other nosodes and oral vaccines.[1]

The first veterinary text to survive comes from Egypt, c. 1900, and is known as the Kahun Papyrus. The original papyrus is very fragmentary and deals with cattle.[2] However, it shows that the art of the veterinary practitioner has an extremely long history. Of the three ailments dealt with, one concerns 'the nest of the worm' for which manual evacuation was recommended, the first known example of such practice.[3] Columella also recommended manual evacuation for maw and tape worms in the horse, and Pelagonius gives many herbal remedies for worms or 'lice in the intestines', and includes the vermifuges wormwood, southernwood and garlic in many other remedies not specifically for worming. Many of Pelagonius' remedies hark back to Columella, and even earlier to Mago of Carthage.[4] The fifteenth-century Alalakh Tablets contain references to what I would suggest is a vermifuge, even though the tablets are not of a veterinary nature. Among the tablets outlining horse feed rations there are two that contain black cumin.[5] Cumin can be used as a mild vermifuge, and black cumin – *Nigella Sativa* – appears as an anthelmintic in the *Dictionary of Assyrian Society*.[6]

From these examples it is clear that internal parasites were a recognised health hazard. All grazing animals have (and had) them. Wherever horses and other animals graze continuously on the same pasture, the worm eggs are passed in dung, hatch into larvae on the grass and are then ingested by animals. Each animal has its own 'worms'. The cycle can be broken, for instance, by grazing in turn, horses, then cattle, then sheep, as the horses, cattle and sheep would not be infected by parasites of the other species. A bad case of worms can make the horse unthrifty, lose weight, have a staring coat, and make him susceptible to colic, which Columella recognised.[7] In a really bad infestation live worms will be passed. In the ancient world the actual cycle of eggs, larvae and mature worms, would not have been understood, as early stages only show up under a microscope. It is certain that large concentrations of horses in studs, and in military holdings, would have had a constant problem with internal (and external) parasites. Horses of the nomadic peoples would have suffered less than horses of settled populations because the herds were continually moving to fresh pastures, and thus the cycle would have been broken.

Another fragmentary veterinary text comes from Ugarit (Ras Shamra) dating to the fourteenth century. The only tablet with enough detail to make veterinary sense out of it states that for a horse with a swollen head and nose it was recommended to insert a plaster of old figs and old raisins, mixed with wheat flour, in the nasal passage.[8]

In the Babylonian Laws it is stated that a 'doctor' of cattle or of donkeys must be paid one-sixth of a shekel if he has successfully treated a serious wound in an animal. But if the animal under treatment dies the 'doctor' pays the owner a quarter of the animal's value.[9]

It is almost certain that there were links between the various ancient cultures that carried over into the veterinary practices. When the Phoenicians established themselves in North Africa, Sicily and Spain their animal husbandry lore would have been transferred into Carthaginian practices, and eventually into the Roman sphere of veterinary practice. From there it was subsequently committed to the body of veterinary literature, some of which still echoes faintly in our modern times.

PSYCHOLOGY – THE HORSE'S MIND

How was it possible to completely negate the horse's natural inclinations as an animal of flight, rather than fight? Why did the horse not bolt away at the first threat of perceived punishment via weapons? For too long it has been accepted that the horse, after initial domestication, became available for use as a weapon in war; but without explaining why. The answers lie in training, control, mental conditioning and capitalising on natural proclivities.

Most horses are amenable animals and, if their training begins early enough, preferably by handling from birth, they become used to obeying their handlers, and later their driving and riding partners. Of course, there are degrees of compliance and unsuitable animals would have been discarded. The Alalakh Tablets hint at practices. Tablet no. 329 lists yearling 'horses belonging to the king, palace, and city quarters', that is, Alalakh's officialdom. Named villages supplied colt and filly foals, and several filly foals are described as 'wild or not broken in for riding'. Five yearlings, not specified as colts or fillies, were received for *mariannu* duties (chariot work). As all other horses did not have the appellation 'wild' it rather indicates that it was usual to handle youngstock from birth.[10]

Temperament comes into selection, to add to conformation already detailed. In his *Cavalry Commander* Xenophon describes the ideal situations that cavalry would work under, and some of the training elements that had a link to temperament. He instructed the city council to double the amount of horses' exercise and to reject slow and vicious animals. Thus warned troopers would have fed their mounts adequately and have cared for them better. Kickers were also to be rejected as they would have been incapable of being kept in line, and would have lagged behind in a charge and rendered the cavalryman useless.[11] Other Xenophonic references and suggestions hint that the Athenian cavalryman was rather dilatory in his equestrian exercises and horse management. A kicker is not necessarily a vicious horse, as horses kick for several reasons. It is a natural reflex action against a predator closing in, as is bucking, which is aimed at dislodging a feline predator. Kicking also happens if a horse is surprised from behind, but of course horses also learn to use these defences against man, and to kick against other horses. Habitual kickers often have their own agenda of intimidation, and would not have been securely under control. Biting his fellows, and man, was also in the aggressive horse's armoury. Where the horse had a real bond with his rider such tactics could have been used to advantage, and directed. A horse owned by the Persian cavalry commander Artybius, who accompanied Darius I in his invasion of Greece, was trained to strike with forehooves and teeth.[12]

The mental conditioning was achieved largely through the control mechanics already discussed when assessing bitting, but also through the trust built between man and horse. Two aspects are important here, and one, to the best of my knowledge, has not yet been considered. It was vital that a cavalryman was completely at ease with his horse, and in action human courage was essential. A horse knows instinctively if his rider is fearful, whether of himself or of his situation. It is said that fear travels down the reins, but a more logical reason is the odour of fear, so faint that a human is unaware of it, but readily picked up and interpreted by a horse. How many routs have been started by horses turning tail because their riders quailed in conflict? Since horses are herd animals this would have had a knock-on effect.

The horse's confidence was also built by engaging in massed mock conflicts in which no harm ensued and in which they had the chance to enjoy speedy manoeuvres. Xenophon recommends that such events were to take place in the Hippodrome.[13] He also advised one-to-one mock practice with button-tipped javelins and spears, and flank-to-flank contact with riders trying to dislodge opposite numbers,[14] a feat not easy to execute as the physicality would have induced horses to separate, unless a rider's outside leg clamped the horse close to his adversary. These and other movements ensured horse and man worked in concert. Transferred to the battlefield the horse would have engaged confidently. In action Xenophon recommends each regiment to have seasoned cavalrymen in the van and in the rear, so that in attack or retreat the unit is well led.[15] The less experienced horses and men would thus have been contained in the unit 'herd'.

EQUINE RESPONSES IN ACTION

In action it might be expected that horses would have flinched, but, once committed to a charge, speed would have excited the horses, which would in effect have been racing their fellows. Horses would not have realised that javelins and arrows came from a still reasonably distant enemy. Horses do not generally associate missiles with the distant man, unless they come in such quick succession as to pose a continuing threat. Close-order launches are different. Excitement, plus any natural aggression the horses possessed, would have overridden the immediate possibility of fear. Fighting horses, not necessarily stallions, bite and kick each other regardless of pain until one overpowers the other and drives it off. These fights are usually over territorial encroachment, food, resentment of a third animal joining a pair, or with stallions over mares. Such fights can be damaging and relentless. A similar attitude prevailed in battle and a seasoned cavalryman would have capitalised on it, at the same time minimising damage to himself and his horse.

The fact that the same horses went again and again into battle suggests they were anything but docile, and that the herd mentality was utilised by commanders. In general horses do not like having things whirled around their heads, or flashing by them, especially by the head. Bows, swords, javelins, spears, maces and lances were part of early cavalry's armoury. In the nomadic sphere lassos were used. Therefore, defusing a horse by repeated training sessions in which no pain was felt would have built courage. In his first action the horse would have been confident. In the turmoil, speed and excitement, wounds would not immediately have registered, unless they were so crippling as to render the horse useless. He would have carried on, then once action ceased, adrenalin ceased to pump, and pain was felt, the horse would not link a previous occurrence with current pain. This is not because the horse is stupid, but because he does not link delayed actions – wound and pain. Should a blow be inflicted in cold blood, without excitement to mask pain, a horse is very aware of cause and effect. When some horses fight against punishment inflicted, it is not against the pain, but in anger against the inflicter, and over who is going to win. Understanding the horse's mentality was essential to getting the best out of chariot and cavalry horses. In harrying, a horse really came into his own, and here aggression would definitely have played a part. It would not have been a blind chase. A good, smart horse can anticipate movements of any animal, human, equid, or cattle that he pursues, and restrict that animal to the path dictated by his rider, often with no signal from the rider. In this he will definitely use his teeth in aggression, particularly if he is a stallion.[16]

ENDEMIC DISEASE

In the history of the use of the horse in war there have been many endemic diseases that have caused great loss in efficiency and in lives. In consultation with my own equine practitioner I was assured that these diseases would have been prevalent throughout history. Unfortunately, the most that can be garnered from ancient texts is a periodic statement that plague carried off both humans and animals. A Hittite text states: 'if plague breaks out in the *Karas* [camp] and people, horses, and oxen start dying. . .'.[17] Similar texts make it clear that plague was not a rare occurrence.

During the Second World War the main task of the Royal Army Veterinary Corps (RAVC) was to keep operational the remaining cavalry horses which, once mechanisation rendered them redundant as mounts, were used as pack and draught animals. There were also many thousands of mules, horses, ponies and camels. These were vital, owing to shortage of mechanised transport and fuel, and in extremely difficult terrain only animal power could be used. The main areas that these gallant animals worked in mirrored almost exactly the territories over which the armies of the ancient world marched. Fortunately all incidences of disease were fully recorded by the RAVC. This enables us to appreciate the immense difficulties ancient armies had to contend with. Although some animals would undoubtedly have acquired a localised immunity to some diseases, they would have been susceptible to diseases not so readily encountered. Many ailments had a wide territorial base, and in the ancient world scientific knowledge and curative medicines were lacking.

Equines *en masse* are always at a health risk. In ancient times contagion was not understood, so infected animals were not isolated. Moreover, treatments were mostly ineffective. Many diseases are also passed by contact with human handlers, their clothing, equipment, and the horse's feeding utensils. Onset of disease, prior to external evidence, is often shown by raised temperature, respiration and pulse. Easily taken, a raised pulse (normal resting rate is about 36–42 beats per minute) warns that the animal is in trouble. The first recorded incident of pulse taking, although it occurs outside the timeframe of this work, is worth noting, as much equestrian lore was passed down the ages almost unchanged. The eminent *veterinarius* Pelagonius scorned the idea saying:

> Those who think that by touching the ear, or vein, or artery in the side under the shoulder may discover if the horse has fever are ignorant of the true reason because it cannot be told by the appearance of the veins.[18]

The 'ignorant' person was tentatively taking the pulse, a method of aiding diagnosis not accepted until over a thousand years after Pelagonius, in the fourth century AD. This fingertip method enables one to take a pulse if a stethoscope is not available.

Many diseases prevalent in the ancient world's theatres of war were still current in twentieth-century camps. Many had a high equine mortality. Among the worst were glanders, farcy, epizootic lymphangitis, ulcerative lymphangitis, surra, dourine (horse VD), piroplasmosis (biliary fever), encephalomyelitis (sleeping sickness), African horse sickness, strangles (incorrectly called shipping fever), rabies and anthrax.[19] Virgil gives a clear, frightening description of rabies. Some of his symptoms accord well with those given by Hayes, except for the contradiction on thirst. Virgil says the horse 'turns away from water'. In fact thirst in a rabid horse is constant.[20]

Strangles, caused by the *streptococcus equi* bacillus, is extremely invasive. Although it can be caught by individual horses, it is far more prevalent within high concentrations of animals. Pelagonius gives a very modern description of the disease, refering to it seven times, in comparison to the single reference to most other ailments. This indicates that strangles, or as he calls it 'tumour in the jaw', parotitis, or swollen glands, – was common in his day. He notes the horse suffering from strangles has a thick discharge from the throat.[21] Other symptoms include a high temperature, and a hard abscess under the jaw, which, when it ripens and bursts, exudes a thick, yellow, purulent matter. Contagion can be by contact with any of this purulent matter which remains infective for a considerable time. Modern medicines can quickly cure the infected horse, but in the ancient world the disease would often have proved fatal. Stud and army horses were prime carriers. Even if sick horses were left at base, those incubating the disease, but still appearing healthy, would have kept the disease within the massed animals. Strong sunlight has the effect of killing bacteria adhering to surfaces outdoors. Fortunately, if they recover most horses have a certain amount of immunity, and the majority of horses contracting strangles would have been young animals up to the age of six years, although older animals occasionally do contract it. It was not confined to the countries that had most of the tropical diseases mentioned above, but occurred in all climatic zones.[22] Some diseases were more prevalent in certain areas, others cost many lives across a range of territories.

INJURY

Warhorses suffered a variety of wounds and ailments caused by direct conflict, and as a result of 'wear and tear'. The worst, with minimal chance of recovery, was tetanus and/or resulting gas gangrene. These ailments were occasioned by puncture wounds from projectiles – arrows, javelins, spears, stabbings with swords, and from caltrops and stakes in pits that would have caused punctured hooves. Tetanus is nearly always fatal. Only a few horses recover, and only if the attack is slight.[23] In the days of chariotry a wound to one of the team spelt death to the partner, or capture as booty. Biridiya of Megiddo, fighting against Lab'ayu, Prince of Schechem, was forced to abandon his own chariot when one of his team was arrow-shot in an engagement.[24]

Hamstringing, severing the Achilles tendon which incorporates all the tendons and muscles attaching to the calcaneus, a bone in the hock, rendered a horse permanently useless. When David (c. 1004–965) defeated Hadadezer of Zoba he is credited with capturing 1,000 chariots, 7,000 charioteers, and 20,000 foot. All but 100 of the 2,000 chariot horses were hamstrung.[25] The injury is not disputed, but I would challenge the conveniently round and large numbers. Slash wounds, unless they severed any vital artery, muscle, or tendon, were not so dangerous, and in time would have recovered leaving, it is true, massive scarring. I have seen some terrible wounds heal in time.

LAMENESS

Lameness must have accounted for a very high proportion of travel and battle casualties. Causes would have ranged from simple soreness and abrasion of hooves faster than the horn could grow (¼ in to ½ in per month, depending on individual horses and the animal's state of nutrition), to stone bruising to the sole of the hoof caused by gravel, sharp stones, rocks and so on. In some hooves splitting travels up the hoof to the coronet, rendering the horse lame for a much longer period, until the siting is cleared by new, strong growth. In military terms that animal would have been useless, except as meat for the pot.

Although some chariot horses were fitted with yoke saddles in front of the withers, which helped traction via neck and shoulder,[26] the whole system was inefficient and better suited to oxen. When circumstances dictated horses being driven to capacity and beyond, serious trauma would, on occasion, have occurred in the neck and shoulder areas with both nerve and muscle damage.[27]

For chariot horses there was a very real danger of a crashing fall and becoming entangled in the chariot structure, with resultant broken limbs, torn backs and similar injuries. There are recorded examples of this from that other chariot activity, the Roman circus, where such accidents were termed *naufragia* (shipwreck). Sidonius Apollinaris graphically described such a wreck:

> . . . his horses were brought down, a multitude of intruding legs entered the wheels and the twelve spokes were crowded, until a crackle came from those crammed spaces, and the revolving rim shattered the tangled feet.[28]

Chariot warfare would have had similar injuries.

Major lameness would have been caused by ruptured tendons, stress fractures, and injury fractures. Many of the ruptures and stress fractures would have occurred in battle, or in a harrying or retreat, as the line taken would have been dictated by circumstances. Any sudden twists or sharp turns taken, without the ability to steady the horse adequately, would have increased the likelihood of such damage.

Hannibal was hampered by his cavalry horses going lame just prior to the Battle of Trasimene in 217 due to extended travel through marshes.[29] Similar conditions would have occurred wherever animals went through excessively wet conditions. The lameness was most probably mud fever. The lower limbs become sore, inflamed and swollen. Subsequently they scab and slough hair and skin, a condition which can extend to the belly.[30]

COMMON AILMENTS

Many ailments common to massed horses were debilitating rather than immediately life-threatening. Lice, mange, and mild tick fever were prevalent in certain areas. Wild swings in temperature were encountered in two campaigns we will meet – Sargon II's invasion of Urartu in 714, and Alexander the Great's 21,000-mile trek from Macedonia to India and thence back to Babylon. This in particular ran the gamut of territorial and climatic changes. Horses cannot adapt rapidly to climatic change. Some horses would have suffered debilitation in hot climates, as would flatland horses plunged into icy mountain territory, where to exacerbate conditions they had to contend with snow balling in hooves, and had to subsist on a reduced fodder ration.

Heatstroke will cause fatalities if oxygen is not administered in time. The 120 degree Fahrenheit heat of the Iraqi (Assyrian) and Persian Gulf zones would have taken its toll, especially in unacclimated stock. The RAVC did sterling work in this area when shipping horses and mules from Basra to (El) Kentara on the Suez Canal in the Second World War.[31] Heat exhaustion would also have been caused when horses were fully armoured and working in torrid zones. Profuse sweat would have both dehydrated the tissues and drained the essential body salts. Some horses would have had a build-up of lactic acid and been prone to azoturia, or 'tie up syndrome', when muscle damage occurs and the urine appears bloody due to myoglobin in the blood plasma. The horse literally seizes up, and unless work ceases and the horse is treated and given time to recover the damage renders him useless. Pelagonius, and no doubt other vets, recognised an ailment brought on 'by too much running and frequent journeying and not having the chance to urinate'. When the horse did urinate, he thought blood was actually being passed.[32]

Overwork, exhaustion and starvation were warhorses' common companions. They find sporadic entries in ancient texts. The first dates to the reign of Pharaoh Piankhi (751–730) who, after successfully besieging Hermopolis, visited the stables of Namlot of Hermopolis who 'threw himself upon his belly before his majesty'.[33] Angered at Namlot Piankhi said: '. . . it is more grievous to my heart that my horses have suffered hunger than any evil deed thou has done . . .'.[34] Out of all the ancient kings Piankhi was noted for love of horses quite divorced from their utility value.

At the Battle of Gaugamela in 331, and the relentless 75-mile pursuit of a fleeing Darius III (336–330), Alexander lost over 1,000 horses to battle wounds and exhaustion.[35]

CONCLUSION

A great many hazards encountered in modern endurance riding are, fighting apart, very close to operational conditions met with in extended route marches – climate swings, very varied terrain, and horses under pressure, often for extended distances at high speed. This has enabled me to appreciate just what horses of the ancient world had to cope with. Today we have superb veterinary care, shoeing of high order, and the best in equestrian equipment. Feeding the endurance horse now approaches a science, with diets for different levels of competition, and there is a scientific approach to putting horses into demanding events. Horses of the ancient world endured in the worse sense of the word. Lack of suitable harness and saddlery did them no favours, especially as this would have been exacerbated by poor driver and rider skills. Lack of veterinary science with often muddled diagnoses and peculiar treatments only makes us appreciate how well the animals served their masters, despite lack of adequate care. The wastage must have been incredibly high, a fact that does come through on occasion, when records bother to mention the animal stock.

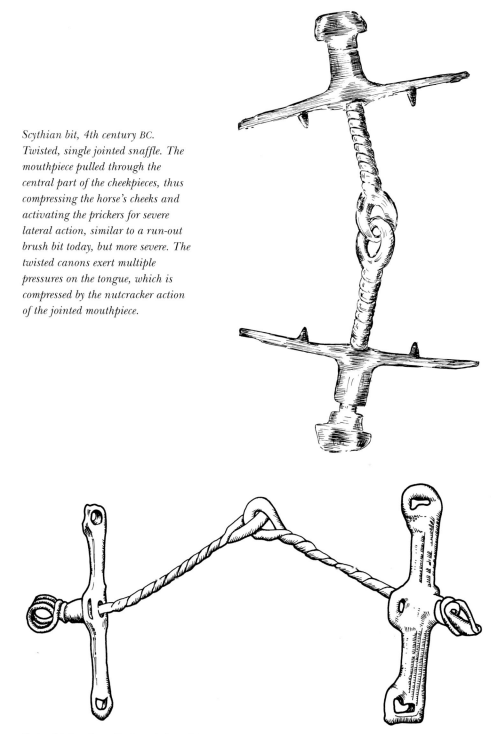

Scythian bit, 4th century BC. Twisted, single jointed snaffle. The mouthpiece pulled through the central part of the cheekpieces, thus compressing the horse's cheeks and activating the prickers for severe lateral action, similar to a run-out brush bit today, but more severe. The twisted canons exert multiple pressures on the tongue, which is compressed by the nutcracker action of the jointed mouthpiece.

Twisted jointed snaffle from Ashur. The extra long canons when activated give nutcracker action and also put pressure on the horse's palate, and compress the tongue. The twists exerted multiple pressures on the tongue. The sliding action of the bit through the cheekpiece compresses the lips. The moderate length cheekpieces exert lateral pressure on the cheeks when the reins indicate a turn to right or left.

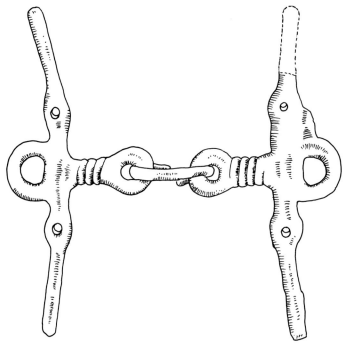

Assyrian three-jointed snaffle from Nimrud. Canons have minimal twists. Solid construction so no compression of lips or cheeks. A much gentler bit than those shown on previous page.

Luristani zoomorphic straight bar square section snaffle that slides through huge cheekpieces. These compress the cheeks when reins are pulled to right or left, but not so much when a direct non-turning pull is exerted. The square section mouthpieces exerts excessive pressure on the tongue.

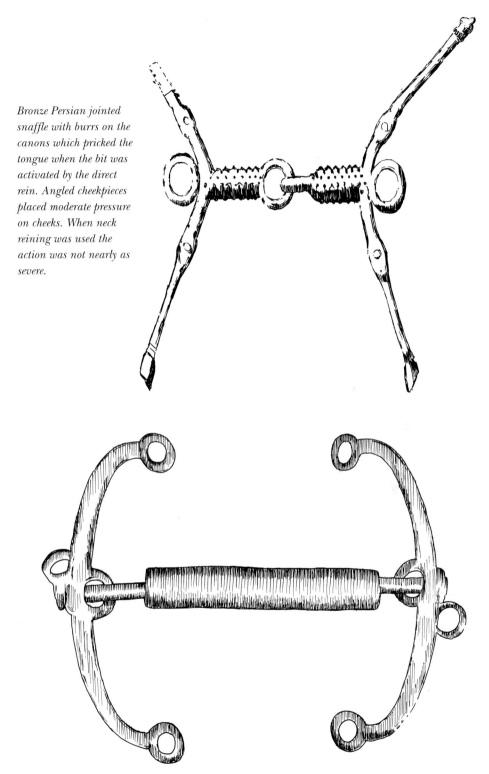

Bronze Persian jointed snaffle with burrs on the canons which pricked the tongue when the bit was activated by the direct rein. Angled cheekpieces placed moderate pressure on cheeks. When neck reining was used the action was not nearly as severe.

Greek straight bar snaffle bit, from Olympia, c. 550–490 BC. The roller bar prevented the horse from grasping the bit with his teeth, as some few horses tried to do to avoid control.

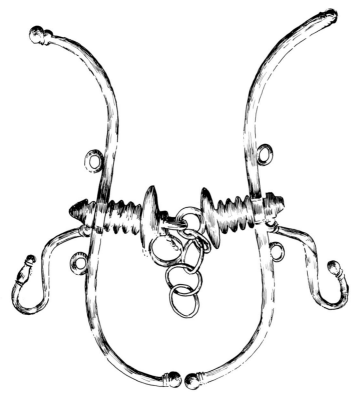

Greek jointed snaffle bit, 4th century BC, with rings dependent from centre. These are flanked by two sharp edged discs and the canons are made with very sharp burrs. This bit was exceptionally severe. It would have induced the horse to keep his mouth open to avoid excessive mouth mutilation. The dependent rings encourage a horse to salivate and thus keep the mouth tender. However, on this bit blood would probably have flowed.

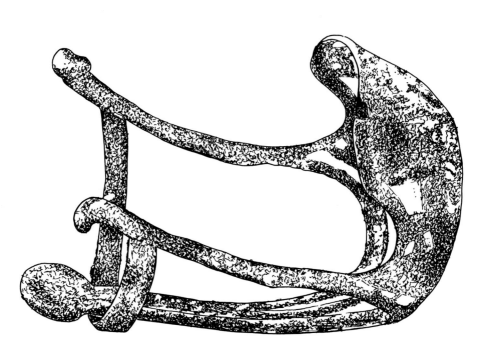

Muzzle used for a) preventing the horse from biting b) keeping the mouth closed (if used with the above bit – it is likely as they come from the same grave – the full action of that bit would have been activated. The animal that wore these would no doubt have had a very mutilated mouth.

CHAPTER 8

Egypt – Her Allies
and Her Enemies

Literature and frescoes show the importance of the horse in war to the Egyptian military. Equestrian participation is highlighted in the records of the great military Pharaoh Tuthmose III, who expanded Egypt's territories in Syria and Naharin (Mitanni). His great-grandson Akhenaton (Amenophis IV) was so besotted with his new religion of the sun that he neglected his army and lost much of Egypt's northern territories. The self-congratulatory records from Ramses II's reign give detailed information of two cultures at war – Egypt and Hattusas. As the scenes unfold they show the equestrian capabilities, similarities, and differences, and indicate that an underlying structure was in place. Contemporary sources show the advantages of horsepower to Tuthmose and Ramses, and the consequences of its lack under Akhenaton.

Under Tuthmose III Egypt began a period of brilliance that lasted until the reign of Akhenaton. At a pharaoh's accession it was customary to make a show of force to establish his rule. The further he made inroads in lands beyond Egypt the better the chance for continued peace within the country.[1] In the cases of Tuthmose III and Ramses II that meant long years of campaigning, significantly in Canaan and Syria where the great powers of the day had a major influence over the numerous city states. Tuthmose's armies were enmeshed with those of Mitanni and her Syrian satellites. Ramses fought the Hittites intermittently for twenty or so years with no final settlement until an accord was reached for mutual respect of boundaries. It was sealed with a marriage alliance between Ramses and a Hittite princess.[2]

THE BACKGROUND TO EQUESTRIAN PARTICIPATION

By the sixteenth century chariotry was an essential part of the armies of the Near East. The Mitannians, a people of Hurrian and Indo-Aryan ancestry, had expanded into north Mesopotamia and eastern Syria, bringing with them a considerable equestrian expertise, culled mainly from their Indo-Aryan associations. Much of their success in the Fertile Crescent was owed to the horse and chariot.[3] The well-known Hittite horse training text was written by Kikkuli of Mitanni. The Hittites emanating from Anatolia stemmed from invading Indo-Europeans and indigenous Hurrians.[4] Canaan and Syria were invaded by the Mitannians and then by the Hittites. Their thriving equestrian scene is illustrated from Egyptian booty and tribute lists.

MITANNIAN INFRASTRUCTURE

By the fifteenth century many Syrian towns were subservient to Mitanni, as was Assyria.[5] From Alalakh in Syria and Nuzi (modern Kirkuk) hoards of tablets have been found. Many of these shed light on Mitanni's equestrian infrastructure. It is to be expected that these city states furnished their Mitannian overlords with tools of war when called on to do so.

Alalakh provided fodder rations for the horses of the Great King of Mitanni on the occasion of his visit.[6] Census lists[7] reveal which towns and villages could supply *mariannu*, and by extension the requisite horses and vehicles. Some *mariannu* owned chariots, others did not. Some tablets specifically refer to horses,[8] giving the locations where horses came from, their numbers, and most importantly, those that were rendered to the city for *mariannu* duties. Out of 64 business houses 11 were described as having cartwrights making wagons, chariots, and carts.[9] In the list of householders, the large village of Tuhul with 179 houses had an unspecified number of 'chariot sheds' and 4 'houses of their relatives who own chariots/wagons'.[10] Of 74 householders in Zalaki village 2 are shown as 'having chariots'.[11] Other census tablets list armed forces.[12] Of one group of 1,006, 76 either fight from or are owners of chariots. Of another group of 1,436 warriors, 80 are charioteers.[13] These tablets show that Alalakh could put a considerable chariot force into the field, and that backing this was ongoing breeding of horses for war, and ancillary trades that kept the military efficient.

The tablets from Nuzi name many breeds, including the Akannu, bred locally in Hanigalbat (Mitanni) and Markunas; the Arkamanu which was a breed/colour; the Baritanna;[14] the Zilukannu; and 'a fine colt of the Ziramannu breed coloured Zilukannu' is noted.[15] Confusingly, several breeds also denote colours. Were these true breeds, or strains that with selective breeding bred true to colour? For example, a palomino, only a coat colour, needs one chestnut and one palomino parent. Were they pure breeds with but one coat colour? For instance, Suffolk Punches are always chestnut. I suggest that breed purity as we understand it had not yet occurred, but *types* had. Indeed, true breed purity, with the exception perhaps of the Arabian, as noted in the fourteenth century AD *Naceri*,[16] did not become the norm until the nineteenth century. Naturally there were areas where, because of isolation, a true breed did evolve, and was kept pure until migrations and military expansions introduced it to stock of other strains.

As well as homebreds, horses were also imported from Mitanni, Markunas, and Nulle, and bought from horsetraders. One tablet notes horsetrader(s) supplying twenty head to the palace at Nuzi.[17] A horsedealer could expect to receive up to 10 minas of copper for one horse, so noted in a sale contract.[18]

Breeding horses for military and spectacle use was carried on by the palace, as is shown by the appointment of an Overseer of Herds, and references to foals, mares, and stallions.[19] Private studs owned by the wealthy also existed. These were not restricted to men: one text records the theft of 'horses removed from the herd' owned by a woman named Azua.[20] Individuals also contributed horses to the palace for possible military use.[21]

Training at Nuzi started in a horse's first year (that is, before it was a yearling), and by their third year (that is, as a two-year-old) the horse was used in chariot work. The average age of chariot horses ranged from four to nine years, with only one older individual, a ten-year-old.[22] Maybe full battle action was not experienced until almost maturity. Even so, the short lifespan was in part due to being worked too young. In particular, limb joints, back muscles, and shoulders would have been traumatised.

Although most horses were harnessed, there is clear textual and figurative evidence that mounted men served in some military capacity.[23] An order from the king was for 'the *Sukallu* [royal messenger] and *Sangu* [temple administrative official] to ride forth on a pair of good horses'. Another tablet stipulates 'horseriders'. Two more texts indicate men who are supplied with a single horse as members of mounted armed units. These acted as messengers, couriers, and scouts.[24]

Chariot horses were armoured. This protection, the *Parasanna*, was constructed of a leather or hair pad covering the withers to loin area. The pad was sheathed in layered leather overlaid with scales, the whole called the *Sariam*.[25] This had corner tails of copper, called the 'limbs'.[26] Their only purpose must have been to anchor down by their weight the whole bard. Wool and goatskin were supplied,[27] whose purposes were to protect against heat and chafing metal, absorb sweat, and prevent soreness. The head, poll, and upper neck were covered with a similarly constructed *girpisu*.[28]

Battle casualties are reflected by the '35 horses which cannot be harnessed because they were crippled and/or feverish'[29] and others that were 'crippled, burned, feverish, or wounded'.[30]

The turnover of stock must have been high, with breeding for war and pomp a large part of the economy. In the Ishtar city festival about 1,200 horses took part. From one locale alone 536 charioteers were fielded, indicating that over 1,000 horses could also be supplied.[31]

Alalakh and Nuzi show that Mitanni could call on considerable chariot and scouting forces. With the breeding stocks to back supply it is understandable why Tuthmose's battle haul from Megiddo was so large. The infrastructure of the equestrian side of war must have been repeated on a scale according to each city's importance and wealth throughout the many city states of the ancient world.

EGYPT'S ARMY

From the Hyksos period Egypt learned that she needed a buffer zone to deter invaders. In the New Kingdom the Egyptian army underwent considerable reorganisation, including the introduction of a standing army. Much of this was the work of Tuthmose III. The pharaoh was Commander-in-Chief, while his vizier was Minister for War. A Council of War made up of senior officers advised the pharaoh in the field. The army was organised in divisions, each of approximately 5,000 men and complete in itself, comprised of chariotry and infantry.[32]

Upper and Lower Egypt each had its own standing corps; on campaign there were three or four divisions, with extra men augmenting the standing army. Infantry units were reinforced by separate companies of elite troops and chariot warriors.[33]

The chariotry had its own hierarchy. It was administered by the Master of the Horse. Stablemasters were responsible for grazing and stable care. Doubtless there was a department for the training of men and horses.[34] The military scribe Hori referred to his position in the pharaoh's stable as:

Groom of his Majesty, follower of the Sovereign, trainer of the steeds of the King. . . . [Writing to a fellow scribe he continued:] I am experienced in every rank. My father taught me, he knew and instructed [?] [me] very often. I know how to hold the reins, beyond thy skill indeed! There is no brave man who can measure himself with me! I am initiated in the decrees [?] of Montu.[35]

The force was divided into squadrons of twenty-five chariots, each squadron commanded by a Charioteer of the Residence. The senior officer of the corps was the Lt Cdr of Chariotry. Each chariot contained two men, the driver and the fighter, the latter equipped with bow, arrows, javelin, shield, and no doubt a sword. The most senior driver was the First Charioteer of His Majesty. In action, according to Faulkner, it appears the engagement was normally opened by a charge of chariots (see below for alternative). In a victory chariots harried the defeated.[36]

Early chariots were patterned on those of the Canaanites, from whom they were imported by Egypt as tribute, gifts, and spoil. The chariots were very light with four-spoked wheels. Later, as shown on the sides of Tuthmose IV's (1411–1403) chariot, Egypt experimented with an eight-spoked wheel, but soon discarded it in favour of six-spoked wheels.[37]

CHARIOTS – DID THEY CHARGE *EN MASSE* OR NOT?

I would like to put forward arguments, from an equestrian point of view, against the accepted massed chariot charge picture. Apart from the psychological factor whereby horses instil fear, or at least apprehension, into people unused to them, chariots could be used in several ways, as mobile archery platforms, as the earliest form of mounted infantry, rapidly delivering warriors to the site where they were most needed, as mobile flanking screens for a marching army, and for attack by the medium- and long-range missiles carried, the javelins and arrows coming in on the flanks of a massed enemy, but from a safe distance. Swords or other cutting or bludgeoning weapons carried would have been for a last-ditch hand-to-hand encounter. If chariots were ever used in massed frontal attacks the encounter was surely very costly in injured and dead horses and smashed chariots. However, a quote suggesting that a chariot did charge into the fighting is graphically described in 'The vassal Treaties of Esarhaddon (680–669) under clause 90', which threatens dire results if vassals do not toe the line: '. . . just as this chariot is spattered with blood up to its running board, so may they spatter your chariots in the midst of your enemy with your own blood'.[38] Although appearing to confirm a charge, it is more likely to have been royal hyperbole, to which Assyrian kings were definitely addicted.

Undoubtedly individual and/or small numbers of chariots did enter into the thick of fighting, either from battle ardour, horses bolting or being uncontrolled, or even human stupidity, and in a rout of an enemy when a field could have been covered with fleeing chariots and pursuing victors in a very loose or no formation as horses ran at their individual best speeds. If ever launched, en masse chariots would have rapidly dispersed and have become individual fighting platforms, again the factor being the individual horse team's speed. It is strongly to be doubted that the head-on charge was the normal method of chariot warfare. The horse was far too valuable to be risked in great numbers. Added to that, although a massed charge would have excited horses, there would always have been some less aggressive horses that veered away from the intimidation of opposing horses, and in so doing they would have created chaos. Horses do not willingly crash into each other, and if a horse had gone repeatedly into charge it would have lost its initial assurance.

One only has to consider the fragile structure of Egyptian chariots to realise that less costly battle employment was more usual. The lightweight rear-axled Egyptian chariot was designed for speed and could turn rapidly with safety. Enmeshed in a massed charge its manoeuvrability would have been compromised. Even the sturdier Hittite and Assyrian vehicles would have been subject to shattering in multi-vehicle pile-ups. There are several other practical reasons for doubting the frontal assaults. If used *en masse* the front rank would have taken the brunt of the collision with opposing vehicles, and the rear ranks would bog down in a welter of rear-end smashes, as once launched into speed it would have been impossible to brake quickly. Combined with the sheer weight of equippages, it would have been inconceivable to be able to prevent mass self-destruction, or 'own goals'. Nor would the following infantry have been very effective climbing over the chaos of thrashing hooves! A shot warrior or driver did not totally incapacitate the equippage, but a horse shot in a vulnerable part, and/or brought down, rendered the whole unit not only useless, but a hazard to its own side. The reliefs we see of chariot casualties are of horses arrow-shot in the side, and such horses falling. We do not see such horses shot in the chest or head. Some chariots are overturned as the injured horse(s) crash to the ground. Hundreds of chariots could not have manoeuvred efficiently on a limited field, or stayed cohesive on an extended plain.

The stability of the chariot as a mobile firing platform has now to be analysed. To give a ride smooth enough to permit accurate shooting or javelin launch means that the horses had either to be going flat out and with absolutely no checking of their speed to maintain uniform stability, or to be kept to a hand canter, which is hardly a 'charge', being slower than medium trot. At the full gallop, although the speed ensured stability, it would have been impossible to turn quickly, thus negating rear-axle utility. At hand canter (about 7 mph) it would have been easy for an accurate bead to be drawn on the unit, and its horses or crew disabled. The two gaits mentioned are those at which the horse moves extremely steadily, with the least upward and downward thrust. Employment of either of these options, *if they were to give stability,* necessitated a completely level surface that was also of uniform construction, with no changes in depth of tilth or sand, and neither stony, nor slippery. The drag on wheels also had to be uniform. Any jerkiness in forward progression would have put extra strains on the neck and shoulder muscles and nerves of the paired horses. I had the chance of a ride in a two-horse Roman-style chariot. It was drawn by two Lusitano stallions, and was driven at a fast gallop on a pasture of very long and thick grass, which, like most pastures, was not completely smooth, although so appearing at a casual glance. I found I had to hang on to the front of the chariot box frame to avoid being pitched out of the open rear. The driver, used to the motion, also maintained stability by the tension he kept on the horses' mouths via the reins.

Chariots needed maintenance, and a scene of a chariot workshop is shown on the 18th Dynasty tomb of Hapu.[39] The *Anastasi Papyrus I* refers to a *maher's* (*mariannu*-chariot warrior) tethered horse being cut loose, galloping off without his driver, and then smashing up the chariot, which had to be repaired in the armour workshops.[40]

THE HITTITE ARMY

The main elements of the Hittite military were a standing army, augmented when necessary by levies from the citizenry and the provinces. Accurate numerical assessment of Hittite forces is difficult. Records show forces of 200 to 600 men, bolstered by 20–60 chariots. At least 6 units of 1,000 each are also recorded. International treaties bound both parties to assist each other in times of war. The King of Kizzutwatna was obliged to supply 1,000 foot and 100 chariot teams. Enemies such as Azzi and Assuwa could put 10,000 foot and 1,000 chariots into the field, making it highly likely that the Hittites could field similar numbers,[41] plus troops and chariots from allies and peoples subjected to a military levy after a Hittite takeover. Kizzutwatna is of equestrian interest, lying as it did in the eastern part of the Cilician Plain.[42] Cilicia (Coa/Kue/Que) was a long-time provider of quality horses to Solomon,[43] and to the Persians.[44] Togarmah in Tabal (in Cappadocia) in Anatolia also exported horses to Tyre[45] and to Assyria,[46] and Cappadocia was renowned in Roman times for its horses.[47] Harsanna in south-east Anatolia was also noted for its horses.[48] Among the Hittites, agriculture, especially horse and cattlebreeding, was the economic basis of their culture.[49]

The key Hittite force was chariotry.[50] Early Hittite chariots carried two men, the *kartappu* (driver), who carried a shield, and a *šuš* (warrior), armed with bow and arrows.[51] The *šuš kusig* was an elite chariot fighter, a member of a corps surrounding the king.[52] By the Battle of Kadesh spears, lances and javelins had been added, as had a third man. Scale armour protected horse and man.[53] The horse divisions had their own hierarchy: the Lord of Horses (*en anše kur ra*); Chief of the Golden Chariot Fighters (*Gal šuš kusig*); Chief of the Chariot Drivers (*Gal kartappu*); Chief Groom (*Gal Salasha*). However, these may not have been field commands,[54] but did show that horses had their own personnel. Some texts are unclear whether an official was 'Master of Horses' or 'horsetroops'.[55] One could mean a non-combat, the other a combat official. Master of Horse should not be confused with Master of Horses. The former was a very high-ranking appointment, as in Egypt; the latter could be more of a 'hands-on' Head Lad position.

Training of chariot fighters was undertaken by the *Uralla* (training sergeant).[56] One text mentions Ispudasinara who was placed over Suppiuman and Marassa, both of whom were 'overseers of 1,000 fighters'. A trainer taught weaponry, and the 'sharpening wheel [?]'. After training the fighters were allocated to their respective units.[57] I would suggest the phrase 'sharpening wheel' indicated proficiency in fighting aboard a manoeuvring chariot. At times this could have been difficult, the fighter(s) having to compensate for unlevel movements and adjust their weapon casts accordingly. Coupled with the Kikkuli horse-training programme it appears that Hittite men and horses went into battle very fit.

So far, Hittite texts have not revealed how their army acquired its horses. Beal says there is no evidence of horses as tribute; he suggests avenues of acquisition may have been by booty, tax in kind, and the increase (that is, on foals dropped) of privately owned horse herds, or perhaps the army bred its own horses.[58] Booty certainly provided considerable numbers. One campaign against Assuwa yielded 600 teams (1,200 horses).[59] Lack of evidence does not mean that no tribute horses were levied. Obligations of vassal states to provide troops and horses were in essence tribute. As so much to do with horses is universal, other nations' practices are a possible guide. We have seen the Nuzi and Alalakh systems. The *Hittite Laws* make it clear that private studs and ownership of horses were widespread. Each category of horse and each age range had its value at law. Stealing a horse cost the thief restitution of fifteen horses, split into several age categories.[60] Hiring a horse cost one silver shekel a month.[61] If it died in the care of a hirer or borrower full value restitution was due.[62] With these factors in view the military most probably acquired its horses from many sources – purchase, horsetraders, levies, hire. Nevertheless, out of all the major nations of the era I cannot think that only Hattusas did not demand tribute horses.

THE RIDDEN HORSE

The ridden horse appears in very small numbers in the fifteenth to thirteenth centuries. As with Nuzi there are records of ridden horses from Hattusas. The term *pithallu*, meaning cavalryman in neo-Assyrian, is recorded in Hittite texts from the thirteenth century, where it means riders and messengers.[63] Over time many words underwent changes in specifics while retaining the general meaning.

Sasson, writing on Mari, Beal on the Hittites, Schulman on Egypt and Kendal on Nuzi, leave the question open as to whether there was a small cavalry presence in the respective armies.[64]

Three Egyptian riders are labelled as scouts on the Kadesh reliefs at Abu Simbel. The plaque of an Egyptian mounted warrior armed with a mace and a bow, already noted, more than suggests that even if not cavalry in the sense of units, a mounted armed man could and did fight on horseback, although his primary job was scouting. It would be strange to think that scouts never got surprised on a reconnaissance. They most certainly would have fought if their horses' speed was insufficient, or if their avenues of escape were blocked.

From the accumulation of textual, pictorial and modelled artifacts depicting horses and riders from numerous sources it would appear that military and social riding was far more widespread than is realised and acknowledged. For every isolated representation, no doubt many riders and horses went unrecorded, especially as their riders were not high in the military hierarchy. True, the chariot was the prime use of horses. It lent dignity to a ruler; and it would not have done for a ruler, often equated with a god, or at least his representative, to fall off his horse. Horses are no respecters of status. In a superstitious age such a fall could have been a bad omen. Another reason for the very slow uptake of massed military riding, was that equestrians were still in the learning phase. For men unused to riding, to have to master their own bodies, their horses' minds and bodies, and also to be able to manoeuvre and fight on a battlefield without the help of advanced tack was a leap too far. It was safer to be ensconced in a chariot box with long-range weapons. Added to that, with many battles taking place on level chariot terrain there was little incentive to change. Later we shall see that the Assyrians, campaigning in mountainous districts, realised the need for mounted troops. The encroachment of Cimmerians and

Scythians undoubtedly hastened the transference from wheels to horseback.

TUTHMOSE III –
MEGIDDO AND ITS LONG-TERM EFFECT ON HORSEBREEDING

Mitanni had whittled away the territories gained by Tuthmose I, who had set up a boundary stela on the west bank of the Euphrates.[65] The first part of Tuthmose III's reign was as co-regent with Hatshepsut, but on assuming independent power he moved on Canaan and Syria in the first of seventeen campaigns to reassert Egypt's authority. Megiddo was the key. It commanded the narrow hill pass linking the plain of Esdraelon and the valley of Jezreel. If he held Megiddo he would hold the rich territories in the Fertile Crescent and the route to Mesopotamia. Thus imperilled, the King of Kadesh on the Orontes, backed by Mitanni, moved south to bar the Egyptian advance in 1468.[66]

One of Tuthmose III's inscriptions describes the run up to the Battle of Megiddo. After leaving Egypt he marched rapidly to Gaza and thence to the environs of Megiddo, where he called a council of war, saying:

> that . . . enemy, the chief of Kadesh has come and entered into Megiddo . . . he has gathered to himself the chiefs of all countries which are on the water of Egypt [that is, subject to] and as far as Naharin consisting of the countries of the Kharu, the Kode, their horses, their troops . . .

Against the advice of his officers the pharaoh chose the narrow pass of Megiddo, 'where horse went behind horse and man behind man'. Debouching safely from the defile and with the element of surprise, the Egyptians found the confederation of Asiatics encamped only a few hundred yards in front of them. The Egyptian battle array was the classic one of left and right wings, while the centre was led by the pharaoh in his electrum chariot. Launched at dawn the actual fighting was summed up thus: 'Then his Majesty prevailed against them at the head of his army, and they fled to Megiddo in fear.'

Unfortunately, as so often, the chariotry (and later the cavalry) failed to harry, instead joining in a general scramble for loot, allowing the kings of Megiddo and Kadesh to escape and reach temporary safety inside the city. This debacle cost Tuthmose a seven-month siege before

Megiddo fell.[67] The equid spoils from Megiddo were huge, bolstered by annual tribute from Syria and Canaan. Nubia also drew Tuthmose and he extended his dominion as far as Napata, installing his own governor, known as the King's Son of Kush.[68]

Long-term Egyptian Horse Acquisition and Breeding

Let us look behind the scenes as to how Egyptian army horses were supplied, not only in the 18th Dynasty, but on a permanent basis throughout Egypt's history. I am starting with Tuthmose III as I consider the spoils of Megiddo so unusual, and the progeny of those 2,041 mares so very important for Egypt, as were the constant increments from Syria and elsewhere. Tuthmose reigned for a further thirty-two years after Megiddo. That is time enough to totally change the course of Egypt's equine history and create a strong breeding tradition.

The horse is not indigenous to Egypt, and although earlier equine remains have been found at Buhen, a mass breeding policy is only indicated by the Megiddo spoils. Over the succeeding centuries horses continued to arrive as tribute from Syria, Hattusas, and Libya. In the reign of the Nubian Piankhi (751–730) there are numerous references to the horses which were offered to him when he moved north with his army. In the Delta fifteen dynasts, knowing Piankhi's love of horses, were quick to offer him the best from their stables.[69] Piankhi founded a horse cult. The tombs of the Nubian 23rd Dynasty contained sixteen horses, four for each king. These were the only ancient Egyptian *equid cult* burials.[70]

With Egypt extending her territories north into Syria, and south to Nubia it is probable that stud farms were established within Egypt to sustain her needs, with new blood being injected by imports. From very few references from other cultures we see that Egypt turned from being a major importer, to an exporter of stock. Twice in the Bible reference is made to Jewish kings seeking horses from Egypt. First named is Solomon,[71] then Hehoiachin of Judah, who was seeking to rebel against Babylonian captivity.[72] About 500 years separate these requests. Assyria regularly imported the prized horses of Kush. There were several sources, direct from Nubia, from studs set up throughout Egypt and no doubt Syria, and from the trading depots set up by Tiglath-Pileser III (745–727) and Sargon II on Egypt's northern border. It is possible that Kusean horses were being imported by Assyria from the reign of Tiglath-Pileser III, as relations between Piankhi and his successor Shabako and Assyria were cordial.[73] However, the first specific reference occurs in the reign of Sargon II, who obtained twelve large horses from Musri (Egypt) from Silkanni of Musri as a *Tamartu* gift which were noted as superior to any in Assyria.[74] Silkanni of Musri was Osorkon IV, who reigned from Tanis *c.* 730–715. In 714 Shabako reconquered most of Egypt.[75] Thereafter, Sennacherib and Ashurbanipal benefited from this breed. No doubt Ashurbanipal helped himself in his two successful campaigns against a weakened Egypt. Kusean studs (horses from Kush) flourished throughout Assyria, as noted in much of the *Royal Correspondence of the Assyrian Empire.*

After the Assyrian visitations Egypt was subjected to a continuing foreign presence, first with the Persians, then with Alexander the Great, followed by Ptolemy, his successor in Egypt and founder of the Ptolemaic Dynasty. All of these had an equestrian background. Ptolemaic Egypt imported from many sources – Cyrenaica, Carthage, Sicily, Italy, Syria, Palestine, Caria, Lycia, and Asia Minor, and later, from Seleucid territory, smuggled into Egypt by dealers.[76]

It is significant that Egyptian horses, which came to be regarded as superior and large from the late eighth century BC, the time of Piankhi and his successor, were bred in Kush, and/or came from a breed emanating from there, *and* that in the history of medieval Egypt the principal breeding grounds of the superior and large Nubian Dongola horse, which stood 15–15.2 hh, was the Upper Nile Valley, where it continued to flourish until modern times.[77] In the fourteenth century AD Nubia exported horses to Sumatra which had strong links with India.[78]

Some breeds can trace their ancestry for hundreds of years. Did the horses of Kush have their distant origins in the 18th Dynasty with its constant and massive increments of bloodstock, the descendants of which Piankhi the Nubian, who ruled from Napata, took back to his native land? Although such projected links are extremely tenuous they are possible. We can take the Arabian breed as an example of extreme lineage longevity. As early as the second century AD the poet Oppian refers to the Erembian horse and the Erembian lion, the latter from Arabia Felix! From the fifth century AD the North Hejaz was noted for Arabian horses. In the twelfth century AD Amir Usamāh ibn Munqidh extolled the virtues of Arabians. Abou Bekr ibn Bedr wrote a treatise on stud and veterinary science in which he listed all the Arabian horses at the stud of the Mamluk Sultan of Egypt, El Nacer (AD 1290–1340). During the Indian Mughal era from the reign of Akbar in the sixteenth century AD, Arabian horses were considered the best for cavalry and racing. Thereafter, the Arabian makes frequent appearances in history, a span of about 2,000 years, and maybe more.[79] Another breed, the

Mongolian pony, has not changed at all in 800 years, going from early representations and comparing modern specimens.

AKHENATON, 1350–1334

During the reign of Akhenaton (Amenophis IV) there was a deterioration, in military terms, with territorial infighting and contraction in Canaan and Syria. The group of tablets known as the *Amarna Letters* provide illuminating reading. They cover approximately thirty years and include the end of the reign of Amenophis III (1386–1349) and that of Akhenaton. Diplomacy and friendship between Egypt and Kadasman Enlil and his successor Burna Burias of Babylon (1380–1350), and Assur Uballit of Assyria (1365–1330) was sealed with reciprocal gifts, among which were many gifts of horses and chariots. However, Assur Uballit's covering letter had a sting. He complained of the inadequacy of the gold sent by Akhenaton and stressed he was the equal of Mitanni.[80]

The positions of Mitanni and Egypt had changed from war to alliance. Amenophis III had married a sister of Tushratta of Mitanni (1385–1360). He negotiated for the marriage of his daughter Taduhepa and Akhenaton. Signal among the gifts from Tushratta were two horses and a chariot from 'the booty of the land of Hatti' from a recent engagement between Mitanni and the Hittites. There was also a plethora of gifts of additional horses and chariots. The rich train of gifts accompanying Taduhepa included 'four beautiful horses that run swiftly', a chariot completely covered in 320 shekels' weight of gold, a leather bard and two bronze chamfrons for horses, plus miscellaneous harness covered in gold and silver and studded with gems.[81] Roux in *Ancient Iraq* says it was Tushratta's daughter who was married first to Amenophis III and then to Akhenaton, but the *Amarna Letters* have Tushratta mentioning his sister and then his daughter. These gifts may have cemented alliances and pleased Akhenaton, who was known to be addicted to fast driving around his new capital of Akhetaten (El Amarna),[82] but the political map was about to change.

On the horizon the Hittites were becoming more powerful, displacing Mitanni. Plagued by internal royal factions Mitanni was unable to maintain a strong presence.[83] Assyria broke free from Mitannian overlordship. Akhenaton was inundated with letters from petty rulers and Egyptian officials requesting horses, chariots, infantry and archers to maintain an Egyptian presence in Canaan and Syria. Overall hung the imminent inroads of the Hittites into Akhenaton's northern possessions. Astride the political fence the new territory of Amurru arose under Abdi

Asirta and his son Aziru. While Syrian rulers and governors, such as Rib Haddi of Byblos, accused Aziru of being a Hittite ally, Aziru protested his loyalty to Egypt.[84]

A clutch of letters from Akizzi of Qatna, the citizens of Tunip, and Abdi Asirta reflect the confused situation in north Syria. Akizzi warned the pharaoh that he had been approached by Aitukama of Kadesh, backed by Hatti, to defect and ally with Kadesh against Egypt. Qatna was attacked, burnt, and her troops captured. Upu, the district around Damascus, was torched and the rulers of Ruhuzzi, Lapana, and Amqu (Beka) wrote to Aitukama, telling him to come to seize Upu. Akizzi begged for horses, chariots, and troops, as not only had the King of Hatti attacked, but he was in fear of Aziru who had assaulted and demanded ransoms for his Qatna captives. Tunip sent an even stronger request for troops and chariots to enable them to hold out against Aziru who had made a strike on Nii and captured the garrison town of Sumur. Tunip's citizens complained that in twenty years of writing to Akhenaton he 'did nothing about these things'. Abdi Asirtu defended himself saying he 'guards all Amurru for the King' and that 'the mayors [of the complaining towns] lie'.[85]

Rib Haddi of Byblos wrote repeatedly to Akhenaton, his vizier Haya, and Amanappa, an Egyptian official. In nearly all his letters he asked for considerable numbers of horses, chariots and infantry to resist Abdi Asirta, whose forces were strengthened with the Apiru, who were roving bands of displaced persons. The Apiru problem escalated. Byblos was threatened. They had already killed the rulers of Irqata (Tell Arqa) and Arasni (uncertain location), and seized Ardata (Arde) and 'the King of Hatti [Suppiliulumas I, 1380–1346] has seized all the countries that are vassals of the King of Mitanni'.[86] Of his towns only Gubla (Byblos) and Batruna were left to Rib Haddi. His men deserted him. He warded off an assassination attempt. He pleaded for food as starvation threatened, and complained that he had no money to buy horses, and that Sumur and Aka each had received thirty teams of horses. When Sumur fell to Abdi Asirta, Amanappa appropriated ten pairs of horses for himself. In a despairing letter Rib Haddi called on Amanappa for an elite force strengthened with chariotry to break the Apiru and Amurru horse and foot blockade of Byblos.[87] Eventually Akhenaton ordered Beirut, Sidon and Tyre to aid Byblos,[88] ignoring the fact that Tyre had already fallen.[89]

At the death of Abdi Asirta, his sons, especially Aziru, took up the fight against Sumur, Byblos, and Irqata.[90] When eventually Egyptian horses and chariots were sent, Abdi Asirta's sons captured them and sold the charioteers and soldiers into slavery.[91] To add stupidity to inaction Akhenaton finally wrote to Rib Haddi telling him to be on guard, drawing the justified riposte from Rib Haddi as to how he could do this without the means.[92] Desertions to Aziru continued. He then allied with the Hittites who mobilised to take Byblos.[93]

Rib Haddi took the pharaoh to task, saying his father led troops in person and was successful 'in a day and you have done nothing'.[94] Old and sick Rib Haddi's letters ceased, and Ili-Rapih continued in like vein, as did the ruler of Tyre.[95] Aziru had the gall to write to the pharaoh professing his loyalty, asking that Amurru be ceded to him, accusing others of disloyalty, and adding his requests for horses, chariots and foot. Akhenaton's reply threatened execution unless he proved his loyalty by sending known traitors, and coming himself, to Egypt. Aziru prevaricated, saying Hittite forces threatened Amurru from Nuhasse (an area north-east of Hamah and north of Qatna) and south of Halab (Aleppo).[96]

The *Amarna Letters* close with more cities accusing each other of disloyalty. Others said their troops and chariots were ready to fight the Hittites and the cities that had defected from Egypt. In Akhenaton's weak reign Egypt lost much in Canaan and Syria. The 19th Dynasty pharaohs Seti I (1308–1291) and Ramses II (1290–1224) reversed the decline.

RAMSES II AND THE BATTLE OF KADESH

Seti I was the first to pit an Egyptian army against that of the Hittites. He campaigned to regain Canaanite and Syrian territories. His son Ramses II continued the struggle for twenty years or so. From now on royal steeds were regularly identified with the prefix of either 'The Great First Span' or 'The Great Span of his Majesty'. Seti I drove 'Amon Assigns to him the Victory', and 'Anath is Satisfied'.[97] I feel this is an example of several teams being present for royal use, as would be expected. Ramses II certainly had several teams at Kadesh: 'Victory in Thebes', 'Mut is Satisfied', and 'Meriamon'.[98]

Seti had come to an agreement with Muwatallis of Hattusas (1306–1282), by which the Hittite retained Amurru and Kadesh, and Egypt kept her territories in Canaan and Upi.[99] This was unsatisfactory to Ramses who in his second campaign into Syria recruited an army of 20,000. Its four divisions each bore the name of the city from which it had been recruited: Amun from Thebes, Re from Heliopolis, Ptah from Memphis, and from the Delta Residence, possibly Tanis, Sutekh.[100] Ramses notes the numbers of Hittite chariots, which makes his own part in the battle that much more extraordinary and courageous. The numbers of Egyptian chariots are not stated. From the following résumé of the run up to, and the succeeding, battle it is clear that horses, both driven and mounted, played a crucial part in the events.

The Koller Papyrus gives us an insight into the preparation of the chariotry and the care the horses could expect. The text was written by one army scribe, Amenope, to another, Paibes, writing about the time of Ramses II:

Take good heed to make ready the array [?] of horses which is [bound] for Syria, together with their stable-men, and likewise their grooms; their cats . . . ed and filled with provender and straw, rubbed down twice over; their corn-bags [?] filled with Kyllestis bread [a small loaf about 8–12 oz] a single ass [?] in charge of [every] two men. Their chariots are of *bry*-wood [?] filled with all kinds of weapons of warfare; eighty arrows in the quiver, the lance [?], the sword, the dagger, the . . . whip of *t3g*-wood furnished with lashes, the chariot club, the staff [?] of watchfulness, the javelin of Kheta, the rein-looser, the chariot their facings [of] bronze of six-fold alloy, graven with chiselling . . . ed, and . . . ed. Their cuirasses are placed beside them. The bows are adjusted [?] to their strings, their wood being tested in drawing, their bindings [?] consisting of clean . . . leather [?]. The pole is of *t3g*-wood . . . ed, shaped [?], fitted with leather, finished off [?], oiled and polished.[101]

Ramses left Egypt in the spring of 1285. Leading Amun he pushed rapidly ahead of the other divisions to where the high ground fell into the plain around Kadesh. Near Shabtuna, around 7½ miles south of Kadesh, two Shasu Bedouin spies in Hittite pay came to Ramses and told him the Hittites had retreated to Aleppo. The Egyptians camped east of the River Orontes. On the river's west bank stood Kadesh. So far there was no trace of the Hittites, then two Hittite scouts were captured and brought to the camp. Under torture they revealed the Hittites' presence hidden to the north-east of Kadesh. Now knowing his danger Ramses' vizier sent a mounted messenger to order Ptah to hasten. Crossing the Orontes Ramses left his other divisions on the east, strung out towards the south. Re then crossed the river with its van 1½ miles to the rear of Amun. Ptah and Sutekh were moving up slowly. Suddenly, 2,500 Hittite chariots swept around the south side of Kadesh and hit Re coming up. Re panicked, broke and fled to the Egyptian camp, Amun too joining the flight. Hittite chariots enveloped the camp. Ramses, left with only his elite guard, launched such a whirlwind charge that he gained enough time to see the Hittite's weak spot where their chariot line was thinnest on their extreme right. 'Victory in Thebes' galloped so fast that the impact drove this section of the Hittite line into the Orontes.

Now the *bête noire* of commanders gave Ramses a respite. The Hittite chariot division, pouring into the now deserted camp, stopped to pillage. They paid dearly: a band of crack Canaanite reserves came up from the town of Amor and massacred the plundering Hittites. Reprieved by the fresh troops, the Egyptians rallied. With Ramses at their head the Egyptian chariotry charged six times in a three-hour engagement. Seeing the battle turning against him Muwatallis sent in 1,000 Hittite reserve chariots, but too late. Ptah coming up hit the rear of the Hittites who fled into Kadesh city.

The Kadesh inscriptions make no mention of a second day of battle, but the Poem of Kadesh does, even though the decisive actions were on the first day. Ramses again took to the field 'when earth grew light', but renewed fighting went against the Hittites and 'the wretched Chief of Khatti sent and did homage'. The poem also gives us more personal details. In the inscriptions Ramses states: 'His majesty halted in the rout, then he charged into the foe, the vanquished of Kheta, being alone by himself and none other with him. . . .' The poem puts Ramses in a more generous light. His acknowledgements went to horses and men:

I defeated millions of foreign countries, being alone, being on 'Victory in Thebes' and 'Mut is Contented' my great horses. They it is whom I found to support me when I was alone fighting many foreign countries. I will persist in making them eat food in my presence every day when I am in my palace. They it is whom I found in the midst of the battle together with the charioteer Menna my shield bearer, and with my household butlers who were beside me, the witnesses to me as regards the fighting, behold I found them.[102]

This is a far more fitting epitaph to his courage than taking all the credit to himself.

Kadesh was the first recorded battle in which infantry was absent. The Hittites did not send their foot in, and the significant Egyptian sections were from Ramses' chariotry. Scouting from the Egyptian side was deficient at the start; the Hittites relied on their scouts to keep them advised on a continuing basis. Although only the Egyptian messenger is specifically noted there must have been a corps of such horses and men to keep the commanders of divisions in touch with each other. Some 2,500 teams of horses sweeping around from the north-east to the south of Kadesh could not have been travelling that fast if they expected to keep their cohesion and full impact on Re. As they hit Re on the march it would have been a broadside hit on an extended line, and therefore more vulnerable to penetration, especially as the bulk of the 5,000 Egyptians would have been foot.

The sound of 5,000 horses and the rumble of wheels would have given brief warning before they appeared, but not enough for Re to form battle dispositions. Having recently worked on a television documentary on *Horses in War* in which chariots were used, but only a token two units, I can vouch for the noise factor. With just two, two-horse teams the noise was impressive. The huge Hittite chariot force must have produced a deafening roar and reverberation that would have elicited, if not panic among their enemy, at least apprehension, a factor not so far considered.

From the inscriptions it seems as if the four Egyptian divisions were marching carelessly, with no adequate, if any, screening of chariotry; but this may simply be an omission from the inscriptions, that reflects Egyptian carelessness. Once alerted, Ramses's crack troops did form up and deliver a telling counter-charge. By that time Hittite cohesion was lost and discipline had disappeared. It is very difficult to get horses galloping full out, and in huge numbers, under control again. With the horses' speed unavoidably being of unequal performance it was also inevitable that the Hittite line would have become strung out as they invested the Egyptian camp. Ramses' claim to 'be all alone' is not to be taken literally. No king, unless he was very stupid, totally exposed himself. An elite corps' duty was as much protective screening of the king as that of a fighting force. I think the most that can be said is that Ramses' courage and the speed of his horses, undoubtedly of superior stock, outstripped his elite teams on both occasions when he is recorded as charging – that is, the initial charge, and the six assaults after regrouping when Ptah had arrived to bolster numbers and morale. Allowing for hyperbole, it is likely that the pharaoh's multiple charges, with his elite guard, were against a scattered Hittite chariotry into which they could pour concerted fire while maintaining a gallop to keep themselves from being sitting ducks.

CHAPTER 9

Assyrian Equestrian Infrastructure

SUPPLIES OF EQUIDS

Once Assyria achieved her independence from Mitanni there was an ever-present need to maintain it. Assyria's heartland was a rich agricultural area of corn and pasture. Her mercantile network was wide. To her north-west, north, and north-east were mountain ranges inhabited by fierce hill tribes. Within the mountains and their valley pastures were products essential to Assyria – minerals and metals, wood for building, and horses for her army. To prevent encroachment on her rich lands, protect her trading network, and to acquire these products, militarism escalated.[1] It is this factor that Assyrian kings boasted of in their annals.

Three areas were prominent in equestrianism. Two, which comprised many small countries and city states, were Syria and Anatolia. The third was Urartu and her adjacent Iranian lands. Assyria warred against all three on many occasions. Some territories became incorporated into the empire as Assyrian provinces. At the height of her military power some Assyrian kings, such as Tiglath-Pileser III and Sargon II, campaigned in each area at some time during their reigns, as well as in countries not especially noted for horses. The annals record the rich equid pickings.

Major expansion started under Tiglath-Pileser I. He campaigned against the Mushki (Phrygians) and against a coalition of the Kings of Nairi to the south of Lake Van, an area later subsumed into Urartu. From there 'he led away great herds of horses, mules, grazing cattle and the flocks of their pastures in countless numbers'.[2] Anatolia also felt the might of Assyrian chariotry and foot. Melid (Malatya/Melitene) fell to him. It was to fall to Urartu, and again to Assyria in succeeding centuries. Under Tiglath-Pileser I, Assyria's army developed, especially in the chariot division and in horses for draught.[3] After such an able king Assyria declined, until it became reinvigorated from the tenth century onwards by a succession of strong monarchs.

INTRODUCTION OF CAVALRY TO THE ASSYRIAN ARMY

Another major boost to the Assyrian army was the introduction of cavalry by the energetic Tukulti Ninurta II (890–884). Although his reign was short he campaigned continuously.[4] In his expedition northwards against Nairi, Gilzani, and the Shubari, he collected a rich haul of tribute horses. Ami-ba'li of Nairi is singled out in connection with his tribute which consisted of furnishing horses to Tukulti Ninurta's bodyguards. It is significant that it was from the mountainous Urartean lands that Assyria's first cavalry horses were acquired, and that Tukulti Ninurta had found mountain trails too difficult for his chariots.[5]

Although it has been considered that true cavalry units were first formed in Assyria, there is a strong probability that cavalry was already part of the armament of the powerful Urartean people whose territory was more suited to the ridden than to the driven horse. In the change from driving to riding horses it would have taken considerable time to have become a significant branch of any army. The Vannic inscriptions give us some idea of this change. In the reign of Menua of Urartu (810–785) considerable numbers of cavalry were already used, as Menua kept a standing army of 65 chariots, 15,700 foot and numerous cavalry. In one expedition he led 1,600 chariots, 9,174 cavalry, and 2,704 archers.[6] With Urartean expertise in equestrianism it is to be expected that such a huge group of cavalry was no recent innovation. From the equid booty lists in the Assyrian annals it also seems likely that Assyria learned much from their Vannic enemies in the north.

URARTU –

THE MISLEADING SIDE OF THE ASSYRIAN EQUESTRIAN COIN

Sargon II's great campaign of 714 against Urartu was only one of many that had their beginnings in the reign of Shalmaneser I (1274–1245), whose annals record the (fictitious) rebellion of Nairi/Urartu against Assyria. Urartu had never been under Assyrian domination. In this instance Urartu was the aggressor, prompting Shalmaneser's retaliation. Thereafter, Shalmaneser periodically raided Urartu. Although he claimed great conquests, levied tribute, and wreaked devastation, once Assyrian forces had gone there was little hope of annual tribute being paid without another *razzia*. As Urartu was rich in the commodities Assyria needed – mineral wealth, horses and meat livestock from the valleys, etc. – raids and campaigns became a feature of Assyrian and Urartean life. As Assyria grew in military and commercial power, so too did Urartu. By the end of the ninth century Urartean influence stretched westward from the Caspian Sea to the Mediterranean, and to the River Orontes, and eastwards and south beyond Lake Urmia. Unlike Assyria, who turned defeated countries into Assyrian provinces and practised mass deportations and resettlements of peoples far from their original homeland, Urartu federated with her neighbours and allies. By such a policy Urartu had access to numerous trade routes and commercial opportunities, links Assyria also claimed.[7]

As Sargon so graphically records, Urartean and neighbouring Mannean territory produced excellent horses and horsemen in vast numbers.[8] This huge swathe of territory, comprising what later was known as Armenia and western Iran, continued to be the repository of quality horses throughout the ancient world. It provided the later empires of the Persians and the Seleucids with their warhorses. Both Xenophon and Strabo comment on the area's horses.[9]

By way of tribute in the reign of Menua, Urartu also acquired horses from the Colchians. This campaign opened the way for a trade route from the south of Urartu to Erzerum and to Trapezus on the Black Sea. Colchian territory lay in the direct path of the Cimmerians. In the eighth century these mounted nomads erupted through the Darial Pass in the Caucasus Mountains and along the east coast of the Black Sea, overrunning Anatolia.[10] Was there a connection between the equestrianism of the Colchians, who may have had prior contacts and learned from these nomads? Most migrating waves operate on a long-term basis. In the case of horsemen and pastoralists one impetus was to seek new pastures, usually because they were being pushed by a similar wave. As invaders they had to fight to hold new territory. The Cimmerians in turn were pushed by the Scythians. In the time of Rusa I (735–714) Urartu was attacked in the same year (714) by the Cimmerians and by Sargon. The Cimmerians were to stay in Urartu's Mannean neighbourhood. The royal correspondence of Esarhaddon (680–669) records that he had ordered out his cavalry and *Daku* (shock troops) against them.[11] Later, his son Ashurbanipal (668–627) campaigned against both Mannai and the Cimmerians who had invaded Assyrian territory.[12] By this time the chariot was coming to the end of its predominance in Near Eastern armies in favour of cavalry. This must certainly have been influenced by appreciation of the horse's greater usefulness in all types of terrain when ridden, and by the lengthy incursions of horsed nomads.

A huge many-columned Urartean inscription from Argishti I's reign (785–753) records several years of his campaigns against Assyria and other peoples.[13] In the careful tallying of Urartean gains, not counting captured civilians, horses feature as the prime booty, preceding other animals in the tally. Numbers vary from a low of 25 to a high of 17,942, but mostly range in the high hundreds and several thousand in each entry. Significantly after an attack on Assyria 987 cavalry were 'led away'.[14] Without actually specifying they were Assyrian cavalry it is most probable they were, as this number is sandwiched between records of several attacks on Assyria. These Urartean booty lists fill in the gaps left in the grandiose Assyrian annals, and show Assyria sustained considerable losses in livestock, losses presumably too unflattering to her king to record. Huge gains and losses by warring countries explain some of the need, apart from sheer belligerence, for campaigns and raids. No people could sustain such continual losses in manpower, horses, and meat on the hoof.

NEO-ASSYRIA

The Neo-Assyrian period from Assurnasirpal II (883–859) to Ashurbanipal is rich in sources and we can trace the kings' military peregrinations in some detail. It is also the period when cavalry was increasingly used, sometimes with a high ratio to chariotry. The detailed reliefs and paintwork revealed by excavators record the armaments of the Assyrians and their enemies. The horse and its related equipment is central to many reliefs. The chariots are far heavier than those of the Egyptians. By Ashurbanipal's reign they had become very much heavier for they now carried four men. Cavalry expertise improved from the two-man team of warrior and horsehandler, both seated very precariously behind the horse's motion, to the cavalry of Sargon II and later kings which were seated independently in a more balanced and secure fashion. Using this balanced seat cavalry was now wholly a strike force, with each rider a combat trooper. It lessened the need for horses per unit, or alternatively allowed the strike force to be doubled. I would opt for the latter situation because the acquisition of horses rose dramatically in numbers over that of previous reigns, particularly from lands beyond the Zagros Mountains. This escalation in cavalry horse numbers, not only of the Assyrians, is backed up by the inscriptions from the reigns of the Urarteans Menua and Argishti noted above.

ASSYRIAN HORSE LEVIES

With cavalry becoming increasingly important, and chariotry remaining the senior arm of the Assyrian army, a look at how the bulk of the military animals, aside from booty, were procured is needed.

Tablets termed 'Horse Reports' from the Kouyunjik (Nineveh) archive, most probably from the reign of Esarhaddon, throw a great deal of light onto the system of acquisition. A series of letters, twenty in all, written in the first three months of the year by Nabu-sumu-iddina (seventeen letters) and Nadinu (three letters), and possibly the same person, tally animals acquired by the government at Nineveh. There were three main collection points, at Kalhu (Nimrud), Nineveh and Dur Sarruken. The letters are probably from a single year and thus illustrate the annual gathering in of stock prior to the campaign season. They cover horses levied from Assyria proper, from its provinces and from high officials, several of whom were provincial governors.[15] Levies are also shown from the Tell Billa texts from the site near Mosul.[16] The indication that these levies of horses (and mules) were also made on a provincial basis comes from two allied texts from Lahiru and Borsippa.[17]

Levies from the empire were known as *bitqu*,[18] and the officials responsible for them were the *musarkisus*, who were appointed by central government and assigned to their provinces where they collected the horses. They were assisted by *saknus* who received and cared for the animals. *Musarkisus* were subdivided into those collecting for various army units such as chariotry and cavalry, the king's cavalry bodyguard, and the palace chariotry.[19] Horses and mules so gathered on a provincial basis were then ready for issue to chariotry, cavalry or baggage (in the case of mules). Horses were also sometimes referred to as *sibtu*, and Postgate suggests this is not the levying of the increase tax, as with cattle, sheep, etc., but is concerned with an 'increase horse' which he considers to have been a stallion reserved for breeding purposes. I suggest it is a levy on youngstock, and when appearing with horses coming in as a tax obligation as 'of the increase' it means the normal tax, plus a percentage or a stipulated number per stud or herd of the stock born at the stud from which other horses were levied, on the tithing principle. In the *Royal Correspondence* there are many entries dealing with levies of horses and it is the Kusean horses that often have 'of the increase of the land of Kusi', and not the Mesean horses which came from east of Assyria. I consider this points to breeding Kusean horses in studs dotted around the empire. Other horses noted above are 'riding horses' indicating grade horses (mixed blood) of no particular breed, and the Mesean horses from Mesu, and neighbouring lands. This would not preclude studs of other horses also operating within the empire, but maybe not with the same prestige as the Kusean of which *sibtu* was demanded. It also implies a shortage of this particular type/breed.

The Tribute System

Another means of acquisition was from the *madattu* (tribute) levied on Assyrian-dominated territories, that yet had a local ruler, nominally in power, but closely supervised by an Assyrian appointee. It was usual for *madattu* horses to be presented by either the territory's ruler or one of his high officials such as an emissary.[20] Along with the tribute horses there would have been an additional quota termed *namurta* horses. Theoretically they were 'freely' given in return for an audience with the king, but in reality drew a customary imposition or expectation. *Namurta* horses were also received from within Assyria from men seeking audience and wealthy enough to be in a horseowning category.[21] On occasion *namurta* horses were real free gifts.

There were several other definitions for horses used to describe the equids' current situation. *Iskaru* horses were those owned by the state and billeted with their charioteers and cavalrymen in the season when the army was stood down, usually the winter. At the start of the campaign season horses and men would have reported for duty. *Nakamtu* horses were those held in reserve. *Ma'assu* horses were those resting in between campaigns. Apart from the *iskaru* animals horses were held in government-run establishments ready for issue to their respective units.[22] Such holdings would possibly have been subdivided into areas for reserve horses ready for issue, and farms with pastureland and supervisory staff for the resting animals, many of whom would have needed time to regain condition lost on campaign, and/or recover from ailments incurred, but not so severe as to render them useless for further action; for example, minor lameness and wounds not in vital parts.

From the various equine military departments Assyria kept its army supplied, but there were never enough horses within the empire to replace those lost to action, disease, and old age. Tribute did not always come in. Assyria considered this as rebellion and an armed force would be sent to collect it. The records show that on other occasions *razzias* were undertaken for the sole purpose of acquiring horses. Esarhaddon sent an expedition to Media;[23] Tiglath-Pileser III sent his general Assur-Daninanni against Media and raised 5,000 horses.[24] When Tabal 'was indifferent towards Assyria's achievements' Tiglath-Pileser III deposed Uassurme and put his own man in place, and among the punitive measures 2,000 horses were taken. When Kummuhi in Anatolia withheld its tribute, tax and gifts, Sargon II invaded it and their horses, chariotry, cavalry, archers and foot were forced to serve Assyria's interests under Sargon's appointed governor.[25] The Medes too withheld their tribute and were likewise invaded.[26] These areas were the major suppliers of horses, the booty/tribute taken amounting to thousands of animals each year, in contrast to significantly lower numbers from other areas of the empire and its tributary countries.

The 'Horse Reports' show, apart from a few mules, that the main types/breeds acquired were the Kusean and the Mesean. Both were used for chariotry.[27] Cavalry horses often appear in the *Royal Correspondence* as 'riding horses'.[28] They appear in the 'Horse Reports' as *Pēthallu* (cavalry) with no breed designation. Of a total of 787+ cavalry horses the *Turtan* (Commander-in-Chief) provided 243. He was probably the Governor of Harran,[29] one of the major cities of the Assyrian Empire. Of the remainder in the Nineveh documents the greatest number came from Syria: Arpad supplied 104; Hatarikka 67+; Guzana 67; Kullania 38. Other Syrian cities, such as Damascus, also provided a few cavalry horses. Some of these city states contributed only cavalry horses, others both harness and riding animals. Zamua across the Zagros in Iran sent forty-seven cavalry horses. Iran was already noted for its horses. Syria had the trade from Tabal and Que. The port of Tyre handled some shipments from Anatolia, and Egypt had long supplied horses. Others no doubt came into Assyria with the commercial caravans, as well as with the retinues of the emissaries accompanying tribute.

In succeeding centuries, both BC and AD, Syria was noted for superior horses. According to Strabo, Seleucus Nicator had a Syrian royal stud of 30,000 mares and 300 stallions.[30] In the medieval period Damascus was the Syrian Mamlūk capital. The Mamlūks were the superlative horsemen of the era.[31] Unfortunately, nothing can be gained as to what these Assyrian acquisitions of Syrian cavalry horses looked like, or what were their attributes, but clues are there. Anatolia produced great numbers of quality horses. Those from Tabal were large,[32] and the Cilician stock was renowned from as far back as Solomon's era, and onwards into the Persian Empire.[33] Just prior to Tiglath-Pileser III's era Urartu held many of the territories known for good horses. In the reign of Sarduri II (753–735) Arpad and Hatarikka, Cilicia, much of central Anatolia and the important city of Carcemish on the Euphrates were subject to Urartu.[34] As Urartu thereby controlled the trade routes north of Assyria it is quite possible, and very likely probable, that horses formed part of the commercial transactions to augment tribute paid to Urartu. This would have added to the genetic mix in the type of animals available to Syria, Cilicia, etc., as well as having an influence on the Urartean breeds, and those of their allies beyond the Zagros. This is taking the view that travel and commerce in equids was not all one way into Urartu.

ASSYRIAN HORSE TRADE

One of the Neo-Assyrian professions was that of horsetrader – *Tamkar Sise* – a term not found before the reign of Tiglath-Pileser III.[35] When this ruler reorganised the army and took Assyria to new military heights it is conceivable that horsetraders became much more important as the need for horses grew, especially when cavalry expanded under Sargon II. A special type of trader, confining himself to one commodity was necessary to fill the shortfall in horses. There are tablets from Sargon II's era which indicate the presence of horsetraders from Syria and Urartu, the latter in Assyrian pay was probably procuring cavalry horses from Mannean territory. A Samarian horse trainer and breeder was employed by Sennacherib (704–681) for his son, and a Nubian (Kushite) official known as Kusaya, the rein holder, had sixteen stablemen under him. With the good relations between Tiglath-Pileser III and the Egyptian Piankhi and Shabako with Sargon, horse trade between the two countries flourished.[36] Two specific details from the reigns of Sargon II and Esarhaddon concern selling and purchase. Sargon had written to Adadittia about horsetraders from Kannua. They had arrived in Urzuhina offering 70 horses for sale, but Adadittia informed the merchant Shari that he desired 200 horses. They were to be of fine appearance and his whole string was to be presented for sale.[37] A letter to Esarhaddon from his official Ninibahiddina says that Ahesha and Belittadin, the agents of Nabushallim of the city of Bit Dakuru (in Babylonia and under Assyrian domination) had arrived with money for the purchase of horses. The official required to know Esarhaddon's wishes in the matter.[38]

ASSYRIA ASCENDANT

Tiglath-Pileser III reversed Urartean supremacy. He recounted his Urartean and other victories with their equid and other acquisitions, gained from Tabal, Urartu and Media, to the tune of several thousand head.[39] In 712 the last King of Melid, Tarkhu-Nazi, and 5,000 of his subjects were taken captive by Sargon II, and his capital of Togarmah was destroyed. This was in retaliation for his father Sulumal having allied with Urartu against Assyria.[40] Going by the dates it may be that the Sulumal of the Armenian history may have been the Uassurme of the Assyrian records of Tiglath-Pileser III. Melid and Tabal, of which Togarmah was the capital are in Cappadocia (see page xviii).

It was not only Assyria that staged *razzias* for horses. Urartu also augmented their horse stocks this way. Argishti I, in overrunning

Dayaeni, an Assyrian territory, took a huge haul of prisoners, and carried off 4,426 horses, and thousands of large and small cattle.[41]

SIZE OF HORSES

One of the prime requirements for a military horse was a decent size. This is related to height and body mass, with enough bone to carry or draw a considerable weight, and to withstand hard usage. Lack of any of these would have rendered horses unsuitable for the military. Postgate remarks that the Assyrian carvings show no difference between chariot and cavalry horses.[42] It is true that they all appear the same, but that is only because artists followed artistic conventions; Egyptian horses were depicted in a similarly stylised way. In the thousands of animals used there would have been wide variations, even if the group type was similar. Nevertheless, the Assyrian horses appear to have solid, well-fleshed and muscled conformation, with limbs showing good bone and clearly defined tendons. The dry head and fine throatlatch shows good breeding. Overall they appear to be of compact, tough conformation, with none of the softness that would have been disastrous to animals on campaign. However, in the reigns of Shalmanezer III and Assurnasipal II the horses, unfortunately, are depicted very badly in respect of conformation. In the reign of Ashurbanipal, horses, equipment, chariots and weaponry are all shown with great accuracy, and the horses' anatomy is beautifully portrayed.

The Kushite stock was often labelled 'large',[43] and the horses from Mesu, according to Dalley, were small.[44] The 'Horse Report's' table shows that yoke horses came from the Kusean and the Mesu types. Surely a general type would have been required in the chariot divisions? It is not impossible that two types, small and large, came from Mesu, but it is unlikely that the Assyrians would have settled for small horses for their cavalry when the animals had to carry substantial weights of men equipped with weapons and armour.

Mesu in Iran, along with Mannai, Parsua and Gizilbundu are located in the valley of the River Jaghati which flows into the south of Lake Urmia.[45] I do not see why these Mesu horses were necessarily small. The horses of the Mannean Ullusunu rendered as tribute to Sargon II were 'large draft' (that is, yoke) horses, and those of the Medes from not too far south are noted as 'mighty steeds'.[46] Other countries were noted for their large horses, such as Susa in Elam and Tabal in Anatolia.[47] Quite clearly large cavalry and yoke horses were in demand. A general idea of 'large' comes from the approximately 15 hh Buhen horse (150 cm at withers), *c.* 1650, and from a similar date from Malyan in Fars, north-west Iran, where bones showed a similar height for the largest of the three horses.[48] In a horsebreeding timeframe, without the impetus for growth given by modern balanced nutrition, it is likely that the huge horses that the Medes were famous for in not much later times, which were bred on the Nisayan Plain south of Ecbatana (Hamadan) were the same, or of very similar, stamp to the 'mighty steeds' described by the Assyrians in the reign of Ashurbanipal. In 612 Nineveh fell to the Medes. Nevertheless, one factor for the Nisaean size was highly nutritious alfafa (lucerne/Median clover) which has a protein content up to 27 per cent green, and hay at 16 to 18 per cent. The total digestible nutrient of this is about half these figures. Fed on such fodder horses were able to reach their genetic potential. Many horses undernourished in their early years never reach potential height or body mass.[49]

THE ASSYRIAN ARMY

The component parts of the Assyrian army were diverse. At its core was a standing army. There was a permanent royal bodyguard, and established garrisons at major Assyrian and provincial locations. Logistical back-up was provided by a pioneer corps for road hacking and building, and for facilitating river crossings. A baggage train carried provisions and other impedimenta, and presumably extra weapons, and a siege train hauled the engines of war. Scribes and priests were essential non-military additions.[50] The largest numerical group of the military were conscripts serving their annual *ilku* obligations to the king and state. These were drawn from the whole empire. However, the equestrian conscripts were mostly drawn from Assyrian nationals and served under a permanent Assyrian captain. A captain in a chariot corps commanded a fifty-strong unit.[51]

As well as troops from the Assyrian heartland and the provinces, equestrian units (and foot) were also added into the Assyrian army from foreign enemies after successful campaigns. Many instances illustrate this, especially from the Levant in the time of Shalmaneser III and Sargon II. Moreover, they indicate that cavalry came into prominence under Sargon II. This is shown by the ratio of chariots to cavalry. This ratio also suggests how the two arms worked in concert. Shalmaneser III captured chariots and cavalry in 853 from Damascus and Hamath in the ratio of one chariot to one cavalryman. Twelve years later he took three chariots from Damascus for every cavalryman. Dalley submits that this indicated the Syrians held chariotry to be superior to cavalry.[52]

By stages the roles were reversed. Sargon II's Babylonian governor fielded one chariot to ten cavalrymen. The Syrian enemies continued to field considerable numbers of equestrian units. Some cities had large units of both arms, some only had chariotry. The less affluent cities had no equestrian units. From Carcemish Sargon II took 50 chariots and 200 cavalry (and 300 foot); from Hamath 200 chariots and 600 cavalry. These units went straight into the royal army, the *Kisir Sarruti*. At the fall of Samaria in 722, after a three-year siege, a fifty-strong chariot corps was added to the royal army. Unlike other equestrian units from both Syria and other foreigners, it was allowed to keep its city identity. The equestrian units from Carcemish and Hamath, although drawn into the royal army, and not into the provincial establishments, as were many other foreigners, did not keep their city names but were broken up before being assigned.[53] One reason suggested for allowing the Samarians to remain as a city unit is that they may have been mercenaries and willing to fight for Assyria.[54] The Bible, in its usual euphemistic way, refers to mercenaries from both Samaria and Jerusalem fighting in the army of Assyria. The prophet Ezekiel describes two sisters, Oholah (Samaria) and Oholibah (Jerusalem) prostituting themselves to Assyria.[55]

ASSYRIAN CHARIOT AND CAVALRY WARFARE

As mentioned earlier (pages 175–77), I do not think it feasible for two enemies to meet head-on in a massed charge. However, the Assyrian army's main strength did lie in its chariotry. There is no clear indication of exactly how this force was deployed. The weaponry of the Assyrian fighting man in the chariot consisted of bow, arrows, sword and a long spear. This indicates long-range assault and close-order combat. Most battle reliefs with Assyrian chariots depict them coming in from all directions and being used at both short and long range. Against an army composed mainly of infantry, a charge of chariots could be effective, since unless the infantry was extremely well disciplined, as in the later Roman army, a mass of horses thundering towards them would have been extremely intimidating. Added to that, in the heightened chaos of battle, when cohesion would in all probability have been lost, the horses, which for the Assyrians were all stallions, as shown by their complete tackle, would have been aroused. Two things undisciplined stallions do is bite and strike with the forefoot, or forefeet. A strike with a forefoot is perfectly possible without the horse appreciably breaking stride.[56] Warhorses down the centuries had their aggressive instincts channelled, especially in India.[57] Similarly, against an enemy weak in chariot numbers, as would have been the case in many of Assyria's foes who did not have her huge military capacity, nor the Assyrians' aggression, a charge of chariots could have been used. I suggest that in the pre-campaign calculations a percentage of losses from the chariot, horse, and cavalry numbers would have been envisaged and considered expendable.

The limitation of chariotry is shown in the fight between Ahab of Samaria, Israel, and Ben-Hadad of Damascus, Syria (the Hadadezer of Shalmaneser III's Battle of Qarqar). The account in I Kings 20 shows a clear example of chariots being hampered, defeated and scattered, a situation in which cavalry was more useful as an escape mechanism. Ahab, after being required to submit to Syria – or being besieged by the Syrians, who were camped at Succoth – pre-empted the Syrian siege. He marched out at noon against the Syrians to the valley of Succoth, about 26 miles east of Samaria, hemmed in by the River Jordan to the west, the River Jabbok to the south, mountains east and north-east, and ravines to the north. The Syrians were unable to utilise their chariot force, but the more mobile cavalry was able to escape with Ben-Hadad mounted on a horse. The following year the Syrians went against Israel, this time at Aphek, but although they chose flat, good chariot territory, were again beaten.[58]

These same kings had earlier joined forces against Shalmaneser III in 853 at the Battle of Qarqar, where Ahab of Samaria, Hadadezer of Damascus, and Irhuleni of Hamath, deployed by far the largest contingents of chariots and cavalry among the coalition armies (see below, page 105).

Another way of utilising chariots and cavalry in concert has been noted by Dalley, using the reliefs and ratios of chariots to cavalry. Where combat is one to one and one to two she suggests the horsemen accompanied the chariots, as shown on the Syrian reliefs.[59] This method would certainly not be suitable if the chariots were supposed to open hostilities with a charge. It is to be expected that a cavalry horse would travel much more quickly and nimbly than a hitched pair with a restraining neck yoke impeding full and continued speed. It would also present a number of small fighting units, rather than a concerted mass. I would suggest that the terrain, and the nature and size of the enemy, would have dictated the specific way units were arranged and used. Whatever the system, cohesion would inevitably have been lost. Possibly the only cavalry force to have kept cohesion was that of Cromwell's army who charged at 'a good round trot', not a very great speed, but one designed to maximise concerted weight and firepower, this being via the gun which needed close range at that date, not by arrows which required long-range assault.

THE FLUCTUATION IN ANIMAL LOSSES AND GAINS IN THE MILITARY SPHERE

From Nimrud comes an account of mules, donkeys and oxen held at one unspecified location. It shows receipts from taxes, booty and tribute in several phases. Most information is about donkeys. Total holdings are tabulated at intervals, 470 donkeys in two corrals, 412 in another. In yet another section, out of 202 animals, 72 have died, the balance being issued to named people, several employed by messengers. Other uses were as pack and draught donkeys. Several unspecified animals (blanks in the tablets) but presumably donkeys, were also issued to messengers to ride. From an obliterated enumeration, of which 34 at least have died, 153 remain in the corrals. Of 93 oxen, 53 had died.[60]

This mortality rate is extremely high and has a bearing on equid and bovine longevity in general, and in particular on animals in military use. We are never given the numbers of Assyrian horses that died in action, and only the occasional specific reference to enemy horses killed. In Sargon II's eighth campaign against Urartu and its allies, he refers to Mettati of Zikirtu and the neighbouring kings, in the course of which 'I filled the gullies with their horses'.[61] And against Merodach Baladan he boasts 'his warriors, horses broken to the yoke I decimated with arrows . . .'.[62]

It is almost certain that there was a similar mortality in action and in the gruelling work expended in going to and from action. This would have necessitated the continual need for large numbers of tribute, and other assessed and stipulated acquisitions coming into the central administration, and to other designated collection points at Kalhu, Nineveh and Ashur. To these were added the equines garnered in considerable but fluctuating numbers from booty horses, those bred at studs, and those purchased as noted above, plus loose horses rounded up after a battle.

An estimate of potential increase in numbers from studs could have been envisaged, but there was always the lowering factor due to barren, infertile and aborting mares, the variability of stallions' fertility, and endemic disease hazards. Although we do not have specifics of stud locations it is certain that these must have operated throughout the empire as horses of specific types are recorded as coming in via various levies from external and internal sources throughout the *Royal Correspondence of the Assyrian Empire* from the reign of Sargon II to that of Esarhaddon. In the reign of Esarhaddon, one levy of ninety-eight horses, mostly from Lahiru, consisted of Kusean, Nisaean and part-bred horses by Kusean stallions out of Assyrian mares.[63] Another letter to the king noted the levies from Karnie, Daana, Arpad and Isana, which totalled 44

Kusean, 104 riding horses and 30 mules.[64] For example, the Kusean horses featured in many levies are often set out as 6 Kusean and 3, of the increase of the horses of Kusi, of Daana.[65] This suggests that 6 mature Kusean and 3 Kusean youngstock, or at least the progeny of Kusean stock held in a stud at Daana, as part of the levy.

ARMY PROVISIONING

It was from Assyria's agricultural economy that the army was largely provisioned, mainly in foodstuffs for animals and men. In addition to comestibles, other army provisions such as clothing for the men, and leather for harness, for chariots, and later for cavalry horses also came from pastoral sources. The timber for chariots and carts and other army engines, and the metals for component parts, and for bits, would mostly have come from imported and/or tribute sources. Weaponry and armour for both horse and man would have been from domestic and foreign sources, particularly in the case of armour composed of fabric or wool overlaid with leather, with metal superimposed on the whole, as described in the Nuzi Tablets discussed in the text describing Mitannian militarism.

Acquisition of corn (or barley) was raised by a tax called *Nusahe*, and acquisition of straw by the tax called *Sibsu*.[66] Postgate's superb work on *Taxation and Conscription in the Assyrian Empire* does not mention the other fodder component, hay. Barley straw, while satisfactory for brickmaking, has poor nutritional qualities. Hay, cut from pasture set aside until the crop was taken, then grazed, was a necessary foodstuff. We know that a considerable amount of hay was raised in the Roman period. Regulations were passed over hay contracts, and deductions from troopers' pay for it appear in army records.[67] At Batnae in Osroene a rick collapsed and smothered fifty army grooms.[68] Batnae is midway between the Euphrates and its subsidiary the Belias, north-east of Til Barsip. Such a huge rick indicates that the riverine lands produced great quantities of hay. I suggest that the 'Watered land of the Assyrian king'[69] was irrigated or maybe lay in a flood plain very suitable for hay production. In the East Anglian Cambridgeshire Fens river meadows flooded in the winter are hay-mown in summer, then grazed until the water levels rise in winter. Are these artificial Assyrian meadows like those developed in England in the seventeenth and eighteenth centuries AD?[70]

A way of procuring meat for the army, and other government departments, was through the *sibtu*, which was an exaction on the increase in the herd.[71]

Rock art at Aravan near Ferghana, 1st century BC. Ferghana is in the Uranian Swathe where hot blood horses were present by 1000 BC at the latest. This painting shows a stallion about to cover a mare.

Scythian horses and horsemen showing various equestrian activities. Top row, left: getting a horse to fall on the ground; centre: roping a horse prior to gelding; right: hobbling, to limit movement. Lower row, left: chasing a horse; centre: horses grazing; right: lassoing a horse.

Outline of Nisaean horse showing heavy-bodied conformation and ram head. As shown on the Apadana frieze at Persepolis.

Greek marble frieze, re-used on the Acropolis at Xanthos, c. 450 BC, showing horse with groom, who, if adult, indicates that the stallion was well over 16 hh. Conformation is well and accurately sculpted, except for the head, which is too small for the massive body. (© British Museum)

Aramean stone relief from the palace of King Kapara, mid-10th century BC, Tell Halaf (Guzana), north-east Syria. This early cavalryman is so crudely executed that little can be ascertained as to equid specifics other than the dating of cavalry. Rider's seat is still well back toward the loin area, and therefore behind the movement. (© British Museum)

Mesopotamian terracotta mould of rider, 2000–1600 BC. The donkey seat is well back on horse's loins: judging from the position of the reins it could well have been used in conjunction with a nose ring, as it was still too early for metal bitting. Stallion wears girthed up and fringed saddlecloth. (© British Museum)

The Armento Rider, Greek, c. 560–550 BC, from Armento, Basiclica, southern Italy. This Greek cavalryman now uses a balanced seat and rides using direct rein. The horse is crudely represented and ill-formed. (© British Museum)

Greek horsemen from west frieze of the Parthenon, Athens, c. 438–432 BC, showing quality horses with good, compact conformation and robust physique. (© British Museum)

Ostrich fan from the tomb of Tutankhamun. King at war with war dog beneath chariot and enemies under horses' hooves. (© Egyptian National Museum, Cairo/Bridgeman Art Library)

Battle of Kadesh: Ramses II rides down Hittite charioteers. Note two disabled horses arrowshot in the side. Also note how the use of the terret puts extra tension on the reins. (© The British Library)

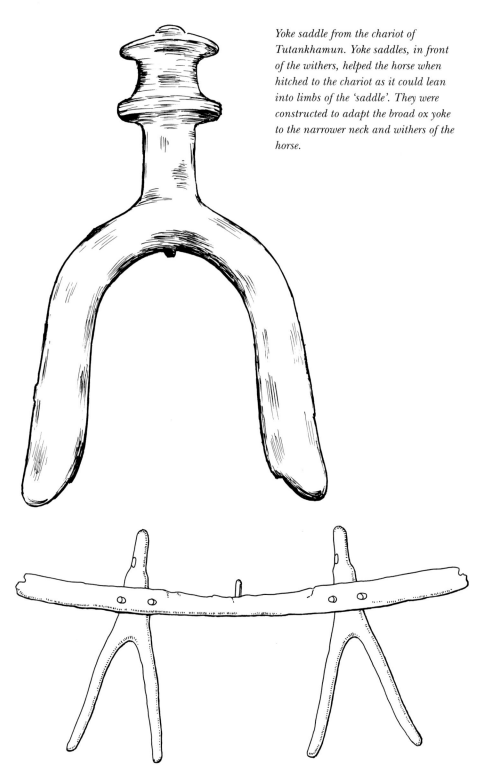

Yoke saddle from the chariot of Tutankhamun. Yoke saddles, in front of the withers, helped the horse when hitched to the chariot as it could lean into limbs of the 'saddle'. They were constructed to adapt the broad ox yoke to the narrower neck and withers of the horse.

A double hitch yoke with yoke saddles from Kurgan V at Pazyryk, burials in the Altai. About 1000 years separates these two examples.

Riding horse saddle and fittings from the Pazyryk burials in the Altai. Above: saddle with ornate felt cover edged in leather, together with ornate breastcollar, girth and crupper. Below: the saddle in place showing the raised front arch and the smaller rear arch, which is almost obscured by the rider's gorytus (bow and arrow case).

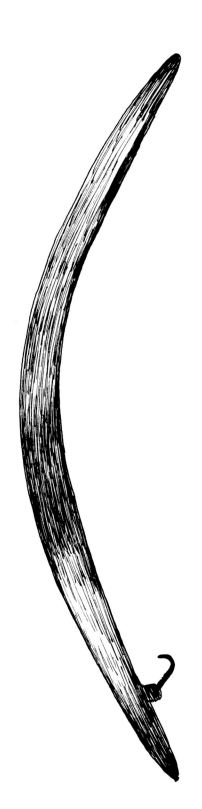
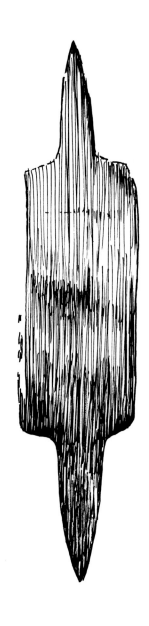

Bow arch (top) and a saddle spacer (bottom). The former was the precursor of the pommel, the latter kept the two stuffed cushions saddle construction quite rigid and prevented pressure on the spine and subsequent fistulous withers.

HORSES ON CAMPAIGN

In the main, lack of sources prevents a reconstruction of military tactics and strategy.[72] The inscriptions and reliefs tell us how successful Assyria was. They do not tell us exactly how the equid components of the army were used, except in the broadest sense of chariotry and cavalry, and the combining of these two elements. There are clues, not all necessarily from Assyrian sources. Open battle reliefs are rare. Two from Ashurbanipal's reign are the Battle of the River Ulai against the Elamites, and a war against the Arabs. The Elamite army was mostly composed of infantry, a few cavalry, and a limited number of heavy battle cars with ten to sixteen spokes per wheel and holding many soldiers, and chariots with eight-spoked wheels. The battle cars were too cumbersome for speed. The Assyrians were mainly foot and heavy-armed cavalry, the latter seen driving the Elamites to the river where men and horses are shown drowning. All the drowned horses are cavalry mounts. Significantly Assyrian chariots are absent from this stage of the battle.[73]

Against the Arabs, who lacked horses but rode camels and had infantry, Ashurbanipal's chariotry and cavalry were used to effect.[74] When records indicate a worthy feat, such as an advance over mountains by Sargon II in his chariot, accompanied by 1,000 elite cavalry and foot soldiers as a rapid strike force against Urzana of Musasir in 714, we only know that Urzana fled and Musasir was put under siege. Sargon dismounted from his chariot and went on horseback where the terrain was unfavourable for wheeled vehicles but suitable for riding, and on foot when even riding was too difficult.[75] We do not know how the action took place. It is therefore impossible to be precise about deployment in battle.

Rarely was the Assyrian army at home. The reigns of Shalmaneser III and Sargon II show Assyria at its most antagonistic. Shalmaneser's military peregrinations are notable for his repeated crossings of the Euphrates into Syria, and his periodic campaigns eastward against Urartu, and southward to Babylonia. In an eleven-year period from 860 to 849 his armies attacked Urartu in 860 and 857, Babylonia in 851, and Syria in 859, 858, 857, 854, 853, 850 and 849. Nor were these the only actions in that period.[76] In the reign of Sargon II, only three years – 712, 708 and 706 – are noted in his annals as 'the king stayed in the land', but his magnates (that is, military commanders) conducted numerous campaigns on his behalf.[77]

The remarkable features of these campaigns are the tremendous distances covered, not only on a single campaign but more significantly on an accumulative and usually annual basis. The two campaigns that give us much information about the Assyrians and their current antagonists are the Battle of Qarqar in 853, and Sargon II's campaign of

714 against Urartu. Both campaigns are rich in equid and equestrian content, but the information available is more about the Assyrians' acquisitions and enemies encountered than about the actual engagements. Hence the equestrian information and analysis given above at least fleshed out the equestrian units of the Assyrians, Levantine, Urartean and Mannean armies. Specific battlefield tactics have not been revealed. Other Sargonic campaigns give a fairly detailed breakdown of the infrastructure of military equine organisation linked to empire expansion. In 713 Tabal and Cilicia were annexed and turned into provinces.[78] It has already been noted that these areas were prime horsebreeding locales. Another Assyrian annexation was Melid in Kummuhu in 712,[79] which became a major supplier of large horses to Assyria,[80] in this instance from the reign of Ashurbanipal.

On these campaigns, especially the first two, very different climatic and territorial aspects pertained. Assyria's heartland is mostly flat, and in summer temperatures can rise to 120 degrees Fahrenheit. Syria has expanses of hot, dry desert and also broken hill country. Qarqar is situated in the Madi Sirhan. At other extremes Sargon went into a mountainous area. He started his campaign against Urartu in late May when the mountains were still snow-capped and the rivers running fast and deep with meltwaters. He came in through the valley of the Wasna Su, south-east of Lake Urmia. His sappers cut roads over mountains and then through dense jungle clothing the lower mountain slopes. Although his army feasted in the lowlands on ripening grain and fruit, the stresses of travel in continually shifting hazards – such as repeated river crossings, scaling rugged heights where ice still lay, and descending into humid lowlands – took their toll. Each variation in the climatic and topographic aspects put certain stresses on the physique of animals and men, especially on draught horses. These stresses would have been far more pronounced in the Urartean venture where so many variables were encountered, and horses had no time to become used to differing conditions in their travels.[81]

SHALMANESER III

Assyria could put a huge army into the field when necessary, calling on more than twenty provinces. In 845 Shalmaneser recorded an army of 120,000 for one of his many Euphrates crossings. Governors of provinces could also raise huge numbers: one fielded 20,000 archers and 1,500 cavalry.[82] However, this does not indicate the ratio of horse to foot across the whole empire, only that the Assyrians were able to put very large numbers of cavalry and chariotry into the field.

THE BATTLE OF QARQAR

Shalmaneser III gave a detailed account of the coalition of twelve kings ranged against him at Qarqar in 853. Hostilities between Syria and Israel were suspended to face the common enemy, Assyria. The three main Levantine kings bringing chariotry and/or cavalry were Hadadezer of Damascus, Irhuleni of Hamath and Ahab of Samaria.

	Chariotry	*Cavalry*	*Infantry*
Damascus	1,200	1,200	20,000
Hamath	700	700	10,000
Samaria	2,000	–	10,000

The animal power from the other kings amounted to only a total of 40 chariots and 1,000 camels. Their combined infantry was many thousands in excess of the 11,900 total that is clear from the inscriptions, some of the figures being obliterated. Shalmaneser boasted of 14,000 enemy dead, and captured the enemies' chariots, their draught stock, and their cavalry.[83] This was a significant increment to equid stocks for the Assyrian army. Shalmaneser is silent on his equid (or indeed any) losses.

SARGON II AGAINST URARTU

Soon after leaving Nimrud in late May 714 Sargon began to encounter very rough going as he headed for Urartu. The Upper Zab was in flood from snow meltwaters, and the Lower Zab too proved difficult, as was the Buia (Wasna Su) which he was forced to cross twenty-six times on account of the terrain. In preparation for attacking Zikirtu and Andia for a third time in his reign, he reviewed his army, chariotry and cavalry in the Plain of Sumbi, south-west of Lake Urmia. In the forbidding Zagros range the most difficult peak was Mount Simirra (Kandil Dagh) where the pioneer corps had to cut a road to enable the horses, chariots and foot to advance.[84] Sargon's mounted couriers had fanned out, summoning kings and chieftains from as far away as six days' journey from the Mannean mountain frontier fortress of Sinihinu where they were to come to offer submission and tribute. Ullusunu of Mannea was the first to arrive. In the course of three 'durbars' held as he advanced, Sargon's chariotry, cavalry, baggage, and 'walking larder' had been enlarged to the sum of 4,609 horses, numerous mules, Bactrian camels, cattle and sheep from Ullusunu, Talta of Ellipi, Bel-Apal-Iddina of Allabria, and forty-five city chieftains of the 'Mighty Medes'.[85]

The first clash was in Zikirtu, north-east of Lake Urmia. Metatti of Zikirtu withdrew his main forces and retreated across the Khwaja Dagh, but his rearguard was slaughtered. Sargon then moved onto Uishdish in Mannea. Ursa (Rusa) of Urartu had drawn up his army in a defile in the Sahend Mountains, in a plain that was dotted by low hills that screened his host. Sargon states, rather grandiosely, that in spite of fatigue, thirst and the difficulty of deploying his troops, and his inability to watch the rear of the straggling army, he was unafraid of the mail-clad host awaiting him, and despised their cavalry. His own royal cavalry division, under the command of Sin Ahi Usur, but with Sargon in the lead, plunged into the fray. A maelstrom of killing ensued. A victorious Sargon then recounted his spoils: 'Them and their horses I captured, 260 of his [Ursa's] royal seed, who [constituted] his cavalry, I captured with my own hand. Ursa fled on a mare.'[86]

From Ushkaia he went to the Urartean border and deep into Zaranda, which was horse country. The people there were famed for their equestrian skills in rounding up young colts, breaking them to ride and drive, before they went into Ursa's royal army. Around Aniashtania, north-east of Lake Urmia, was where the Urartean royal herds of horses grazed. Sargon destroyed this city and seventeen other cities.[87] Further north-east of the lake was the city of Tarmakisa in the rich plain of Dalai where the grain and pasture lands lay, also for the royal horses. From there his army marched back and around the lake's northern shore to Ulhu, set in a fertile, well-drained land of orchards, grain fields and pasture. This whole area he overwhelmed 'with the chariots and horses of my destructive advance'. Fifty-seven cities were destroyed and the horse pastures 'made like ploughland'.[88]

In the mountainous districts over which this whole campaign traversed there was always the threat of resistance and ambush. Several of Urartu's northern strongholds were not attacked, and once the army turned southwards for home there was always a threat from the rear.[89] It was then that Urzana of Musasir, an ally of Rusa, revolted by withholding tribute and submission. Sargon took a flying column of 1,000 heavy cavalry armed with bow, lance and shield, exchanged his chariot for a charger, and turned eastward to Musasir. Urzana, taken by surprise and with no time to form solid resistance, fled. Musasir was invested and systematically stripped of its huge wealth (it was a religious centre). Tons of precious metals, arsenals of weapons, trains of mules, donkeys, cattle and sheep, plus other valuable objects, the whole family and over 6,000 of Urzana's people, were soon on their way to Assyria.[90] Sargon's losses were 1 charioteer, 2 cavalrymen, and 3 sappers killed.[91]

Assyria claimed victory in both the Qarqar and Urartean campaigns. In reality it was something less, as neither campaign was decisive. Once the

Assyrian hosts had gone, both the Levant and Urartu returned fairly rapidly to their previous situation. Shalmaneser's repeated crossings of the Euphrates showed that Syria was hardly permanently subdued, and not until twelve years later was the outcome settled in Assyria's favour.[92] Less than a year after Sargon's departure from Urartu it had recovered and once more was militarily aggressive.[93] The Anatolian states still paid tribute to Urartu. Argishti II repeatedly provoked Assyria, but he had a more pressing enemy to deal with as the Cimmerians were encroaching, and in 708 won a battle against Urartu, but on Cimmerian soil. They then pressed onwards to Phrygia. There they were repulsed, changed course towards Assyria, and in 705 fought in Tabal against Sargon. Assyria claimed victory, but Sargon was killed in the battle.[94]

CHAPTER 10

The Persian
Empire

Herodotus' *Histories* give us much valuable information on the Medes and Persians. He pays particular attention to the equestrian features of Persian armies. Much of his information was gleaned from eye witnesses involved in Xerxes I's (486–465) expedition of 481–479, or from people who had been in contact with them. Xenophon's writings are also revealing. Xenophon served as a mercenary under Cyrus the Younger, who challenged his brother Artaxerxes II (405/4–359/8) for the Persian throne. He had first-hand experience of the Persian military. Many of his literary works reflect Greek and Persian aspects of equestrianism, as well as his own recommendations. Especially valuable equestrian sources reflecting Persian details are *The Anabasis – Persian Expedition*, *The Cavalry Commander*, *The Hellenica*, and *The Cyropaedia*. I would suggest that the historical elements, his own equestrian expertise, and his military advice on such matters, were an amalgam of his own Greek traditions, what he had absorbed from the Persians, his observations on his hazardous trek back to Greece after the Battle of Cunaxa in 401, and his service with Sparta thereafter.

PRELUDE TO EMPIRE

The Indo-European migrations of the second millennium and earlier, stemming from the Eurasian Steppes spread their equestrian legacy in many lands, among them Iran.[1] Some of these movements came in via the Caucasus;[2] others equate in area with territory comprising today's Kazakhstan, Turkmenistan, Uzbekistan, Tadzhikistan and Kirghistan. Franz Hancar calls this Turan. In the first millennium it bred a superior type of riding horse.[3] This area supplied horses throughout much of the ancient and medieval world's history. A large part came under the sway of the Persian and Alexandrian empires. By the early first millennium Iranian tribes, among them the Medes and Persians, were well entrenched in the territories that now bear their name.[4]

The Persian Empire

MEDES AND ASSYRIANS

Land beyond the Zagros was a bar to permanent Assyrian expansion. Nevertheless, Assyrians repeatedly raided into and beyond these mountains. They considered the Medes a 'Mighty People',[5] and coveted their famous horses. Median Nishai (Nisaya), home of the Nisaean horses, paid tribute to Assyria.[6] In Sargon II's eighth campaign, forty-five Median chiefs, and on another occasion thirty-four Median districts, paid tribute. Kings even launched campaigns to capture prized Median chargers, their numbers often running into many thousands at a time.[7] By the mid-eighth century the Medes had formed a confederation of tribes, and less than a century later under their King Kyaxares (625–585) attacked Assyria, taking Nineveh in 612 and Harran in 610. By 590 they had brought Mannea and Urartu, both famous for horses, within their boundaries, and then their armies moved into eastern Anatolia and conducted a five-year war against the Lydians. Diplomacy, politics, and might were used in furthering their expansion. Royal marriages took place: Astyages (585–550), Kyaxares' son, married the Lydian king's daughter, and a Median princess married the Babylonian Nebuchadnezzar (605–561).[8] Lydia, a country in Asia Minor with its capital at Sardis, had grown to prominence and wealth from agriculture and mineral resources under the Mermnad royal house, of which Croesus (560–546) was the last king, whom Cyrus the Great was to meet on the battlefield.[9] Lydia was noted for its superb cavalry.[10]

MEDES AND PERSIANS

In 550 the Medes were conquered by the Achaemenid King of Persia, Cyrus II (the Great, 560–530) in a long-drawn-out war against Astyages.[11] Median territories were incorporated into the fledgling Persian Empire. By the end of the next decade Cyrus' empire surpassed in extent that of the Assyrians. After annexing the Median territories he targeted Lydia, followed by the Ionian Greeks and all of Asia Minor. In the east Parthia, Areia, eastern Iran, Sogdia, Bactria, Afghanistan and part of India were also incorporated into the Persian Empire.[12] From these people Persia drew much of its cavalry. Some areas north-east of Persia were in the Turanian homeland of excellent horses.[13]

Cyrus was succeeded by his son Cambyses (530–522), who, in his short reign, acquired Egypt, Libya, Cyrene, Barca and Cyprus.[14] In Egypt a courier brought Cambyses news of a revolt and usurpation of his throne in Media by a magus impersonating his brother Smerdis whom he had already murdered.[15] According to Herodotus, Cambyses' death was from

109

a self-inflicted wound; in his haste to be on his way to depose the usurper an unsheathed sword tip pierced his thigh as he clumsily mounted his horse. Over a three-week period the wound went gangrenous and mortified.[16]

DARIUS I (522–486)

Darius I of the Achaemenid lateral line, with, as he put it, 'the aid of a few men', slew the usurper Gaumata at the Median stronghold of Sikayauvatis in Nisaya and seized the throne.[17] One of the first perquisites he inherited from Cambyses were the Nisaean horsebreeding grounds. When Darius spoke of Parsa (Persis) having good horses[18] he was perhaps speaking of Median imports, not indigenous stock (see Xenophon's *Cyropaedia* below).

Immediately after his accession in September 522 Darius was faced with revolts throughout his empire. The Behistun Inscription lists nineteen battles fought, all but two dated. By the end of November 521 he had overthrown nine kings.[19] Many leaders and their chief followers who were captured were executed after their mutilated bodies had been exhibited at various key locations.[20] The 'few men', all Persian, who aided Darius are listed as, Intaphrenes (Intaphernes), son of Vayaspara, Otanes, son of Thukra, Gobryas, son of Mardonius, Hydarnes, son of Bagabigna, Megabyzus, son of Datuvahya, and Ardumanis, son of Vakauka. Royal protection was to be offered to all these men, and their families, by future kings.[21] As Herodotus has it, these six, plus Darius, formed a pact to overthrow Gaumata, and from among them should be chosen the one to ascend the Persian throne. Otanes withdrew, saying he wished neither to rule nor be ruled. The other six agreed in essence that the choice should be left to their horses. The rider of the first horse to neigh after the sun rose would be king.[22] The way Herodotus expands on the contest is very theatrical, but absolutely true as to how an entire horse will behave. Scholars believe in the agreement between the six for a variety of reasons: the kingship had reascended into Heaven and a sign was needed from the Sun God via the animal sacred to him, and from the practice of hippomancy.[23] The horse played an enormous part in the life of the Persians. Many of their names incorporated the word for horse – *aspa* – as we have already seen.

Darius' clever groom, Oebares, led a mare in oestrus to the meeting place, tied her up, and then brought along Darius' stallion and allowed him to mount her. Next morning with the six horses present Darius' horse, anticipating covering the mare, whinnied. The Persians had another, but basically similar tale. The groom got the scent of the mare in oestrus on his hand and surreptitiously let the horse sniff it at the appropriate moment.[24] The mare would have left scent traces on the ground where she had been tied.

The following are the campaigns against rebels. Many were run concurrently and must have taxed Darius' military resources in man and animal power. For the latter he used camels in addition to horses.[25]

Date	Battle against/rebellion of
522	
29 September	Slew Gaumata
13 December	Elam and Babylonian rebellion. Fought Babylon
18 December	twice
29 December	Arachosia
? (no date)	Elam – second revolt
31 December	Armenia – campaign led by Vaumisa
521	
12 January	Media
21 February	Arachosia
8 March	Parthia and Hyrcania
8 May	Media
20 May	Armenia – campaign led by Dadarsi
24 May	Persia
30 May	Armenia – campaign led by Dadarsi
11 June	Armenia – campaign led by Vaumisa
20 June	Armenia – campaign led by Dadarsi
? (no date)	Sagartia
11 July	Parthia
15 July	Persia
28 November	Babylon.[26]

Elam again rebelled in autumn 521,[27] and in 520/519 Darius warred against the Scythians, captured their leader Skunkha, and set his own appointee over them.[28] Darius lists twenty-three peoples subject to him.[29] Herodotus names twenty satrapies with the annual tribute payable to the Great King.[30] Herodotus' list is more accurate, as Darius' list contains some peoples who, although he went against them, such as the Saka, did not see their territories become satrapies.[31]

In 516 Darius crossed the Hellespont for a lengthy campaign against the Scythians north of the Black Sea in order to prevent trading in grain supplies to Greece.[32] The Persians never closed with the Scythians who kept a day's march ahead, destroying forage and blocking wells.[33] Darius' army, including cavalry, was a formidably large force, according to Herodotus, numbering 700,000 which was probably somewhat exaggerated. Animals and men suffered greatly. When the Scythian cavalry's advance guard approached, but still encamped at a day's distance, the Persian cavalry gave ineffectual chase. So the 'war' progressed until a desperate Darius dispatched a rider to the Scythian King Idanthyrsus asking him why he 'kept running away' and demanding the earth and water tokens of submission. Idanthyrsus replied that he was following normal nomadic life as he had no towns or farmland to protect; he promised a fight if Darius found and destroyed the Scythian burial grounds.

The Persians' only help on their foraging forays were the baggage donkeys. These brayed so loudly that they scared the Scythians' horses who, unaccustomed to 'long ears', bolted. After hundreds of miles and two months of frustration, expensive in men and animals, Darius withdrew back across the Hellespont. The donkeys, tied in the deserted Persian camp, noisily screened Darius' withdrawal, fooling the Scythians into thinking the camp was inhabited.[34] The 'donkey warrior' aspect is tinged with humour, but horses can show unreasoning fear of animals they consider strange, and there are many such instances recorded, for example with camels and elephants, as well as with donkeys.

BATTLE OF MARATHON

In 492 the Persian Wars between Greece and Persia began. The high commands in the Persian army went to Darius' nephews Megabates, Mardonius and Artaphernes. Thrace and the Macedonians submitted early to Mardonius,[35] but later a Thracian tribe, the Brygi, attacked Mardonius' camp. In the ensuing fight Persian losses were heavy, and Mardonius was wounded. In addition, storms in the northern Aegean around Athos wrecked a large part of the Persian fleet, causing Mardonius to cross back to Asia.[36]

Undeterred, Darius proceeded with his preparations for war against Greece, especially Athens, which earlier had burnt Sardis.[37] He sent envoys to various Greek cities demanding earth and water submission tokens to sound out those favourable to Persia. Horse transports were built and the fleet brought up to strength.[38] Datis, a Mede, was Commander-in-Chief of the new expedition, replacing Mardonius. The Persian land and naval forces met in Cilicia, horses and troops embarked, and the fleet sailed for Ionia, crossed to Delos, thence to Eretria and a brief, harsh and successful campaign, before landing at Marathon where the plain offered ideal cavalry terrain.[39] On learning that the Persians were disembarking the Athenians moved fast, reaching the southern end of the plain before the Persians.[40] Datis probably chose the north-east end of the plain as good grazing was available.[41] The Athenians fielded a much smaller army than that of the Persians, theirs numbering only 10,000, and they had no cavalry,[42] the arm in which the Persians put great faith. However, cavalry played no part in the ensuing battle since it was either away being watered, or had been re-embarked to make a pre-emptive dash for an unprotected Athens.[43] On an extended front, weak in the centre but strong on the wings, the Athenians charged. The Persians, thinking the enemy crazy, drove into their centre, but were routed on the wings. The Athenian wings then joined and cut the Persian centre down. Persian losses were 6,400, Greek losses 192.[44] A battle that should have been won was lost, largely for the lack of cavalry.

The defeat at Marathon hardened Darius' resolve to conquer Greece. More ships, horses, men and grain for an even larger army were raised, but death intervened and the plan for the invasion of Greece was inherited by Xerxes I (486–465).[45]

XERXES' GREAT EXPEDITION

Xerxes' campaign against Greece is the only one recorded in great detail when the Achaemenids were at the height of their power.[46] Herodotus gives the background of the diverse equestrian contingents, much on individual equid and equestrian aspects, and an account of the Battle of Plataea. Telling against Greece was the divisiveness among the numerous states. Many sided with Persia, all of which had cavalry to contribute, such as Boeotia (including Thebes), Macedonia and Thessaly.[47] To repel the common enemy, Athens and Sparta, and their allies, saw sense and united.[48]

Xerxes left Susa in the spring of 481, proceeding to Kritalla in Cappadocia where the army was mustering, then he wintered in Sardis. In spring 480 he headed for Europe,[49] with an army greatly exceeding that of Darius. Contingents came from all subject nations: some sent infantry, others cavalry, horse transports, warships, crews, and supplies.[50] The order of march was pack animals with their drivers first, followed by a host of mixed nationalities. Then came a gap to separate the commonality from the king who was preceded by 1,000 elite horsemen, and 1,000 picked spearmen. Then came a group of 10 sacred Nisaean horses and an eight-horse hitch of white horses led by a charioteer, followed by Xerxes riding in a chariot drawn by Nisaean horses and driven by his Persian charioteer, Patiramphes. Behind Xerxes came other 1,000-strong units of spearmen and cavalry, then 10,000 Persian foot and 10,000 Persian horse. After another gap came the mass of the army.[51]

After marching through Lydia, Mysia and into the Troad, watering became a problem: the first river to run dry was the Scamander, so great was the demand on it by men and animals. At Abydos Xerxes reviewed his host and prepared to cross the Hellespont by two bridges he had had constructed. On European soil the army marched through the Chersonese to Doriscus in Thrace. Here Xerxes halted to number his troops. Herodotus admitted imprecision but assessed the total at 700,000 foot, 80,000 horse, and 20,000 for the Arabian camel corps and Libyan chariotry that had crossed from Asia. To these were added the European contingents, and crews and fighting men aboard the ships. The grand total of fighters was 2,641,610. Baggage personnel on land and sea brought the total in excess of 5 million, to which were to be added numbers of eunuchs, soldiers' women, and female cooks.[52] Clearly this is gross exaggeration, a fault common in 'reports' from the ancient to the medieval world. Nevertheless, a total of about 750,000 must have been on the move.[53] Of animal numbers it is impossible to give a valid estimate. Mules, donkeys, cattle and sheep on the hoof for meat, plus the 80,000 cavalry and 20,000 camels and chariot horses, excess ceremonial horses and numerous remounts, probably in their thousands, had to be watered and found grazing for. No doubt merchants and their animals added to overall numbers. An oriental army, as in Mughal India, resembled a moving city, thus limiting each day's progress to very few miles.

UNITS IN THE PERSIAN ARMY

Herodotus names forty-three units of infantry, some very small. The foremost came from Persia and Media. Their main weapons were bows, javelins, spears and swords. Daggers and maces (clubs) also featured. All those who provided infantry were also capable of fielding cavalry, but for his expedition only the following did so: the Persians, equipped with scale armour, trousers, felt cap, wicker shields, bows with cane arrows, and a dagger, some with 'devices of hammered bronze or iron on their heads' (helmets), and the 8,000 nomadic Sagartians, who were equipped with lassos and daggers. India supplied cavalry and chariotry. The Libyans too provided chariotry. Others furnishing cavalry were the Medes, Cissians, Bactrians, Caspians, Caspeirians and Paricanians. Arabians provided the camel cavalry. The three cavalry commanders were Harmanithras, Telhaeus and Pharnuches. The latter remained at Sardis as he fell off his rearing horse when it spooked at a dog. The horse was summarily executed by cutting its forelegs off at the knees. Mardonius commanded the infantry hosts. The description of the fleet was as meticulous as that of foot and horse.[54] Many Median and Persian cavalrymen, especially the higher-ranking nobility, would have been mounted on Nisaean and part-bred Nisaean horses. If the Babylonian stud of Tritanchaemes noted below was representative, Persian contingents from satrapal governors would also have had superior mounts. The Bactrians and Caspians would have had access to the superior Turanian horses.

The war opened at sea. The Greek fleet lay at Artemision in north Euboea. The approaching Persian fleet ran into a storm which lasted three days and wrecked hundreds of ships. In the ensuing naval engagements both sides suffered losses, but the Greeks were worst hit. With half their ships damaged they withdrew.[55] Meanwhile, the Persian land army approached Thermopylae, the gateway to Greece from Thessaly. The pass was too narrow for cavalry to deploy, and the huge Persian army would have been at a disadvantage.[56] A mounted Persian scout reconnoitred and assessed Greek numbers. Xerxes waited four days expecting the Greeks to withdraw. Then he sent in the Medes – they were repulsed with heavy losses. Two more attempts failed. Then a traitor showed the Persians a hill track to Thermopylae. They marched by night and on the morrow Leonidas' 300 Spartans holding the pass fought to the death.[57] The Persians burnt their way through Attica and in Athens set fire to the Acropolis.[58] However, at the naval Battle of Salamis in 480 so great was the defeat of the Persians that Xerxes considered withdrawing his army.

Mardonius offered Xerxes advice, saying the next phase of the war would be won by horse and foot. He encouraged Xerxes to choose between marching on the Peloponnese, or returning to Persia leaving him, Mardonius, with 300,000 foot and horse to complete the subjugation of all Greece. Xerxes withdrew and marched for the Hellespont and crossed into Asia.[59] Again the numbers are inflated, the more likely figures being 60,000 foot and 30,000 horse.[60]

In 479 Mardonius wintered in Macedonia and Thessaly. He sent an offer to Athens, via Alexander of Macedon, proposing a way out for them from the impending war. Athens delayed her answer until Sparta offered to help and then turned down Mardonius' suggestion.[61] Mardonius' answer was to harry Attica, and march on Athens. He reiterated his offer, hoping Athenian resolve had weakened. On hearing that Sparta was sending an army under the regent, Pausanius, Mardonius withdrew from Attica and marched for good Theban cavalry country, but on learning that another 1,000-strong force had already arrived at Megara he headed there, his cavalry pushing ahead, and overran the surrounding country. Herodotus places Megara as the furthest point that the Persians reached.[62]

THE BATTLE OF PLATAEA, 479

In Theban territory Mardonius built a 10-furlong-square fortified encampment as a bolt hole in case the forthcoming battle went against the Persians. He then deployed his army along the River Asopus in Plataean country. The Greeks occupied the lower slopes of Mount Cithaeron. Battle was opened by a Persian cavalry charge under Masistius, who rode a Nisaean charger bridled in gold and splendidly harnessed. First blood went to the Persians with successive squadrons of cavalry causing heavy losses in the Greek ranks. Then on the arrival of a 300-strong Athenian relief force the battle turned. Masistius' horse was shot in the flank. It then reared and threw Masistius, who was overpowered and killed by the Athenians, and his horse seized. An attempt to retrieve his body failed, and after losing many of their cavalry, and now leaderless, the Persians retired. The Greeks then moved down to Plataea as it was better supplied with water.[63] For ten days the armies faced each other, during which time the Persian cavalry blocked and captured a goods convoy of 500 mules, and continually harried the Greeks on the Asopus Ridge with Theban, Median and Persian cavalry.

Running short of provisions and water the Greeks decided to split their forces and on the twelfth night half withdrew southwards to Mount Cithaeron. Next morning the Persians, thinking the Greeks were in retreat (as the remaining Greeks were shielded by knolls), pursued, crossed the Asopus, their cavalry well to the fore, and were soon harrying the Spartan half of the army that had moved out in the night to regroup at Plataea. Pausanias dispatched a rider to the Athenians for help and they closed in, but too slowly, and were overtaken by the Persians' Greek allies.

In the Persian lines the hardest fighting was around Mardonius, mounted on his white charger and surrounded by his 1,000 picked foot. Once he was killed, and his force annihilated, partly due to their lack of defensive armour, the end soon came. Artabazos, a senior Persian officer who had disapproved of Mardonius' campaign from the safety of the palisaded camp, was careful not to get embroiled. Seeing the rout begin he turned about and rapidly led his 40,000 men to the Hellespont and Asia. The heaviest Greek losses were the Megarian and Phliasian hoplites whose ranks had become disordered. Theban cavalry closed in and killed

600. The Persian remnants, protected by Boeotian cavalry, raced for their stockade; this was breached and pillaged. One trophy noted by Herodotus was the elegant bronze manger used by Mardonius' horses.[64]

After the Persian defeat at Plataea the spoils were shared out. Pausanias as leader got ten of everything, 'women, horses, camels, and everything else'.[65] Many of the Persian cavalry not with Artabazos would have escaped and joined him, but many loose horses would have been running riderless over the battlefield, and swelled the victors' spoils.

For future equestrian exploits we have to rely on Xenophon, who lived in an era when Greece was becoming more attuned to horsepower.

BASIC MILITARY ORGANISATION

The Persian military organisation was based on the decimal system. A division was 10,000 men – a myriad; a regiment 1,000, subdivided into 100s, and these into 10s. The ten-man unit was the basic tactical infantry unit. It was drawn up in file, the lead man carrying a 6 ft spear and a *spara*, a large rectangular shield, similar to a medieval pavise. The other nine men were armed with a bow, arrows and a falchion. On occasion the *spara* bearer also had bow and falchion, and the shields were lined up as a shield wall. The famous infantry division, the Immortals, was so called because it was maintained at full 10,000 strength.

Originally, Persia did not possess cavalry, and Cyrus had to form his own Persian cavalry divisions, as cavalry of conquered subject peoples could never be fully trusted.[66] How quickly Cyrus raised his Persian cavalry is not known. He inherited Median cavalry in 550, and within four years he fought Croesus of Lydia who fielded very superior cavalry.[67] The Persian cavalry was also organised on a decimal system. The elite 1,000 cavalrymen were drawn from the 15,000 Persian noblemen known as *Huvaka* – kinsmen. However, the new cavalry had much to learn from their past and future enemies. Bactrian and Saka cavalry were far superior.[68] This is to be expected of the Saka who had a nomadic background, and from the Medes with their equestrian traditions.

THE CYROPAEDIA

Xenophon's novel *The Cyropaedia*, although a mostly fictitious account of Cyrus the Great's life, includes Persian customs and institutions. The first two books give the fictitious early life of Cyrus, much of it spent reputedly at the Median court where he learned to ride, and from which he took part in the hostilities between Media and Assyria.[69] The facts were otherwise, as the Medes had long settled the Assyrian question. Cyrus was an Achaemenid prince from Parsa (Persia), King of Anshan in the heart of Persia,[70] who overthrew Astyages the Median king, thereby being able to immediately incorporate Median cavalry into his service. From Xenophon we learn that in Persia, that is nuclear early Persis, it was rare to see a horse as the mountainous country was ill suited to raising horses,[71] but that the Median cavalry, supplied with the most powerful horses, was the best in the world.[72]

It is Xenophon, no doubt using oral tradition, who credits Cyrus with first raising a Persian cavalry corps, ensuring Persians learned to ride, and decreeing that Persian nobles never travelled on foot, no matter how short the distance, but always rode instead.[73] He describes the panoply of a Persian cavalryman: purple coat, bronze corselet, helmet with white plumes, and weapons of short sword and cornel wood spear. The horse was armoured with bronze chamfron, breastplate, and shoulder pieces which also served as thigh pieces for the rider.[74] A similar passage appears in his book *Horsemanship*, but with the addition of the 'cloth' which was to be designed to give the rider a safer seat, and prevent galling the horse's back.[75] This sounds like a contoured pad saddle rather than a mere saddle cloth. Horse armour as Xenophon described it has been identified on the sarcophagus of Payava found in Lycia. This was donated to the British Museum. Another example was found on a bas relief at Yeniceköy, in the former Persian satrapy of Daskyleion in north-west Asia Minor.[76] It is suggested that this armour, protecting both horse and man, was in use by the Persian military.[77] A similar armour is shown on a Phoenician artifact from Byblos, *c.* eighth to sixth century. It shows a Phoenician horseman and horse with the armour on the horse's breastplate continuing in the form of 'wings' to protect the rider's mid-section. The artifact is held in the Musées Royaux de Bruxelles.[78] The famous Etruscan winged chariot horses held in the Museo Etrusco di Tarquinia, dating to about the second half of the fourth century, suggest a mythical rendering of what was in practice a real piece of equipment. The wings attached to Xenophon's saddle (cloth) had their medieval counterpart in saddle steels for military and jousting use.

Xenophon also projected back to Cyrus the invention of long-axled scythed chariots, with the fighting man and horses mail-clad.[79] Ctesias, a Greek doctor at Artaxerxes II's court, says they were even older. They were in use in India in the mid-fifth century, so it is not known who had originally developed them.[80] Xenophon saw the scythed chariot in the armies of both Cyrus the Younger, and his brother, Artaxerxes II, at the Battle of Cunaxa in 401.[81]

Xenophon recounted Croesus of Lydia's battle of 546 when his cavalry bolted from Cyrus's baggage camels turned into cavalry mounts. In Xenophon's version he elaborates on Cyrus' army contingents, and its large corps of Persian horse and chariotry. His description of the horses' reaction to the camels is far more vivid than that of Herodotus, and far truer to equine responses. Xenophon has some horses bolting, others rearing, yet others in panic crashing into their fellow chargers.[82]

That an infantry army until 550 was so quickly equipped with numerous cavalry and chariotry is hard to accept, unless, as shown above, many Medes were immediately incorporated, under Persian officers, to serve in Cyrus' expansion. *The Cyropaedia* suggests that Xenophon had probably read or known the content of Herodotus' *Histories*, as much of his novel seems based on Herodotus' earlier tales. In the horsemanship department Xenophon can be more readily trusted as the reactions of the animals ring true, as do the uses he foresaw for them. On several occasions he says that the customs of Cyrus' time were still current in his day.[83] Putting thoughts into Cyrus' mind, but in reality one of his recommendations, are comments on the gelding of vicious horses which were then still of service as warhorses.[84] He also attributed to the Persians the usefulness of hunting as preparation for war.[85] This was a feature of every equestrian people and age down to the last days of using cavalry in the early twentieth century AD.

Throughout *The Cyropaedia* Xenophon's ideals are evident, as is his knowledge of how the Persian military was run. The Persian king reputedly equipped himself with a 200-strong stud of horses.[86] This was very small in comparison to the resources later Persian kings could call on. In this case what was probably meant was not a stud, but what a Persian king or prince of his own era could call on for immediate use as his personal stable or string of mounts and chariot horses, as opposed to a stud which is specifically for breeding. Cavalry units noted in *The Cyropaedia* in Persian employ came from Media, Armenia, Hyrcania, Cadusia and the Saka.[87] Such cavalry had a high reputation throughout the Persian Empire. Satraps were required to organise Persian and allied units of cavalry from the respective satrapies.[88] Pure Xenophon, hitched to Herodotus' *Histories*, is an enlargement on the postal system whereby Cyrus, that is, Xenophon as a horseman and/or knowledge of current practice, tried horses' endurance to find out how far and fast they could go before breaking down.[89]

Often dismissed as pure fiction, *The Cyropaedia* appears to be, in many of its parts, an instruction in elements of horsemanship and horsemastership, and a way of telling what Xenophon saw in the Persian army, all wrapped up in a simplistic eulogy of the first great Persian king.

PERSIAN HORSE ACQUISITION

Persian kings and their armies obtained horses from many sources. Other sources can be inferred from the results of successful battles. What is remarkable is how rapidly the Persians became thoroughly proficient horsemen without a tradition of early equestrianism.

Herodotus says that Cyrus's move against the Medes was conducted with only three of the ten Persian clans. The remaining clans were dependent on the prime three which were the Maraphioi, the Maspici, and the Pasargadai, from which the Achaemenids traced their lineage. A dependent clan was the Sagartioi (Sagartians) who under Xerxes, about seventy years later, provided 8,000 cavalry whose prime weapon was the lasso,[90] a very difficult weapon to use which required exceptional expertise in horsemanship, weapon accuracy and timing.

With Armenia's fall to the Medes in 590 their horse-producing areas – so often raided by Assyria in both Mannea and Urartu, particularly the Urartean horsebreeding lands of Aniashtania between Ushkaia and Tarmakisa[91] – also fell to the Medes. Aniashtania lies just a few miles south-west of modern Tabriz.[92] According to Xenophon Armenia continued to provide horses to Persia throughout Achaemenid times.[93] From the Nisayan Plains thousands of horses were produced on an annual basis. When one considers that only the most notable statistics have found their way into literature, it is obvious that the broader base of unremarkable production also has to be considered. Together with the territories that were known from the days of the Assyrians and then the Medes it becomes clear that the expanding Persian Empire was rapidly and extremely well supplied with first-class horses.

The geographer Strabo gives a wealth of equestrian information regarding the Median and Persian eras. He writes in general terms of the Median territory below the Caspian Gates as being very fertile horse-pasture country where Persian kings ran 50,000 mares. He then discusses the Nisaean horses as a separate entity.[94] The plains of Nisaya are over 200 miles south-west of the Caspian Gates, and south of Ecbatana (Hamadan). He also notes that Armenia had excellent horse pasture, that Nisaean horses not inferior to those of the Medes were bred there, and that annually the Satrap of Armenia sent 20,000 foals to the Persian king.[95] Strabo then comments on the style of horsemanship in Armenia, Media and Thessaly, saying they are alike, and that Armenia learned both horsemanship and archery from the Medes.[96] In this he was probably mistaken as Urartu/Armenia was an equestrian nation long before being overrun by the Medes. Nevertheless, both areas probably acquired certain skills from each other. (It should be

noted that modern Armenia is only a small part of the ancient
Armenia/Urartu.)

On Thessaly Strabo may well have been more accurate. The Thessalian
Plains were one of the major horse-raising areas in Greece. As noted above
both Thessaly and Macedonia were used as wintering areas by Mardonius's
army, which included many thousands of Iranian cavalry.[97] Many of the
Iranian and Median cavalry would have been mounted on horses of
Nisaean provenance. In addition to Iranians and Medes, there were
Indian, Saka and Bactrian cavalry.[98] Thessaly and Macedonia would have
enjoyed an input of new horse strains for a period long enough to leave
foals behind from indigenous mares. It is inconceivable that such matings
would not have occurred. Over time there would have been many crosses
to improve certain strains and provide future army mounts. The Persians
at this stage expected to keep these territories, so increase of herds would
have been welcome. Although no doubt some animals retained their 'pure
blood', there would have been a general blurring of breed input.

Cappadocia, a prolific horsebreeding land in Assyrian days, provided a
yearly tribute of 1,500 horses and 2,000 mules to Persia.[99] Cilicia's
tribute was 360 white horses, and from their 500 talents of silver, also as
tribute, 140 were spent on the Cilician cavalry in the Persian army.[100]
Although noted as a satrapy by Herodotus,[101] Cilicia had been constantly
attacked by Babylon, so probably welcomed Cyrus. Instead of an
appointed satrap it maintained its own royal house.[102] As we have seen,
Cilicia had a very long horsebreeding past. In addition to those noted
the peoples who provided cavalry for the expeditions against Greece
were mounted on their own stock. One exceptional non-royal stud was
that owned by Tritantaechmes, Satrap of Babylon, whom Herodotus
credits with a vast stud of 16,000 mares and 800 stallions.[103] Even
allowing for exaggeration, this points to huge wealth and fertile land to
supply the fodder, and the wherewithal to feed the considerable
manpower involved on stud and herding duties. This breeding herd did
not include the satrap's warhorses, presumably progeny of his herds. As
shown by Xenophon satrapal warhorses were used in the king's interests.
Although not appearing in the sources, all satraps and noble Persians
would have had impressive studs to equip their military units when
called on to mobilise.

On an individual level a man granted a cavalryman's fief by the king
had to produce money, food, a horse and its tack, armour for himself of
a cuirass, helmet with a neck guard, a shield, 130 arrows, an iron shield
attachment, a club (mace) and 2 javelins. No horse armour is mentioned
at this date of 422. Later Achaemenid cavalry horses were so
equipped,[104] as shown by Xenophon.

THE ANGARIUM AND THE PERSEPOLIS FORTIFICATION TABLETS

The courier's mount was vital for speedy communications. Herodotus describes the 1,600-mile Royal Post Road from Susa to Sardis. It was equipped with 111 post stations, each set approximately 15 miles apart.[105] At each post couriers and horses were stationed, each unit scheduled to cover its allotted days' distance regardless of weather conditions.[106] Although Herodotus thought this a Persian invention it was inherited from the Assyrians. It is estimated that a galloping courier could cover the distance in a week.[107] However, as it was deemed a safe road, and had a prepared surface, it is possible that, if necessary, the distance could have been covered in considerably less time. This is suggested by the feats of modern endurance horses where 100 miles is regularly covered in ten to twelve hours by riders using the same horse, and where the routes are often over very rough terrain indeed. The nineteenth-century AD American Pony Express demanded that their couriers average 12½ mph, again over tough territory, in parts running the gauntlet of attack from Indians. Staging posts, 10 to 15 miles apart, were often attacked, replacement riders killed and horses stolen. Despite this the ten-day schedule for 1,966 miles was kept. On the occasion of Lincoln's first address to Congress the time taken to carry the news was seven days.[108]

The Persepolis Fortification Tablets, from the reign of Darius I, illustrate aspects of equestrian travel, some of the organisation behind the postal system, and other information relating to horse supply in Persia. The tablets are largely concerned with rations allotted to those serving the king. Those dealing with equestrian matters are nos 1635–1704; special rations for horses, 1757–78; travel rations, 1780 and 1785; letters 1791; and many others ranging through numbers 1834–2062.[109]

Far more information can be garnered than the quotas of grain for individual horses. Rations in exact amounts use the basic units for dry measure of a *bar*, which equates to 10 quarts.[110] This is either 15 lb using English imperial measure or 11 lb 4 oz using the American measure. As the translation was for a University of Chicago publication it may be the American not the imperial measure used. Barley was the grain usually fed to livestock in ancient times. One quart of English measure, using cooked flaked barley from my grain bin, weighed 1 lb 8 oz. Whole grain barley provided by a farmer neighbour, weighed 2 lb per quart dry weight. The legal limit of moisture permitted in grain for sale is 15 per cent. These calculations at least give an idea of the nutrition the Persian horses received. We do not know if crushed or whole barley was fed, but it is likely that it would have been crushed, or milled in some way, as whole barley is extremely hard and difficult for a horse to masticate efficiently, and a large percentage would have passed through undigested.

Rations were issued for a variety of horses: *ber* (mature) horses; young horses, age not stated; yearlings; express horses (*Piradazis*);[111] road horses; going horses; and horses travelling the road – these latter categories were probably the same. The ration indicated for yearlings was 2 quarts per day (qpd).[112] From that the ages of other young horses can be deduced. Where all horses were classified as 'young' some got 1 qpd, others 2 qpd, yet others 3 qpd, so probably the animals represented were foals, yearlings, and two-year-olds.[113] The most usual quantity for a *ber* horse was 3 qpd (a mule got 2 qpd), although on one occasion a *ber* horse, duties unspecified, received 1 *bar* per day.[114] Other tablets indicate that some horses in extremely hard work, or likely to be called on for endurance but not actually being used, were allocated considerably more grain. A mature horse held in reserve at Muran was fed 6 qpd,[115] and others at different locations also received the same.[116]

Many riders and horses recorded carried documents to the king which were issued by Parnakka. He was High Comptroller for, and also uncle of, Darius.[117] The normal rations in these cases appears to be 6 or 5 qpd.[118] A *Baris* horse received 1 *bar* per day when his rider carried sealed documents. A run, ridden by Šakšaka the horseman, was from Persepolis to Susa. Rations were issued for four horses for three days.[119] The distance covered was approximately 300 miles. A similar run, ridden by Urakama, carrying a sealed document, was made with eight of the king's horses, each receiving 1 *bar* per day.[120] This conflicts with some of Herodotus' information, as it implies that Šakšaka rode the whole distance using relays of special horses, and presumably presented a docket for his rations and his new mount at stations. If the three days of rations meant three days for the Persepolis to Susa run it implies express horses were changed every 75 miles, the whole distance completed by one rider using his four allotted horses. Urakama's run suggests he had eight horses for the same distance, and no journey time was mentioned, but each of the eight horses still did a very good distance. No doubt there were occasions when extremely rapid transit of news was vital and special horses were used. It was possible for the same horse, if he was of a special type and suitably trained and fed, to have covered these extended distances at a high average speed.[121]

In a section dealing with special rations – *Hadazanam* – which detailed wine, extra grain, *mitli*, a special cereal product, and *Hamura*(?), eight *Baris* horses got by far the largest wine allocation. The translation reads 5 *Marris* (50 quarts) of wine for five months.[122] Unfortunately it does not say whether it is 5 *Marris* for each of five months, or the total for the period. It could well have been used as a fortifier, and probably diluted, as wines in the ancient world were often cut with water. If so it would be much like the drink of stout given as a pick-me-up to some hunters after a hard day. Possibly those *Baris* horses were those fast horses referred to in the Book of Esther[123] as being specially bred for the Persian courier service. They could also be the Express horses of tablet 1672, which may represent a stud specialising in these horses, as fifty-six animals each got 1 qpd over a period of six months.[124] This is certainly insufficient for a working horse, but could well be maintenance for out of work and/or stud horses on good pasture. In addition to classifications of horses, several other types were mentioned: *Kuttukip*,[125] *Kulla*,[126] *Barra Manus*,[127] and the *Baris*,[128] without any further indication, except in the case of the *Baris* horse, as to what their duties were.

Many locations where moderate numbers of horses were kept were on postal routes, but larger concentrations are indicated as being kept at Persepolis. An official called Ustana, who set the rations for the king's horses at Persepolis,[129] issued large amounts of grain to cover considerable spans of time: 108 *bar* for a three-month period for six horses; 75 *bar* for ten horses for a 25-day stint; and the six months' supply of 1,008 *bar* for the fifty-six Express horses mentioned above.[130] Another issue from Ustana was for 3 *bar* for *Kulla* horses, but with no other information.[131] The specific types/breeds(?) under Ustana's jurisdiction suggests that, including Šakšaka's *Baris* mounts, the equestrian establishment at Persepolis was equipped with a variety of horses to suit all needs. Not noted are the Nisaean horses which were mostly bred further north, just south of Ecbatana.

At Rakkan on the Susa to Persepolis road a considerable number of horses must have been kept, as 593 *bar* (just under 4 tons) of grain were issued for an unspecified number of horses. The receiver was Umartanna of Missaka who was assigned by the king. There are also many entries for horses at Rakkan classified as 'travelling the road'.[132] Another extremely large concentration of royal horses was kept at Karakusan and came under the jurisdiction of Parnakka. He wrote to Harrena who issued '13 sheep and 5 portions to Bakatanna the horseman and his companions who feed [?] [that is, care for] the horses and mules of the king and princes'. At the rate of one sheep per ten men, that is 135 men on the stud herd staff.[133] This indicates an extremely large concentration of horses. As Persepolis and Susa were in the heart of the empire it is likely that this stud or herd was within their boundaries in order to be readily available to royal persons. The tablets' geographical range was wide as rations for as far away as Areia were sanctioned. The modern town of Herat preserves its ancient name. It is about 800 miles north-east of Persepolis. From there Baddarada, called 'the elite guide of Uneyararna', carried a sealed document to the king at Susa.[134]

The Persepolis Fortification Tablets illustrate that there were heavy concentrations of horses within the purlieus of Persepolis and Susa. They are of more use in showing the real equestrian infrastructure than the purely military horsed units. As the tablets only cover one portion of the huge Persian Empire, it can be envisaged that a similar pattern of equestrian data covered all other satrapies, though maybe not in such heavy numbers of horses.

CHAPTER 11

Equestrian Greece

For the equestrian history of Greece we are indebted to archaeologists and historians who place artifacts into the context of time, place and contemporary military happenings. The works of Herodotus, Thucydides, and especially Xenophon are valuable; Pausanias' history of his Greek tour, with his record of past events, is useful as he notes areas that produce notable breeds of horses. Some references to enemy cavalry on Greek, Thessalian and Macedonian soil are important in the long-term status of certain areas and breeds. Some historians consider Thessaly owed her superior warhorses to the Cimmerians and their Thracian kin.[1] The Cimmerians inhabited the Eurasian Steppes, as did the Scythians, and from the mid-eighth century onwards steppe horsemen raided into Urartu, Assyria, Asia Minor and Greece. Not all the incursions were predatory, as nomads increasingly turned to trading with countries south of the steppes.[2] Horse trading was probably a regular occurrence unless rulers were powerful enough to prevent exodus of horses, inevitably seen as potential weapons. Racehorses were imported, so imports can be projected for military use.

Pausanias describes chariot and ridden races, and the mechanics of the starting apparatus. He names owners, breeders, horses, and provenance of teams. Most were within Greece, but horses and drivers also came from Cyrene and Syracuse.[3] A fifth-century Spartan victory used horses from Venetia on the Adriatic which also exported to Sicily.[4] Rather than become enmeshed in the conflicts between Greek city states and colonies in Anatolia, Sicily, North Africa, and Italy, it would be better to take a broader view of Greek equestrian infrastructure. Interesting data relates to Athens, but I suggest similar data could have been applicable to other states. General comments on horses would apply no matter what their provenance. Most information is from the fifth century onwards, but some is from an earlier era.

EARLY EVIDENCE

The earliest Greek work in which horses often appear is Homer's *Iliad*, *c.* eighth century, about the later Bronze Age fall of Mycenaean Troy to

126

mainland Greece. The Trojan Wars were fought in the age of chariots. The epic was written when chariotry was about to be superseded by more mobile and efficient cavalry. Some historians consider the Homeric chariots were mounted infantry,[5] others that chariots were used,[6] the warrior dismounting from chariot or horse to fight. Chariotry is used in the *Iliad* as a taxi, never as a shock weapon. In the thick of fighting it would have been difficult to manoeuvre, but much easier to enter a fracas with a mounted warrior accompanied by his squire who then took his master's horse to safety, but near enough to remount at need.

Contemporary with Mycenaean chariotry the ridden horse starts to appear, albeit rarely. A terracotta statuette from Mycenae, *c.* 1300, and another from Prosymna near Argos, show ridden horses in a Greek military context, even if not in the fullest sense as cavalry. The chariot tablets from Knossos in Crete, *c.* 1400, detail equipment of corselet, chariot and horses (plural) issued to chariot fighters, and a few tablets that record equipment of corselet and horse (singular). This could indicate equipment for a rider. Mycenaean frescoes show horses with warriors standing with them. Two warriors are armoured with corselet, helmet and greaves, and carry swords; one has a long-bladed lance or spear, the weapons of a cavalryman, not a charioteer.[7]

In the eighth century some states raised cavalry. Spartans and Messenians used it in the first Messenian War, *c.* 740–720.[8] In the contemporary reforms of Lycurgus, Xenophon notes the reorganisation of the Spartan army into six regiments of cavalry, and the same of infantry,[9] each troop consisting of fifty men.[10] One hundred and fifty years later Sparta had dispensed with cavalry, presumably as representing individual trooper wealth, and the name *Hippeis* was transferred to a foot guard. Thucydides erroneously stated that Sparta first used cavalry in the Peloponnesian Wars.[11] According to Aristotle, Chalcis, Eretria and Thessaly fielded cavalry in the Lelantine Wars at the end of the eighth century.[12] Greenhalgh maintains that these warriors were not true cavalry, but mounted infantry.[13]

In the Geometric Age, 900–700, Greek warfare was rather disorganised, centring on an individual's prowess, but with the seventh-century hoplite reforms it was the unit that mattered. The larger 80-cm-wide shield, with its double grip, protected the mid-section and the left side, and the overlap from the shield of the man on the right afforded extra protection. A thrusting spear replaced the throwing spear. It was the closely ranked and combined weight of the phalanx that counted in the attack.[14] However, for the wealthy hoplite the horse was useful as he still rode to war, accompanied by his squire, and on site took his place in the phalanx. There are numerous pottery representations of mounted hoplites, and a few of true cavalry.[15]

GROWTH OF CAVALRY

The reformer Solon (630–561) divided the landowning Athenians into four classes, based on agricultural production. The powerful *hippeis*, or cavalry, class, each member with land producing at least 300–500 measures of corn per day, were ranked second highest.[16] Under these reforms each cavalry man provided his own charger, but it is doubtful if an effective cavalry force was raised.[17] In the sixth century the strong Greek confederations were Sparta and Thessaly.[18] Under the tyrant Hippias Athens hired 1,000 Thessalian horse, but in 510 they were defeated by Spartan heavy infantry, and by injury to horses from pits and entrenchments. Thereafter Athenian cavalry declined. Opinion is divided as to whether Athens retained any cavalry, but there are numerous references by ancient authors who note its presence, even if in small numbers.[19] At Plataea the few Athenian horses present were used by couriers.[20]

In the Persian Wars the Greeks were able to learn much equestrianism from the Persians who fielded huge and very well-mounted contingents. They also learned that although unbroken hoplite phalanxes could win them wars, broken infantry was vulnerable to mounted attack, as shown at Plataea when Theban cavalry allied to Persia killed 600 Megarians and Phliasians who neglected to keep ranks when the Persians were routed.[21] With the Persians still to be cleared from Greek colonies in Anatolia, Aristides, an Athenian commander who had fought at Plataea, asked for 1,000 horse, 10,000 hoplites, and 100 triremes to continue the war against Persia.[22]

Once the Persian Wars were over Athens and Sparta renewed hostilities. At Tanagra in Boeotia in 458/7 the 1,000 Thessalian cavalry in Athenian pay deserted to the Spartans and plundered the Athenian baggage train.[23] Shortly thereafter the Athenians raided Thessaly, ostensibly to restore the exiled Thessalian Prince Orestes. Although the Thessalians could not prevail against the heavy infantry their cavalry prevented the Athenians from leaving their camp, capturing the town, or acquiring any campaign spoils.[24] With these multiple lessons Athens realised she needed her own strong cavalry.

Cavalry in the Peloponnesian Wars, 431–404

Thucydides, an Athenian active in the early war years, recorded the interminable conflicts between Athens and Sparta, the constant politicking among Greek states, the battles and their cavalry actions.

Although the hoplite phalanx was the major arm, cavalry was felt to be indispensable. Originally, Athenian forces were reputed to consist of 13,000 hoplites, 16,000 'others', 1,200 cavalry including mounted archers, 1,600 foot archers, and 300 triremes.[25] Thereafter Athenian cavalry usually appears in groups of 200 or 300 horses. Her allies' cavalry is mostly referred to without numerical reference, as was Athens' cavalry on occasion, but enemy cavalry numbers are often quoted.

HORSE TRANSPORTS

There were many occasions when Athenian foot and horse were transported by sea.

Year	Against	Cavalry	Hoplites
2	A raid into the Peloponnese	300	4,000
7	Corinth	200	2,000
8	Cythera (held by Sparta)	A few	4,000
10	Thrace	300	1,200
		(plus allied troops)	

Other occasions were against Perdiccas of Macedon when 300 cavalry landed at Methone on the frontiers of Macedonia. Horses were shipped twice to Sicily in very small numbers with their initial campaign forces, and later when 250 cavalrymen were sent without horses, only the 30 mounted archers had their mounts shipped from Athens.[26]

CAVALRY ACTIONS

Several cavalry actions stand out. Collectively they show the equestrian situation in the war zones, and highlight the major 'cavalry states'. In the early years there was also plenty of action to the north. Even while the Spartans besieged Plataea the Athenians invaded the Chalcidians in northern Greece with 2,000 hoplites and 200 cavalry, but were routed by the Chalcidian cavalry and light troops, losing 430 men including their generals.[27] When Sitalces of Thrace warred on Perdiccas of Macedon he reputedly had 150,000 troops, of which 50,000 were cavalry, mostly from the Odrysae and Getae. However, the Macedonian cavalry was so superior that, although Thucydides omits its strength, it was used, to the exclusion of infantry, in repeated attacks on the Thracians. 'Being excellent horsemen and armed with breastplates [that is, heavy cavalry] no one could stand up to them.' Despite this, because of 'greatly inferior numbers', the Macedonians ceased their attacks. Sitalces continued his depredations, overrunning Chalcidice, Bottiaea and Macedonia, but cold, hunger and treasonable advice from his nephew Seuthes caused him to withdraw.[28]

ATHENS AND BRASIDAS OF SPARTA

Athens made the Spartan-held town of Megara a constant target. In the first year the Athenian army laid the Megarid waste. Annually thereafter they invaded, sometimes with just cavalry, or with the whole army.[29] By the eighth year it was twice a year. Inside Megara there were those prepared to betray it to the Athenians who had brought up a relief force of 4,000 hoplites and 600 cavalry. They took neighbouring Nicaea, but Megara was saved by the Spartan general Brasidas who had bulked his large force with Boeotian aid of 2,200 hoplites and 600 cavalry. Athenian and Boeotian horse clashed, both claiming victory. The Athenians withdrew, declining to fight the superior Spartan numbers. Brasidas returned to Corinth to prepare his expedition to Thrace.[30] Against her normal practice Sparta had raised a moderate cavalry force of 400 and a company of archers,[31] and was often aided by large contingents of horse from the 'cavalry states', notably Boeotia, Thrace and Macedon, especially in the eighth to tenth years when Brasidas coupled fighting with diplomacy.

Athens enjoyed considerable success on Spartan soil. To draw her attention northwards Brasidas sought support from Thrace, which wished to revolt from Athens, and from Macedon, Stagira, Acanthus and Chalcidice.[32]

At Delium in 424 the Athenian general Hippocrates encouraged his men, saying a victory against Boeotia would deny Sparta Boeotian cavalry, without which they would not dare invade Attica. Boeotia fielded 700 hoplites, 10,000-plus light troops, 500 peltasts, and 1,000 cavalry against the Athenian's 700 hoplites and an unnamed number of cavalry on each wing. The Boeotian horse routed the Athenians, and in a hot pursuit cut them down, harrying them till dark when the pursuit was called off.[33]

In the same year Brasidas took Amphipolis, an Athenian colony on the River Strymon.[34] A truce was called between Sparta and Athens, but Brasidas broke it, going to the aid of Mende which was in revolt from Athens.[35] With 3,000 hoplites and 1,000 Macedonian and Chalcidian cavalry and numerous native troops, Brasidas next marched with Perdiccas into Macedon against Arrhabaeus, the independent king of the Lyncestians in Upper Macedonia. Cavalry on both sides charged, the victory going to Brasidas, the Lyncestians suffering huge losses.[36]

A year later, at Amphipolis, an Athenian army under Cleon, with 1,200 hoplites and 300 cavalry, and a larger number of allied troops, met Brasidas' army, which included 1,500 Thracian mercenaries, 2,000 hoplites, Edonian peltasts, and 300 cavalry from Edona, Myrcina and Chalcidice. The Myrcinian and Chalcidian cavalry were prominent in Brasidas's victory. Some 600 Athenians lay dead: Spartan losses were incredibly low – seven killed – but Brasidas was mortally wounded.[37]

As the war dragged on into its twelfth year Athens contravened the treaty with Sparta and allied with previously neutral Argos, Mantinea and Elis. Athens sent Argos 1,000 hoplites and 300 cavalry. Throughout the thirteenth year there was fighting in the Peloponnese. Sparta was aided by Boeotia, whose huge army included 500 horse and 500 dismounted men trained to work with cavalry. In 418 at Mantinea the Spartans won a decisive victory. Argive and allied losses totalled 1,100, Spartan losses were 300, plus a few allies. In the debacle Athenian cavalry saved their infantry from annihilation.[38]

SICILY

The major drawbacks to Athenian ambitions in Sicily were that all war materiel had to be shipped in. In addition, Sicily had ample corn supplies and a great number of horses.[39] Although 5,100 hoplites, 480 archers, 700 Rhodian slingers and 120 light troops landed, only 30 horses arrived on the first shipment.[40] Numerous Syracusan cavalry hampered troop movements in open country and Athenian losses to harrying tactics were high. Only the Egestans, who had called on Athens for help in their dispute with the Selinuntines, could supply them with cavalry.[41] Syracuse, with cavalry also from Gela and Camarina, could deploy at least 1,200 horse. To prevent cavalry action their first major engagement was fought in terrain boxed in by houses, trees and marshes on one side, and by cliffs on the other. Although Athenian hoplites prevailed over Syracusan foot, Syracusan cavalry prevented an Athenian pursuit.[42] Realising horses were essential Athens used the winter to recruit reinforcements from Athens, and to gain allies in Sicily.

By the next campaign season 250 cavalrymen from Athens had arrived, with 30 mounted archers. The troopers purchased some mounts and acquired others from Egesta and Catana. Egesta also supplied 300 cavalry, and 100 more came from Naxos and other towns. In their first well-horsed engagement, backed by hoplites, Athens defeated the Syracusan cavalry.[43] Sparta then shipped in considerable land forces to Syracuse. In Sicily cavalry recruitment escalated. In the first infantry engagement under the Spartan general, Gylippus, the Syracusans were defeated, the terrain preventing cavalry action. But at the second battle Syracusan cavalry and javelineers routed the Athenian forces. From then on in spite of huge and repeated hoplite reinforcements, and winning a sea battle, Athenian losses mounted. And their ships were rotting. Syracuse then gained a succession of naval victories. In the final land battle Syracusan cavalry and javelineers won the day with persistent charges on the Athenian flanks. The *coup de grâce* came as Syracusan horse surrounded the Athenian general Demosthenes's detachment, forcing his surrender. Thucydides considered the Sicilian campaign the greatest action in Hellenic history, a brilliant victory to Syracuse, a calamity for Athens.[44]

In 411 Thucydides' record ends. It was continued by Xenophon who fought in the final years. Sparta gained foreign help from the Lydian and Phrygian satraps. When Athens fell the wars ended and, with Spartan support, the short-lived 'Rule of the 30 Tyrants' in Athens began.[45]

THE GREEK HORSEMASTER – HIS WORKS AND CAREER

Only one of Xenophon's works is specifically about the horse, but others give much information on the horse in war. Apart from the end of the Peloponnesian Wars most of his personal experiences date from his mammoth *Anabasis* of 401 and thereafter. In 399 he joined the Spartan army under Thibron. In 398/7 he was exiled from Athens. By 394 he was with King Agesilaus of Sparta, and a lifelong friendship developed between them. In 386 he retired to his Scillus estate from which he was ejected in 370 by the Eleans a year after the Spartan defeat at Leuctra. He resettled permanently in Corinth.[46]

In the *Anabasis – Persian Expedition,* the *Hellenica,* the *Agesilaus,* and the *Cavalry Commander,* we can see many aspects of Athenian, Spartan, Thessalian, Boeotian and Persian cavalry, and how changing sides was a common occurrence, except with the Persians who had a consolidated empire. They made alliances, and broke alliances, according to the Great King's and his satraps' political and territorial exigencies.

Xenophon's literary career most probably began at Scillus (modern Skilous) near Olympia. His experiences and observations of Persian equestrian customs, armour and appreciation of different types of horses owes much to the *Anabasis* period, and to his cavalry service in Ionia in 410, and under Agesilaus.[47] The land around Scillus was good horsebreeding country, and this ultimate horseman surely had a sizeable stud of horses. He wrote from knowledge as breeder, trainer, and cavalryman.

THE ANABASIS

In 401 Xenophon enlisted as a mercenary with Cyrus the Younger in the latter's bid for the Persian throne. Cyrus was defeated by his brother, Artaxerxes II, at the Battle of Cunaxa, south of Babylon in October 401. The 10,000 Greek mercenaries under Clearchus refused to surrender their arms to Artaxerxes,[48] and began the hazardous trek to Greece.[49] Among the mercenaries were men of the *Hippeis* class who owned several horses. The first noted is Lycius of Syracuse who rode to survey the Persian positions after the battle.[50] Tissaphernes, Satrap of Lydia, escorted the Greeks for nearly three weeks, gaining their confidence, especially that of Clearchus. He then inveigled five Greek generals into his tent, seized them, and massacred the twenty captains waiting outside. Native cavalry then cut down all the Greeks they could find on the plain outside the Greek camp.[51] Later, Artaxerxes had the generals executed.[52] The Greeks were in a parlous state: Cyrus's troops had turned against them.

Cavalry was essential for capitalising on any victories the Greeks might have, and to protect their infantry. When new officers replaced those who had been executed, Xenophon emerged as one of the leaders.[53] He quickly organised a small troop of cavalry. Some horses were his and those of Clearchus. Others had been captured, and some were baggage animals. The fifty best were equipped for service under the Athenian Lycius. With these and their Rhodian slingers they could repel attacks, and provide protective screens on the march.[54] Persian horse and foot plagued their rear, but never too close, as the Rhodian slingers' leaden bullets shot twice as far as the Persian slingers' stones. In a second attack when Persian troopers fled from the Greeks' cavalry charge, eighteen Persian cavalrymen were captured, killed and mutilated.[55] Their horses were a welcome bonus. Tissaphernes prevented them crossing the Tigris and taking the road to Lydia and Ionia,[56] so they continued northwards towards mountainous Kurdistan, the territory of the fierce, independent Carduchi.

After seven days of fighting they reached the Armenian border, but across the River Centrites (Buhtan Su) waited the hostile cavalry and infantry. Fortuitously they learned of an unguarded ford upriver. They crossed into Armenia, and into deep winter snowfalls so heavy that some men and animals perished. Tiribazus, Satrap of Western Armenia, hoping to lull them into feeling secure, guaranteed their safety in return for the Greeks doing no harm to houses en route. He planned to attack at a pass, but a pre-emptive strike gained the Greeks booty of twenty horses.[57] More men and animals died as winter closed in, but Xenophon augmented horse stocks from a temporarily occupied village, with seventeen colts destined as tribute for the Persian king. Xenophon took several; the rest went to his officers. He returned one horse, ostensibly as it was destined for sacrifice to the sun,[58] but more likely as it was thin, old and would not survive marching conditions. His cavalry must have been an eclectic range of lowly baggage beasts, Persian Nisaeans, and the smaller, finer Armenian acquisitions, as well as his and Clearchus' Greek mounts.

When eventually they saw the sea they rewarded their guide with money, clothes, jewellery, and 'from the common store' a horse,[59] thus indicating that remounts were available. At the Greek colony of Trapezus the army dispersed into Colchian villages for thirty days, during which they raided the countryside. The Colchians brought gifts of oxen, no doubt hoping the depredations would cease. Sacrifices to Zeus and athletic games were held, including an unusual horse race which entailed galloping down a steep hill to the sea, then scrambling back uphill to much cheering and laughter.[60] Then hugging the coast they plundered their way to Paphlagonia, taking prisoners for sale to raise funds.[61] Now down to 8,100 at Heraclea the army split into three. The cavalry, reduced to about 40 went with Xenophon's detachment. They rejoined at Port Calpe, 100 miles short of the Bosphorus.[62] The land was fertile, but in camp hunger stalked. A foraging party of 2,000 men was turned back by Pharnabazus, Satrap of Phrygia, losing 500 men. Another larger foraging party, with a burial detail, again clashed with the Persians. Greek peltasts attacked and were driven back, but when the phalanx charged the Persians fled, sustaining heavy losses when pursued by Timason's cavalry. The dispersed Persian right wing was pursued by peltasts until they were checked by sight of Persian and Bithynian cavalry, but a last massed Greek charge routed the Persian horse.[63]

Once across the Hellespont, Seuthes, a minor Thracian prince, sought Greek aid to regain his father's Odrysian lands, but once successful withheld the promised pay. Heraclides, Seuthes's spokesman, had stolen it, then agitated against Xenophon until he was accused of making himself rich at his men's expense, forcing Xenophon to defend himself. Meanwhile, Spartan recruiters offered the Greeks employment in their projected war against Pharnabazus and Tissaphernes, their erstwhile allies against Athens in the Peloponnesian Wars. Throughout the *Anabasis* the need for cavalry surfaces. It was used in the occasional head-on action, but its most frequent uses, clearly stated in the Seuthes episode, were to discourage pursuit by enemy cavalry and to gain live plunder of slaves and cattle.[64]

With many clashes with fierce tribes in hostile territory, and the recurring menace of satrapal cavalry, it was some feat to reach safety. The peoples in the transit territories must have been relieved when the Greeks left for Sparta. Throughout, they had behaved much as medieval *écorcheurs*, as dangerous out of employment as mercenaries as when on a war footing.

THE HELLENICA – CONTINUING CONFLICTS

Throughout the *Hellenica*, although horses do not feature as individuals, it is shown how essential they were to Persians, Greeks, and the normally footslogging Spartans.

As Tissaphernes' power in Asia increased the Greeks there called on Sparta for aid. It was not until the *Anabasis* survivors joined him that Thibron felt strong enough to march against Tissaphernes' massed cavalry, eventually wresting many Asiatic cities from Persian control.[65] The Spartan command then went to Dercylides and the Greek army moved into Aeolia and took nine cities. Even with these successes, and to prevent Persian cavalry harassing the Greek cities, peace was agreed between Dercylides and Pharnabazus. The Spartans, joined by cavalry and peltasts from Seuthes of Odrysian Thrace, wintered in Bithynia, which suffered much from their depredations.[66]

Dercylides then crossed to the mainland and marched to the relief of the Chersonese which was under attack from the Thracians,[67] and then recrossed to Asia. Tissaphernes and Pharnabazus joined forces to expel the roving Spartan army. Xenophon comments on the great number of Persian cavalry, Tissaphernes' force on the right, Pharnabazus' on the left. Pharnabazus was eager to attack, but Tissaphernes, mindful of the *Anabasis* mercenaries' valour, preferred to negotiate. Dercylides demanded independence for the Asiatic Greek cities (while still paying tribute to the Persians); but Tissaphernes and Pharnabazus demanded that the Spartan army leave Artaxerxes' territory. A temporary truce was agreed while the matter was referred back to their respective rulers.[68] No more of this is heard until Agesilaus had been King of Sparta for over a year. At Ephesus a similar truce was agreed, and broken by Tissaphernes who sent to Persia for extra forces.[69] Knowing that Agesilaus had no cavalry, and thinking he would march on Caria which was bad cavalry territory, Tissaphernes planned to use the Persian horse to annihilate the Greeks on the Maeander Plain. Instead, augmenting his forces and raising some cavalry, Agesilaus invaded Phrygia.

Near Daskyleion the cavalry of Pharnabazus and Agesilaus met. The Persians initiated the charge. The Greeks took the brunt, all their lances breaking. The Persians, with stronger cornel wood lances, had soon killed twelve men and two horses, routing the Greek horse until the hoplites charged, in turn routing the Persians.[70] Agesilaus then recruited cavalry from wealthy Asiatic Greeks, exempting from personal service any who provided a horse, arms, and an approved rider. Renewed hostilities started with a march on Tissaphernes at Sardis. He had again sent his cavalry to Caria, forcing Agesilaus to march for three days before the Persian horse appeared and cut down any Greeks out plundering until Agesilaus' cavalry came to their relief. The huge number of Persian horse drawn up in battle array, withstood the Greek cavalry charge, but disintegrated under successive waves of hoplites, peltasts, and archers. The peltasts pursued, and plundered the Persian camp. Among the spoils were camels which were sent back to Greece. The way these are singled out indicates they were a novelty, though Xenophon must have seen them earlier in Artaxerxes' army. By staying at Sardis Tissaphernes' behaviour was considered dereliction of duty and his replacement, Tithraustes, had him beheaded, then paid the Spartans 30 talents to leave, sending them into Pharnabazus' Phrygia.[71]

Tithraustes then unsuccessfully tried to bribe the states of mainland Greece to war on Sparta in order to remove Agesilaus from Asia.[72] Instead, Agesilaus marched on Daskyleion and, advised by Spithridates, a disaffected Persian nobleman, allied with Otys, king of neighbouring Paphlagonia. Otys, seeking to break from Persian dominance, boosted Agesilaus' forces with 1,000 horse and 200 peltasts.[73] Xenophon had already noted that Paphlagonian cavalry was considered superior to that of the Persians, and that it had supplied 1,000 horse to Cyrus, showing that the desired break from Artaxerxes was of long standing.[74] Some Persians also came over to Agesilaus.[75]

Wintering in Daskyleion, Agesilaus ravaged the satrapal heartland until, with 400 horse and 2 scythed chariots, Pharnabazus struck Agesilaus's careless foragers, killing 100. The rest fled back to the hoplites.[76] Four days later when the Greeks sacked Pharnabazus' camp in the scramble for booty, Spithridates and the Paphlagonians were denied their share, so they deserted, marching to join Arieus, the Persian satrap at Sardis who had revolted from Artaxerxes.[77] Agesilaus next met with Pharnabazus to persuade him to ally with the Greek cause, but he made it clear he would only defect if the king replaced him with another as satrap.[78] War on the mainland against the major Greek cities called Agesilaus back, and although heavily outnumbered he prevailed,[79] then scored several successes. Against Thessalian troopers who prided themselves on their horsemanship he pitted the considerable cavalry force raised in Asia.[80] He then gained a decisive victory at Coronea in 394 against a coalition from Boeotia, Argos, Athens, Locris, Euboea, Corinth and Aeniane.[81]

Although Xenophon mostly shows the Spartans in a good light and the Persians otherwise, he is critical when Spartan discipline foundered, and gives Persian cavalry due credit when they succeeded. When Thibron sent out plundering parties he neglected to maintain any sort of order, a defect quickly spotted by Struthes, the general dispatched to conduct Persian operations. He brought his cavalry in with orders to round up and drive off stragglers. This drew Thibron's disordered forces to their relief. They were met by Struthes at the head of a compact and numerous body of horse who killed first Thibron, then routed and pursued the rest, killing many.[82]

At the Battle of Leuctra in 371 Xenophon draws the distinction between the Theban cavalry's efficiency, and Sparta's inefficient horse. Boeotians had become battle-hardened and warwise with earlier actions, while the Spartans, with some troopers only riding the horses allotted to them when called for military duty, showed weakness in action. At Leuctra they were useless and fled, and the elite Spartan horse guard was pushed back. As the right wing was repulsed the rest gave way, Spartan losses amounting to 1,400, of which 400 came from Sparta itself.[83]

THE CAVALRY COMMANDER

Although directed at Athenian authorities, Xenophon's *Cavalry Commander* was useful to other Greek states whose cavalry might have been ill prepared. An exception was Thessaly. Xenophon recognised her superior horsemanship, and the remarkable number of horses she could field. Even if his precise figures are awry, the ratio of horse to foot was exceptional. It was only bettered by equestrian nomads. Thessaly could raise 6,000 horse and over 10,000 foot; with her allies the numbers came to 8,000 horse and 20,000 foot.[84] The tone of the *Cavalry Commander* suggests that Athenian cavalry had deteriorated. Xenophon's first comments are those of any good horsemaster. Horses were to be well fed to ensure fitness for speed work of overtaking and escaping; that is, harrying or being harried. Horses' hooves were to be well cared for so they could gallop on rough ground. If they had felt pain they would have been useless. Docile temperament was essential as disobedient horses and kickers helped the enemy.[85] Intimidated horses would have hung back or shied away from the aggressor. More dominant horses would have retaliated with heels, and possibly teeth. Chaos could have resulted. A horse that can be intimidated is not necessarily a coward, but one admitting a pecking order. Some very gentle horses that never dispute among their own kind can exhibit extraordinary courage for a rider with whom they have bonded. Recruitment of troopers was to be continuous to offset those retiring through age or other causes.[86] The same rule would have applied to horse recruits.

TROOPER RECRUITMENT

Recruitment of men was to be by persuasion, or, failing that, it was to be by court order. Guardians opposing their charges joining up were to be warned that they could not get out of keeping horses, but would be better off encouraging their youngsters, as once in the cavalry their practice of buying expensive horses would cease.[87] In Aristophanes' (*c.* 450–383) *The Clouds*, Strepsiades complains that because his son Phidippides is addicted to riding and chariot horses he is up to his ears in debt from purchasing and maintaining the horses. Phidippides is adamant that horses are the most important thing in his life.[88]

Infirmity, age, or lack of means exempted men from cavalry service. If any rider presented and was considered unfit he was to be dismissed.[89] Brilliant horsemanship was to be extolled to encourage recruits to train hard.[90] Xenophon directed that mounting was to be from the 'spring', as many owed their lives to this ability;[91] that is, remounting after falling off, or being pushed off in battle. A spear assisted mounting, which was akin to pole vaulting without the run-up. Another method would have been to grasp the mane, or push off with the left hand around the withers area, combined with a leap; athletic men could have done this fully accoutred, and there is medieval documentary proof of this.[92] Javelin exercises and becoming 'efficient in all the details of horsemanship' were to be assiduously practised.[93] Both horses and men were to be armoured. Xenophon is here talking of the heavy cavalry where horses wore chamfron, breastplate, thigh pieces, and 'the cloth' which was designed to give a secure seat and protect the horse's barrel, and was therefore more than a mere saddlecloth. The thigh pieces and cloth were based on Persian equipment, evidence for which has been found at Daskyleion in Phrygia, as noted in the previous chapter. Xenophon must have seen this used by Pharnabazus' cavalry. The advice that 'the men must be made obedient, or their good horses, horsemanship and fine armour would have been useless' is slightly comical, perhaps indicating privileged youths resenting orders.[94]

CAVALRY COMPOSITION

In the *Athenian Constitution*, written between 328 and 325, Aristotle includes information on early requirements for entering the cavalry. Under Draco (*c.* 621) when the classes were categorised, horsemen ranked second highest. An aspiring cavalry officer had to have an unencumbered estate worth at least 100 minae, and legitimate sons over ten years of age. Later an officer had to be over thirty years old. Under Solon (*c.* 630–561) the estate had to produce 300 measures of dry or liquid comestibles, or 'as some say those who could afford to keep a horse'. According to Aristotle the number of Athenian horse was fixed at 1,200 in the 470s.[95]

Athenian cavalry was raised from the ten tribes of Athens, each led by its own tribal commander, the *phylarch*.[96] Each tribe's 100 cavalry was subdivided into 10 files, each with a competent leader.[97] Two cavalry commanders were elected, plus one for the island of Lemnos.[98] At the time the *Cavalry Commander* was written numbers were thought to have dropped to about 650, but this was based on the wartime costs of 40 talents per year at 1 drachma per man and horse per day,[99] whereas in peacetime this amount provided for the full thousand.[100] Numbers fell dramatically in the third century. Prior to 282/1 they fell to below 200, were then raised to 300, only to fall again in the mid-third century. In the third century the number of tribes was raised to 12, then to 13, and the number of cavalry was fixed by law at 1,000.[101]

GENERAL CARE AND EXERCISE

Most horse training is incorporated into Xenophon's book on horsemanship, and some in the *Cavalry Commander*. By doubling the training exercises and casting out slow, vicious and kicking horses, Xenophon envisaged troopers would be careful when purchasing horses, break them in to a higher standard, and tend them better. Essential hoof care was to stand the horse on large stones while it was being groomed so that when it stamped at flies it rounded the hoof.[102] This may sound odd but it meant that blood supply through exercise benefited the hoof. Xenophon does not mention hoof trimming, but in a dry climate hooves are harder and will withstand abrasive conditions better than hooves with soft laminae that are frequently found in moist climatic areas. Nevertheless, continual use will keep even the hardest hoof pared, and some worn down to the extent that they become sore. Horses were to be regularly exercised, not always in formation, and they were to be galloped over all types of footing. To maintain standards, and to keep the men keen the commander was occasionally to accompany his unit in sham fights in a variety of locations. Colonels were to take part in javelin exercises.[103] Exercise kept animals at optimum fitness. Variety keeps a horse fresh and unlikely to anticipate commands from the rider which could have been disastrous in action.

All units turned out for public spectacles,[104] which were held at four locations: the Lyceum, the Academy, Phalerum and the Hippodrome.[105] Performances differed but all were expected to be brilliant. Horses and riders had to have mastered many techniques, be able to maintain cohesion when marching, crossing rivers, etc., and be courageous in action.[106] Manoeuvres included parading sedately and saluting various deities, followed by a flat-out gallop by regiments, the men positioning their lances between their horses' ears to avoid fouling their weapons; they were to return at a sedate pace,[107] which is not specified, but for spectacle purposes was probably a hand canter. The *antihippasia* sham fights took place in the Hippodrome. Horses filled the breadth of the arena. The corps divided into opposing halves which charged through each other, then turned, one half pursuing, one fleeing by turns. Three charges were made at increasing speed, the final one at full gallop. When riding on hard ground riders were advised to lean back and collect their horses on the rapid turns to prevent them falling. Once on the straight speed increased.[108] Monuments recording victories were set up in the Agora. One noting the victory of the Leontis tribe shows a squadron at full gallop; another dating to the second half of the fourth century or to the early third century records a victory of the Erectheis tribe.[109]

There were common-sense precautions to be taken over avoiding ambushes, and advice on subterfuges to be used to gull the enemy.[110] A trooper had to know his horse's capabilities for overtaking or fleeing enemy cavalry,[111] as did his commander whose knowledge was to be gained by observing individual horses and their condition after strenuous sham fights.[112] Out in the country riding was to be alternated with riders walking to rest their horses' backs, unless the enemy was perhaps lurking near, when the spelling was to be by regiments, leaving those mounted ready for action. Narrow tracks called for advance in column, broad tracks for extended formation. Open ground required battle array. Scouts were to be sent ahead, and in dangerous territory a second scout was to reconnoitre well ahead. Study of local and potential war zones topography was considered essential so that a cavalry commander was not caught napping when a campaign got under way. Spies, merchants, neutral persons, and sham deserters were to be used for gathering intelligence. Guards were always to be posted.[113]

Xenophon appreciated that cavalry needed to work in conjunction with infantry, which should be concealed within and behind the cavalry.[114] There is a homily addressed to the commander-in-chief to care well and generously for his men, and to perfect his own weapon handling, and horsemanship by jumping over walls, ditches, and from banks.[115] According to Xenophon the strongest foe were the Thebans of Boeotia with their numerous cavalry,[116] well remembered from his days with Agesilaus.

The *Cavalry Commander* ends by reiterating advice already given.[117] Battle action is covered from many aspects with set plans for every situation, appearing more as 'battles fought on paper'. Although the advice is sound it appears to preclude the enemy having any clear battle plan of their own.[118] A final piece of advice is to raise 200 mercenary horse. The cost of their horses was to be met from men bound to do cavalry service but willing to pay to opt out, as well as from the elderly who were unfit, and from children who had inherited wealthy estates. The enrolment of foreign residents was to be promoted.[119]

Running throughout the text is the feeling that Athenian cavalrymen had become lax, recruitment difficult and the young men enrolled undisciplined on the march, forging too far ahead of the main body, or lagging behind it,[120] and neglecting to take adequate precautions.[121] The repeated admonishments over exercising, training, and caring for the mounts suggests that Athenian cavalry standards had fallen, and that Xenophon knew only too well the results of such inadequacies.

HORSE VALUES

The discovery at Athens of two large deposits of inscribed tablets and armour tokens from the fourth and third centuries give much information on cavalry administration. In 1965, over 570 tablets were recovered from a well in the courtyard of the Dipylon Gate near the Kerameikos cemetery. In 1975, 145 lead and clay tablets came from the Agora, and would originally have been held at the cavalry headquarters, the *Hipparcheion*, at the north-west corner of the Agora, which was used for cavalry activities and training.[122] The maximum value for horses from these tablets is 1,200 drachmae for the third century, and 700 drachmae for the fourth century, with over 500 tablets for the former and only 17 for the latter. It should not be assumed that all third-century values had risen, or that some horses were so superior to earlier examples. Xenophon sold a horse for 50 darics (1,250 drachmae).[123] Aristophanes quoted 1,200 drachmae for a racehorse,[124] and Lysias 1,200 drachmae for a horse given as security for a loan of this amount;[125] 1,200 drachmae was the conventional value for a quality animal, and the military's ceiling evaluation price.

These tablets indicate there was a wide range of horses in the cavalry. Although cost, or appraisal value, was not always the true worth of a horse, the tablets show the investment in a unit's chargers. Prices range from 1,200 drachmae, reducing by 100 or 50 drachmae to the lowest value of 100 drachmae. Not all inscriptions are complete, but from almost 500 from the third century 44 horses were valued at 300 drachmae, 3 at 250, 12 at 200, 2 at 100; the average was just under 700 drachmae. Of the 17 fourth-century prices the average is just under 400 drachmae, with small-value animals ranging from 250 to 100 drachmae. There were more horses in both groups valued at 500 drachmae. The fifth- and early fourth-century sources record 300 drachmae for a cheap, adequate horse, and 1,200 drachmae for a class animal.[126]

RECRUITMENT OF CAVALRY HORSES

The Kerameikos and Agora tablets indicate that horses were procured from many sources. Studs and stables sold direct to troopers, or through dealers. Some troopers must also have raised their own horses. Well over fifty brands are recorded, and a sample shows that some are linked to provenance. Horses from Pharsalus in Thessaly carried the *boukephalai* brand. Axe-brand horses also came from Thessaly. Macedon was represented by the *caduceus*; Corinth by the *koppe*; Sicyon by the *san-bearing* and Larissa by the *centaur*.[127] Once purchased the horses were subjected to two assessments, or *Dokimasia*, one for condition, and one for performance.[128]

PURCHASE AND MAINTENANCE ALLOWANCES

The *katastasis*, first recorded in the 420s, was the loan to help the recruit purchase his horse. It was a fixed sum, unstated, regardless of the evaluation. When the cavalryman retired it had to be repaid, the loan being passed on to his replacement. It is unclear what arrangement covered horses lost in action – whether the trooper paid the total cost of a new horse – if any allowance was made for depreciation due to injury, as opposed to normal depreciation. It is suggested that the yearly evaluations recorded what – if it did pay out –

Athens was liable for when a horse was lost in action.[129] Many conditions would have rendered the horse militarily valueless and should have been considered in the same way as lost in action. These included chronic lameness, and loss of nerve. The latter would have been dangerous if the horse was kept in the ranks and able to incite panic among the other mounts, possibly even trigger a rout, and could have cost a trooper his life. Long-service troopers would have had many horses during their careers, some of which lasted twenty-five years.[130] The means test limited the state's expenditure.

The *sitos* of a drachma a day, paid monthly, was allowed for maintenance of horse and rider during war; in peace it dropped to four obols per day for the horse.[131] At the condition *dokimasia* an underfed charger cost his rider the *sitos*. Slow horses and those shying out of the ranks were cast out, and branded on the jaw with the sign of the wheel. Mounted skirmishers and infantry that worked with the cavalry were also inspected.[132] A brand prevented a sub-standard horse appearing under another owner. Skirmishers would probably have ridden cheaper horses that were also spare-framed and suited to rapid manoeuvring on the flanks, rear, and out in the country in small mobile detachments, for reconnoitring, setting up an ambush, and harrying the enemy's ranks.

LENGTH OF A CHARGER'S SERVICE

The tablets show that cavalrymen generally changed horses on a regular basis. Some had more than one animal valued in a year.[133] Some tablets relating to mounts of the Erectheis tribe show that six horses appear in four consecutive years. This is indicated by the annual decrease in value. Kleochares of Kephisia had an unbranded chestnut horse valued at 600 drachmae for four years. Kroll says that as unbranded chestnut horses were common this probably represented two horses; he considers it unlikely the same horse retained its value over four years.[134] If it was a seasoned superior horse remaining sound and with full mental capacity I see no reason to automatically drop its annual value, unless it was done because of Athenian army regulations regardless of the animal's condition. There are wide time differences for maximum capabilities being retained.[135] If a man had bonded with a super horse it would be priceless to him. There would have been occasions when riders and horses did not remotely bond, friction resulted, and a different teaming would have benefited both. A cavalry troop was not just horse and human numbers, but individualistic duos that had first to work in concert, before being of any use in a cohesive unit, aspects overlooked by most military historians. Nevertheless, the tablets do show that devaluation normally occurred annually. In third-century Athens this was 100 drachmae, and several horses dropped 200 drachmae a year. Normally only 1,200 drachmae horses maintained their value for as much as three years, because their true value was far higher.[136]

Because inscriptions could be erased and the tablets re-inscribed, a lot of valuable information has been lost.

CHAPTER 12

The Macedonian Empire

PHILIP II (359–336) AND ALEXANDER III (336–323)

Under Philip II Macedon grew from fractured tribal territories to a unified country. Between 354 and 339 Macedon expanded until it stretched from the Lower Danube to the Aegean, and from the Adriatic coast to modern Scutari, the Black Sea and the Dardanelles. Opposing Greek cities were subjugated. Blending militarism with diplomacy Philip tried to end the friction between Greek states, but Athens rejected the peace proposals. At the Battle of Chaeronea in 338 Macedon's army won decisively over Athens and Thebes. In 338/7 the Common Peace among mainland Greek states, called the League of Corinth, was forged. Only Sparta was excluded. It was decided to war on Persia in retaliation for the destruction of Greek temples 150 years earlier. Philip was to lead the army, raised from levies on League states.[1]

In early 336 Philip's advance army of 10,000 Macedonian and mercenary troops under Parmenion, Attalos and Amyntas, crossed the Hellespont into Asia and moved south down the Anatolian coast where Persian-ruled Greek cities rose in revolt. Philip's army would have profited by Persia's internal problems. Artaxerxes III (349/8–338/7) and his successor Arses were both murdered within a year by Bagoas, a eunuch general. Once assured of the Persian throne, Darius III (336–330) eliminated Bagoas. Philip too was assassinated in July 336. Alexander inherited the Persian enterprise. Unrest in Greece, and in Thrace and Illyria among the Triballians and Dardanians, caused a delay. Alexander's cavalry played a significant part in these early appearances.[2]

Philip and Alexander were the first Europeans to make consistent, extensive, and successful use of hard-hitting cavalry. As his prolonged campaigns probed deeper into Asia, Iran and ultimately India, Alexander increasingly used multination cavalry with horses indigenous to their countries. The sheer scale of his enterprise has been lauded by many, questioned by others. What has not been considered sufficiently is the endurance of his cavalry horses, which on occasion were pushed to extremes, and that of the baggage beasts. The latter were essential as transporters of the army's foodstuffs and replacement weaponry. A look at these factors can show the considerable debt Alexander owed to his animal army, which eventually also included camels and elephants.

Arrian's *Anabasis* is the best account of Alexander's campaigns. He based it on reliable sources: Ptolemy Lagos was one of Alexander's generals, and founder of Egypt's Lagide Dynasty; Aristobulus was one of his technical experts. Arrian, a military man and horseman, understood equid usage. He wrote a technical treatise on cavalry and infantry. In this the cavalry horses' manoeuvres can be analysed stride by stride; speed and angle of weapon delivery from horseback can be plotted. Arrian records the difficulties Alexander's cavalry encountered, and how much he relied on aggressive cavalry attacks. Although an admirer of Alexander, Arrian did criticise him over the mutilation of Bessus, the murder of Cleitus and the adoption of Persian customs.[3]

ALEXANDER'S MILITARY AND EQUESTRIAN INHERITANCE

Alexander inherited a strong army. The highly trained phalanx was armed with Philip's invention of the cornel wood *sarissa* (4½–5½ m) with a bladed head and spiked butt.[4] The cavalry had been built up steadily by Philip to about 3,300 heavy and 400 light horse. It was raised from the landed gentry, many of whom had been given estates for services rendered. With the land went the obligation to cavalry service.[5] The elite heavy horse were known as Companion Cavalry. They were divided into *ilai*, each at least 200 strong, with the Royal Squadron, the *Agema*, of 300, which fought around the king. Light horse, the *prodromoi* (scouts) were also called *sarrissaphorai*.[6] Macedonian cavalry were armed with swords and the cavalry *sarissa* whose dimensions were as follows:

Total length 4.87 m formed of tapered cherry wood (cornel).
A solid-bladed butt 53 cm long, weighing 1.235 kg.
A hollow head blade 47 cm long, weighing 0.235 kg.
Total weight 3.610 kg.
Balance point 1.47 m from the butt blade (that is, about 30 per cent)
   behind the grip, 70 per cent before the grip.

This enabled the head to reach well ahead of the horse and cause maximum damage to an opponent, who with a shorter cavalry lance could not come close to his target. Should the shaft break, the butt blade could inflict a stabbing injury. I am indebted to Peter Connolly who crafted a cavalry *sarissa*, based on archaeological data, and had its use tried out by horseman John Duckham. Cavalry were trained to aim the *sarissa* at the enemy trooper's face (or at his horse).[7] Impaling an enemy was not practical as without a retaining cantle or stirrup the resistance could have forced the *sarissa*-wielder over his horse's rump.

CAVALRY FORMATIONS

The Macedonians used the wedge formation, said to originate with the Scythians; the Thracians also adopted this practice. Thessalian cavalry favoured the rhomboid (diamond) formation. Both these had good penetrative qualities and were easier to wheel about than the Greek square.[8] Under Philip and Alexander Macedonian cavalry was used as a major strike force.[9]

QUALITY OF HORSES AND HORSEMANSHIP IN ALEXANDER'S EARLY ENGAGEMENTS

When Alexander crossed into Asia he had about 32,000 foot and 5,100 horse, according to Diodorus Siculus. Left in Macedon with the regent Antipater were 12,000 foot and 1,500 horse. The equid content of the initial 5,100 cavalry were: Macedon, 1,800; Thessaly, 1,800; Greece, 600; and Thrace and Paeonia, 900. Other sources quote from 5,000 to 5,500. Brunt analyses the reasons for the discrepancies. To these must be added those already in Asia, which as the Persian strength lay in cavalry, was probably about 1,000, giving 6,100 available to Alexander.[10]

The main horse supply areas had interesting equestrian data. Herodotus gives clues regarding the excellence of Macedonian, Thessalian and Thracian horses and horsemanship which affected future generations in their respective areas. In Xerxes' army Zeus' sacred chariot was drawn by eight white horses,[11] later identified as mares. The equippage was left at Siris in Paeonia. The Paeonians claimed it had been stolen by 'up country Thracians'.[12] No mention is made of its recovery. As with the Persian cavalry horses that spent considerable time in Macedon, Thessaly and Boeotia,[13] these valuable mares would have been put to stud and benefited future Thracian stock. Unlike the cavalry entires that moved onto further engagements, the mares, if Herodotus is right about their being stolen – and we have no reason to think otherwise as he was so right about much of the detail of Xerxes' and his son Darius' expeditions – could have had considerable genetic input over time in their new 'up country' Thracian home. They are not specifically noted as Nisaean, but mention of them first occurs with descriptions of sacred

Nisaean horses and other Nisaeans drawing Xerxes' chariot.[14] Other references to Nisaeans are to the mount of cavalry commander Masistius,[15] and to Mardonius' white (grey) charger.[16] It is certain that high-ranking Persian officers rode Nisaeans. The preponderance of greys is indicated – white mares, white charger, sacred white horses offered to the Thracian River Strymon (Strouma).[17]

THRACE

The horse was important in Thracian culture. The legendary King Rhesus had 'coursers swift as the wind and white as winter snow'. On a practical level the *Iliad* records Thracian horses as 'huge'. They were sacred to the Thracian sun god; deities are often shown mounted. The Moesians, a Thracian tribe, sacrificed a horse before going into battle.[18] Thracians rode earlier than did the Greeks, to whom the Thracians were known as lovers and breeders of horses. As a symbol of military and economic power the horse was important to tribal chieftains and their retinues.[19] Thrace had commercial contacts with Persia,[20] so it is probable that horsetrading occurred. Horses were parental and political gifts. Kotys I (383–359), a contemporary of Philip II, gave two herds of white horses as part of his daughter's marriage portion.[21] When Xenophon served in the army of Seuthes he was at a banquet when a swift, white horse was presented to the king.[22] Depictions of Thracians' horses are numerous. Those of the hero god, and of warriors on horseback, are conformationally crude, but many rhytons are exquisitely modelled with refined outlines showing what some animals must have resembled. Grattius Faliscus (first century AD) described Thracian horses as easy keepers, excellent performers, but with 'ugly necks and a thin spine curving along their backs'; that is, ewe necks and a roach back.[23] Arrian singles them out:

> Where there are fairly level plains as in Mysia, the country of the Getae [a Thracian tribe], Scythia and Illyria, the stag is hunted by men mounted on Scythian or Illyrian horses. There are slow goers at first . . . but for a hard day's work they can hold out against anything.[24]

This is an enlightening description. In endurance riding the tough, lean horse lasts the distance, while the fretful speed merchant burns itself out. It also suggests that the horses of Thrace had received a fair dose of blood from neighbouring Scythia, as well as direct imports.

To improve and increase Macedonian stocks Philip II imported 20,000 'noble' Scythian mares.[25] Roughly contemporary with Philip were the Scythian Pazyryk burials in the Altai which yielded superior fine-limbed horses about 14.3 hh. We may doubt the 20,000 but accept that Macedon received large draft(s) of mares. 'Noble' infers that these were not stocky steppe ponies, but quality mares capable of producing weight carriers with size and speed. The size, conformation, and golden coats of the Altai horses imply that they were from Turan, partly within the huge Persian Empire. Other Persian artifacts were found, notably a carpet from mound 5 showing horses and riders. These have clearly been adapted to a weave, but based on Persian conformation of Nisaeans as noted above in chapter 6, page 53. Other depictions, notably a warrior riding a saddled horse, show a much finer type of animal. This is in felt on a wall-hanging from mound 5.[26]

The *caduceus* brand appears on the coins of Macedonian kings as early as Alexander I (498–454) and Pausanias (390–389) showing first-class Macedonian chargers were available from an early date.[27] The Companion Cavalry was levied on a district basis and included men from Macedon, Thessaly and other Greek locations. Socrates was a Companion Cavalry squadron leader heading the detachment from Apollonia.[28]

THESSALY

Thessaly is plains country, suitable for raising grazers. The Athenian archives reveal several brands indicating horse-rearing areas. Pherae horses carried an axe brand; those from Larissa a centaur. Pharsalus horses were branded with an ox head, a *boukephalus*. Since Aristophanes' day (*c.* 450–*c.* 383) Pharsalus horses were noted for quality. *Boukephalus* horses were also those with an unusual naturally occurring feature.[29] There is the often repeated tale of Alexander's large, black Thessalian charger, Bucephalus, told by, among others, Plutarch, Arrian, Pliny the Elder and Gellius. Details vary as to the horse's price – Plutarch says 13 talents, Pliny the Elder says 16 talents; both are probably fictitious. The name Bucephalus is also variously ascribed to an ox-head brand, a similar-shaped white mark on his forehead, the shape of his head. However, the important points agree. It was brought to Pella by a Thessalian horse trader from Pharsalus; and turned out to be vicious. But Alexander, aged about twelve years old, noticed how it shied from its own shadow, and by skilful positioning ensured that the shadow fell to its rear, which enabled him to ride it successfully. Bucephalus died, aged 30, in 326 (having remained with

Alexander until this date),[30] which meant that he was foaled in 356, supposedly sharing a birth year with Alexander. No dealer would have kept a twelve-year-old horse past its prime in his yard, nor a stud owner in his paddocks, if it was as vicious as reported, nor price it so high. Shying is common with nervous horses, particularly young horses ridden late in the afternoon when the sun casts long shadows. Rogue horses soon learn that shying can unload a rider, a vice the outcome of which is exacerbated by lack of saddles and stirrups. It is inconceivable that the excessive mileage, the rigours of travel, and frequent hunger and thirst, would have permitted a very old horse to survive, let alone be used in battle. It was probably a young colt, brutally handled and rebelling, with which Alexander struck up a bond. This does happen. Some nervous or recalcitrant horses perform well for a gentle handler, and abominably for a callous one. Far from being specifically named Bucephalus, he was probably known as the Bucephalus horse on account of his provenance and brand.

MILITARY ACTION AND THE CHANGING FACE OF HORSE SUPPLY

After every battle Alexander would have acquired horses from those running loose after their riders had fallen in action, and from captured cavalry. As Macedonians were appointed as satraps in place of defeated Persians, satrapal equid resources became available. Brunt and Griffiths have written on elements of Persian and Iranian cavalry incorporated into Alexander's army, although they do not agree whether it was post 328 or 324.[31] However, not a word is said about the cavalry's equid composition. This must have changed dramatically throughout the campaign years.

BATTLE OF THE RIVER GRANICUS, 334

At the Granicus, Alexander's Companion Cavalry lost 25, plus over 60 from other horsed units, and about 30 foot, set against Persian losses of about 1,000 cavalry and mercenary foot 'surrounded and butchered to a man, and Persian prisoners taken of about 2,000'. Elite Persian dead included satraps, governors, and royal princes. Spithridates, Satrap of Lydia, and Mithrobarzanes, Governor of Cappadocia, were among them. From the early Persian Empire Lydia had notable cavalry, and Cappadocia, the Tabal of the Assyrians, had long been a producer of large horses,[32] so the haul for the Macedonians must have been of superior stock.

BATTLE OF ISSUS, 333

At Issus the River Pinarus largely dictated how the battle unfolded. The sea was on the Macedonian left and on the Persian right. It was only possible for horses to cross the river near its mouth and 3.5 km upriver at a narrow ford. In between, though narrow, it ran between banks too steep for horses, and difficult enough for foot to cross. Alexander's cavalry totalled about 4,500, that of Darius approximately 30,000. Huge numbers are given for the Persian foot by all sources and are clearly fantastic, as are the numbers of Persian losses. Nevertheless, Alexander's horse and foot were greatly outnumbered, but better disciplined than that of the Persians. Cavalry, tactically deployed and cunningly used, played a major part in Macedon's victory. Initially, the only cavalry on Alexander's left were 600 Greeks, with most of the foot in the centre, and archers, javelineers, some Greek foot, and the rest of the cavalry to the right. On the opposite bank Greek mercenaries and Persian foot faced the slowly moving phalangites. Some Persian foot had worked round to Alexander's right, but were blocked by 300 cavalry, javelineers and archers. Darius's cavalry were deployed on both wings, the cataphracts on his right, Hyrcanians and Medes on his left. His royal bodyguard were in the centre around him, placed behind his foot. Once in missile range Alexander, leading the Companion Cavalry, galloped through the ford and hit the Persian left, which crumbled. Meanwhile, the Thessalian heavy horse, screened by infantry, rode to reinforce the Greek horse who had successfully lured Darius' cataphracts across the river. Thinking to overwhelm the Greeks the cataphracts lost their cohesiveness and succumbed to the Thessalians who hit them in the flank. The cataphracts turned and fled across the river, hotly pursued by the Thessalians. The Persian foot also fled. The Companions then struck into the Greek mercenaries. Darius too fled, joining his routed cavalry whose horses under heavily armoured cataphracts suffered immensely.

Macedonian losses were about 150 cavalry, 302 foot, and 4,500 wounded; Persian losses were approximately 15,000. Arrian notes Persian losses from each arm 'were equally severe'.[33] The haul in Persian cavalry horses would have been huge, and certainly would have more than replaced dead and injured Macedonian horses. There would also have been vast numbers of baggage beasts and remounts in the Persian camp. No man of high rank went to war with but one charger. A high proportion of Persian warhorses would have been of the Median Nisaean breed, heavy, muscled, large weight carriers.

THE BATTLE OF GAUGAMELA, 331

In 331 Alexander returned from his sojourn in Egypt, crossed the Euphrates at Thapsacus and headed for the Tigris, intending to use a less intensively hot route to Babylon. The route was provided with horse fodder and supplies for the army. Persian scouts captured en route told Alexander that Darius had moved up from Babylon and was waiting on the Tigris. After a forced march the Macedonians reached and crossed the Tigris unopposed. There was no sign of the Persian guard, nor of Darius. Four days later scouts sighted about 1,000 Persian cavalry. Taking the *Agema*, one *ile* of Companions and the Paeonian light horse, Alexander galloped for the open ground where the Persians had been seen. Without a blow struck the Persians fled, hotly pursued. Most got away; a few on slow horses were killed. Some were captured with their mounts. From these Alexander heard that Darius was at Gaugamela, north of Arbela. Learning from the restricted terrain at Issus, Darius had had the ground levelled for cavalry and the 200 four-horse scythed chariots in which he placed his mistaken trust.

NUMBERS AT GAUGAMELA

Alexander's cavalry had increased to about 7,000. His foot numbered approximately 40,000. Darius had amassed a huge army, reputedly 40,000 horse and 1,000,000 foot. The Persian figures, especially for foot, are fictitious. The sources' lowest figure is 200,000. Marsden calculated that the Persian horse totalled about 34,000. The right wing main line under Mazaeus, Satrap of Cilicia, had 12,000, with 3,000 in advance of it. The left wing under Bessus, Satrap of Bactria, had 16,000, with 3,000 deployed in front. Darius, surrounded by kinsmen cavalry, was in the centre. Marsden is not specific about the foot, which 'were in any case of extraordinarily little significance'.

Darius' horses largely came from the noted horse-raising territories collectively called Turan, which have been discussed in the Caballine Canvas section. Much of this swathe was in the ancient kingdoms of Bactria, Sogdia and Arachosia. Most of Bessus' cavalry would have been of Turanian stock. Many contingents served under Mazaeus. The Median, Hyrcanian and Parthian horses came from south of the Caspian Sea. West of the Caspian horses with high reputations both before and after the Persian era came from Cappadocia and Armenia. Syria also provided cavalry. Strabo recorded that later, Seleucis Nicator, who succeeded Alexander in Iran and Syria, had a huge royal stud at Apameia on the

Orontes with 30,000 mares and 300 stallions, colt-breakers and instructors in heavy armed warfare. Much of the equid wealth would have been in place well before the end of the Persian era. Both Bessus and Mazaeus had Sacae and Scythian cavalry. The Persian kings annually levied 20,000 foals from Armenia as they raised Nisaean horses equal to those of Media. The Albanians, a Scythian tribe, also in Mazaeus' command, fought on fully armoured horses, as did the Scythians whom Arrian notes as being 'provided with defensive armour, both horses and men'.[34]

Alexander deployed his army with the bulk of his foot in the centre front, with two Greek units behind. To the right was the wedge of Companion Cavalry under Philotas, with the *Agema* under Cleitus. Obliquely to them were the *Prodromoi* under Aretas and the Paeonians under Ariston, backed by three foot units of archers, Agrianians, and Macedonians, with a unit of mercenary cavalry under Menidas, and Agrianians, archers and javelineers under Balacras. The left comprised cavalry units from allied Greeks, 1,800 Thessalians under Parmenion and, obliquely to them in a wedge, mercenary cavalry at its head, allied Greek and Odrysian (Thracian) horse behind, backed by javelineers, archers and mercenary Achaeans. Arrian singles out the Thessalians, especially the contingent from Pharsalus, which was the best and largest.[35]

Cavalry was crucial at Gaugamela. After cresting the ridge overlooking Gaugamela, Alexander saw the Persians 4 miles away. While officers consulted on a plan of action, light infantry and Companion Cavalry reconnoitred the battle site. Both armies waited under arms overnight. Arrian emphasises the demoralising effect of this on the Persians. A horse's strength is sapped by continuous weight-bearing, as well as by the more active endurance, and the Persian heavy cavalry were equipped as cataphracts.

Alexander opened hostilities with his Royal Squadron attacking slightly to the right. Darius, whose line outflanked that of the Macedonians, countered by trying to encircle them. Even though Scythian cavalry had already engaged Alexander's forward units, he pressed on, intent on covering the cleared ground to deny Darius' chariots an advantage. Menidas' 600 mercenary cavalry were ordered to attack the Scythians, but they were hit hard, the weight of Scythian and Bactrian horse pushing them back, until Ariston's Paeonians joined the mercenaries and countered the enemy, some of whom fled. Bessus then sent in his remaining Bactrians, whose total force of 8,000 outnumbered all Alexander's cavalry. Fully armoured Scythian horses and men revealed the Macedonian weakness in defensive equipment. In fierce fighting the Macedonians were hard hit, but refused to give ground. Squadron by squadron they attacked until the enemy formation broke.

The chariots proved totally ineffective as missiles rained down on the horses. What few escaped had their reins grabbed, drivers hauled out of the chariots and the horses killed. A few chariots escaped and plunged into the Macedonian foot which parted ranks, the horses galloping through to be 'dealt with' by the Royal Guard and the grooms. A captured few formed part of the battle spoils. Meanwhile, as the Persian cavalry tried to envelop Alexander a gap opened in Darius' front. Alexander's wedge of Companion Cavalry and heavy foot shot through, straight for Darius, the cavalry's *sarissas* – aimed directly at the enemy's faces – inflicting terrible injuries. Darius fled, leading the Persian rout.

On the Macedonian left Persian cavalry had broken through and made for the baggage park, only to be attacked by the phalanx which turned about and hit their rear. Many were killed, others fled. Mazaeus' command, unaware that Darius had fled, tried to envelop the Macedonian right, coming in so hard on the Thessalians' flank that Parmenion sent a galloper to Alexander for aid. According to Arrian, Alexander broke off his pursuit of Darius and galloped to the rescue, hitting the Persians who were trying to escape. The hardest fighting ensued with the Parthians, Indians, and the finest Persian cavalry units, in a fierce hand-to-hand melee. Sixty Companion Cavalry perished, and others were wounded. Those Persians who managed to fight through Alexander's wedge galloped off to safety. On the point of engaging Mazaeus' right Alexander found the Thessalians had fought magnificently and routed the Persians. Parmenion made for the Persian camp to secure baggage, elephants and camels, and Alexander took off after Darius. In the pursuit his horses suffered severely. Over 1,000 died from battle wounds and exhaustion. Of these nearly half came from the Companion Cavalry. A major inconsistency arises here. Alexander could hardly have begun his pursuit of Darius. The failing of cavalry in general to quite literally get carried away is not one that a man of Alexander's military stamp was guilty of. Marsden suggests the urgent message arrived when Alexander was hotly engaged, and thus he left once he had broken the Persian centre, and before Darius' flight. The sources give different numbers of dead and wounded. Arrian says 100 Macedonian dead. More realistic figures give 500. Persian losses are variously given. Arrian notes 300,000, other sources 40,000, 60,000, and even 90,000.[36]

Reinforcements and Replacements

After every major battle Alexander's animal acquisitions more than made up for losses. After the Granicus he moved down the Anatolian coast. At

Aspendus he demanded all the horses that were there raised for Darius.[37] After Issus Parmenion took over 7,000 pack animals that Darius had in Damascus.[38] After Gaugamela, with Alexander now master of the Persian Empire, reinforcements and replacements were on a huge scale. He acquired a supply network throughout Babylonia. Some idea of Babylonian riches are given by Herodotus. Arrian and Curtius Rufus also note Babylonian and other acquisitions. As these are agriculturally based they would not have changed markedly from the early days of the Persian Empire. Huge numbers of horses are quoted. We may question the exaggerated and too precise specifics, but accept the fact of prodigious supply.

Cyrus the Great's Satrap of Babylon, Tritantaechmes, had a huge personal stud of 16,000 mares and 800 stallions, and in addition to tribute Babylon supplied the whole Persian army with comestibles for four months of the year.[39] After Gaugamela the contents of Darius' baggage park, which included camels and elephants, fell to Alexander.[40] Babylon welcomed the victorious Alexander with gifts of herds of horses and cattle.[41]

From the Median Plains Alexander had the 50,000 Nisaean mares said to remain from earlier herds of 150,000.[42] As the annual foal crop from these mares reached maturity Alexander's cavalry would have received a massive and continual input, and also have undergone a radical change in horse type. In Bactria Alexander re-equipped his cavalry with fresh horses to replace losses from exhaustion in crossing the Caucasus (Hindu Kush) and in marching to and from the River Oxus.[43] When Uxian hill tribes demanded payment from Alexander to pass through the Persian Gates his response was to launch a massive night raid. He seized the pass before the Uxians could reach it. For their temerity he imposed an annual tribute of 100 horses, 500 mules, and 30,000 sheep.[44]

As early as 333, after Issus some Persians who had surrendered were drafted into Alexander's army.[45] Arrian does not specify whether they were horse or foot. Common sense suggests there were some of each, but as the Persian horse were the superior arm it is likely that such troops would have been those recommending themselves to Alexander.

Apart from acquisition of new animals by the above means, after Gaugamela when he was Persia's master he could draw on the cavalry and their horses from Iranians and other subject peoples of the Persian Empire. These included Scythians, Daae, Bactrians and Sogdians.[46] However, the Bactrian and Sogdian satrapies had still to be pacified.[47]

Cavalry reinforcements had also come from home with 300 from Macedon and 200 from Thessaly.[48] At Ecbatana (Hamadan) when Alexander dismissed his Thessalian cavalry some men re-enlisted, the rest sold their mounts (to other troopers) before travelling home.[49] Elephants that joined the army on several occasions, some coming from Darius,[50] must have helped desensitise the cavalry horses prior to their advance into India. Once in India, Taxiles also gave Alexander many elephants and 700 Indian cavalry.[51]

PRACTICALITIES BEHIND THE ACHIEVEMENTS

Terrain and Climate

Between 336 and his death at Babylon in 323, Alexander's campaigns covered about 17,000 miles. The farthest northern point reached was Chojend, close to Ferghana from which came the best horses. The farthest point east was the River Hyphasis (modern Beas) in the Punjab. From Macedon to India, and back to Babylon via the Indus, the horrendous Gedrosian Desert (modern Makran), Carmania, Persis, and into Babylonia, the army toiled through numerous agricultural and climatic zones. These included arid, infertile areas, lush expanses, deserts, grassy plains and soaring mountains. Climate would have had a significant impact on the condition of cavalry horses and other animals. It ranged from temperate in Macedon, dry and hot in Greece, hot also in Syria but laced with their heavy winter rains. Egypt had excessive dry heat; parts of Mesopotamia rose to 120 degrees F, and the major river valleys were swelteringly humid. Persia had extremes of summer heat and winter cold. India differed from anything previously encountered, from the ice and snow of the Hindu Kush, to the heat, humidity, and lushness of lowlands, the intensely dry heat of sandy plains, and the inundations of the monsoon period.

Supply

Alexander knew the supply problems he would encounter initially. When his aims extended beyond the core of the Persian Empire into Bactria and India, it is doubtful he had much idea of what to expect in terms of terrain, climate and provisions. In the early stages supplies were carried by ship to nearby ports, then offloaded onto baggage animals. Up to thirty days' supply could be transported. Each baggage animal could carry about 250 lb.[52] In Engels' excellent work on the logistics of Alexander's army, there are nevertheless certain anomalies in the equid content. Most of what he says regarding equines was culled from early twentieth-century army veterinary manuals, in which the animals dealt with were of mostly middleweight hunter stamp which consumed rather larger quantities than would a horse on marching rations in the ancient world. The army's daily grain, fodder, and water requirements allowed each animal 10 lb grain, 10 lb long feed, and 80 lb water (8 gallons). One day out of seven was to be allocated for grazing to top up nutrition, and rest animals' backs. Two surprising comments then occurred: all feeding had to be done during the day because horses would not graze at night; and cavalry horses would not be regularly used to carry baggage as it would break their spirit.[53] Given the chance all herbivores graze at night, particularly in excessively hot weather because they seek shade and doze in the heat; and a well-broken horse will carry any burden you put on it without damaging its spirit. Horses have no sense of self-importance, which is not to be confused with dominance. The feed/water requirements would have been the maximum needed for the average daily stint; the water is on the high side except for excessively hot conditions and/or under maximum usage in high-speed lengthy pursuits.

Harvests

The early marches into the Persian Empire were planned to coincide with regional harvest dates. Once through areas about which there was accurate information there were spells when the army stayed put long enough for information to be gathered on forward provisioning, and plans made for routing accordingly. Alliances were made and depots stocked in advance of massed troop movements. In areas where provisions were scant the army divided to avoid depleting resources. When necessary forced marches were made to conserve rations.[54] Harvest dates and soil fertility varied. The average ancient yield of grain per acre was about 5 cwt, but in the fertile, heavily agricultural areas of the Nile, Mesopotamia, the Lower Helmund Valley, and the Indus, yields were higher. In Persia ancient yields were 20 bushels per acre; today it is between 8 and 11 bushels. Rhagae (near modern Tehran) was a major grain-producing area. In general, farming was then far more productive, with more land under cultivation. Harvest dates fell in April to May in Seistan and the Lower Helmund Valley; in mid-May for Egypt; in June for Thrace, Syria, Phoenicia and Mesopotamia; in June to July for Persia, Uxian territory, and north of Susa; in July to August for the Anatolian Plateau, Phrygia, Cappadocia, and the Hindu Kush villages; and in August for Arachosia, and for Afghanistan in the Kandahar to Kabul region.[55]

MARCHING RATES, PROVISIONS AND HAZARDS

The daily average march rate for the whole army was about 15 miles, at a rate of 3 mph or so. The distance covered often fell below this in difficult regions. The longest recorded daily distance for the whole army for one week covering the distance from Gaza to Pelusium was 19½ miles per day. Smaller detachments frequently moved faster.[56]

It is not until Persia was under Alexander's control after Gaugamela, that Arrian begins a detailed portrayal of the pressures encountered in terrain and temperatures increasingly hostile to good animal and human management. Previously, deaths in battle are noted. Now the spotlight falls on attrition from overexertion. Combined with this was the uncertainty of obtaining provisions, and, in some areas, water. Alexander made heavy demands on his cavalry, especially on the crack force of Companions. Sometimes detachments were sizeable, but often smaller numbers were employed for greater speed. When necessary Alexander operated in winter cold, summer heat, even through waterless deserts. Under abnormal conditions the cavalry was nearly always to the fore, and in some cases the only troops used. There was no way that ideal rations were always fed. Even though a baggage beast carried many days' supply, it also ate its way through this. Its 250 lb load of grain diminished by multiples of ten, plus the 3 lb per man, according to how many animals and men it fed, in addition to itself. It is doubtful if long feed was carried in any quantity, and only a modicum of water. All animals would have had to rely on grazing, and in winter hay, and water en route. The records frequently indicate occasions when horses got scant water and feed. In winter conditions with no grazing, or at best minimal amounts of poor quality grass, animals would have run up very light from overwork and undernourishment. For the excessively hard treks horses could not eat enough in one day to replace the calories expended. As many of these stints were over several days the cumulative effects would have weakened animals, made them inefficient, and prone to stumbling, lameness, and other muscle and joint trauma. No wonder Alexander was often in need of replacements.

A clutch of notable endurance rides, in which unfortunately many horses were lost, covered considerable distances, and were run at consistently high speeds. The 75-mile pursuit of Darius after Gaugamela achieved 46 mpd (average) over the time taken.[57] Later, again chasing Darius, Alexander covered about 200 miles between Ecbatana and Rhagae in eleven days, stopped for a five-day rest, then took up the pursuit in earnest after two important Persians brought news that Darius had been seized by Bessus, Nabarzanes and Barsaentes, Satrap of Arachosia and Drangiana. Bessus also usurped the royal power. In a close reading of Arrian, adding the days, nights and part-days, in five days of hard riding Alexander covered between 170 and 210 miles. He arrived at Damghan or Sharud (the difference in the mileage), largely riding through uninhabited waterless desert, only to find that Darius had been murdered and Bessus had escaped.

In the final stages of this pursuit Alexander dispensed with infantry except for 500 of the best, whom he mounted on cavalry horses.[58] The speed never dropped below 33 mpd, and one 45-mile stretch took only twelve hours.[59] The speeds are not that remarkable,[60] but without water, adequate food, and almost no rest, and with unshod hooves on abrasive sand, and in the absence of decent tack, it was a truly great achievement. Dehydration was probably the worst killer. Alexander then ordered Ptolemy to take three *ilai* of his Companion Cavalry, mounted javelineers, Philotas's infantry, half the archers, and the Agrianians, and make contact with Spitamenes and Dataphernes, who had indicated they would arrest and hand over Bessus. In four days Ptolemy rode from the River Oxus to Nautaka, a distance normally a ten-day ride. Bessus was sent to Bactra for execution.[61]

INDIA

Battle of the River Hydaspes, 326

The people of Taxila welcomed Alexander, and there he learned that the army of Porus, King of the Pauravas, was waiting across the River Hydaspes. All fordable places were blocked. It was summer 326 and the river was high from mountain meltwater and monsoon rain. With ample provisions Alexander dug in to wait until the water level dropped. Meanwhile, he split his army into constantly moving detachments so that Porus did not know where the Macedonians would try to cross. At night cavalry moved noisily along the river bank. Porus reciprocated until it became so normal that he dropped his guard and kept his cavalry in camp, only posting lookouts. Then Alexander struck. Eighteen miles away was a thickly wooded site offering concealment for a crossing. Craterus, with cavalry and foot, was left in the main position with orders to stay put until Porus moved to attack Alexander, or was clearly in retreat. Porus' army, although powerful, well equipped and efficient, held no worries for Alexander, except for the elephants which he feared would disrupt the cavalry horses. Alexander's command contained the elite cavalry, the *Agema*, and three *ilai* of the Companions, Bactrian, Sogdian, Scythian horse, and mounted archers of the Daae. All the foreign contingents, acquired since Gaugamela, had a reputation for superior horsemanship. Infantry came from the Guards under Seleucus', Cleitus', and Coenus' battalions, Agrianians, and foot archers. A providential thunderstorm masked night preparations. The dawn crossing was hidden until it was past a mid-stream island. Then enemy patrols sent gallopers to Porus.

Meanwhile, the Macedonians were in a predicament. They had landed on a large island separated from the far bank by a narrow, deep channel, the waters of which came chest high to the men, neck high to the horses as they waded through. On landing Alexander deployed his 5,000 cavalry on the right, the mounted archers in the van, with 6,000 foot in the rear. Foot archers, Agrianians and javelineers were posted on each flank of the heavy infantry.

Arrian considered Alexander's intentions were to open hostilities with a cavalry charge. If it failed to turn Porus's main forces troopers could then fight a delaying action till the infantry arrived; if the Indians broke, the cavalry could have harried them mercilessly. As there were several versions of the opening attack, Arrian followed Ptolemy. As he accompanied Alexander his version was probably the most reliable. Too late to oppose the crossing, Porus' son arrived with 2,000 horse and 120 chariots, against which the Daae archers were sent in to soften them up. Then, realising this was only an advance contingent, Alexander's cavalry charged squadron by squadron until the Indians broke and fled; 400 Indian cavalry, including Porus' son, were killed. All their chariots were captured as they bogged down in the mire.

To impede Craterus' crossing Porus left a small contingent with enough elephants to disrupt his cavalry, and marched on Alexander with 4,000 horse, 300 chariots, 200 elephants, and 30,000 foot. He relied on his elephants – placed 100 ft apart in advance of his heavy infantry – to panic the Macedonian horses. His foot were to have halted Alexander's infantry advance, which would then have been trampled by the elephants. Infantry outflanked the elephants on both wings; on their flanks were the Indian horse screened by chariotry.

While Porus' army deployed, Alexander checked so the foot could close up with his cavalry and get a second wind; his cavalry manoeuvred continuously along the Macedonian front. Refusing to be drawn into a frontal attack, and risk being trampled by elephants, Alexander moved part of his horse towards Porus' left wing, thus drawing the Indian horse to counter the Macedonians, whose heavy infantry were to hold hard, until the cavalry had disrupted the Indian horse and foot. The action opened with 1,000 Daae archers charging and shooting on the Indian left wing, immediately followed by the charge of the Companions before the Indian horse could recover from the hail of arrows. To meet the weight of the Macedonian thrust all the Indian horse moved to support their left, at which, as ordered, the foot under Coenus closed on the enemy rear. Compelled to split their forces, part of the Indian horse about-faced to repel Coenus. As they wheeled, Alexander charged. The Indians fell back on the elephants whose mahouts drove them forward against Alexander's horses. The Macedonian foot loosed missiles at the mahouts and elephants, which trampled many underfoot, while the infantry on both sides fought hand-to-hand.

A second time the Indian horse were pushed back to the elephants, and suffered heavy casualties from repeated Macedonian cavalry charges, and from their own elephants which, injured, bewildered, and many without mahouts, ran amok trampling Indian and Macedonian alike. The Indians jammed together suffered more, as the Macedonians with room to manoeuvre avoided their blundering charges, but still peppered them with javelins. As the elephants backed away, Alexander's cavalry surrounded the massed Indians; his infantry then closed in forming a shield wall and the slaughter began. Survivors, seeing a gap in the encircling cavalry, fled, to be pursued by Craterus' fresh cavalry who were now coming up to relieve Alexander's horse in the pursuit.

Unlike Darius, Porus fought aboard his elephant until the end, when he was wounded. Only then did he turn and ride off. In victory Alexander treated Porus with the dignity reserved for a great warrior, reinstating him as a vassal king and sealing a bond of friendship. After the battle two cities were founded near the battleground: Nicaea for his victory, and Bucephela for his companion Bucephalus who had carried him on his campaigns for a decade. Reputedly thirty years old he died at the Hydaspes of old age or, as some say, from wounds received in this, Alexander's final, battle.[62]

After the Hydaspes there were several operations to bring the Punjabi tribes into submission. The most troublesome were the independent Cathaei around modern Amritsar. Alexander next moved to the Hyphasis (Beas) in search of further conquests. There the army mutinied, refusing to go further, despite Alexander's blandishments.[63]

EXODUS FROM INDIA – THE GEDROSIAN DESERT

On the march through Gedrosia the army was tested to its utmost. Arrian's powerful portrayal shows he appreciated the effects of nature's worst aspects on men, and particularly on the horses and mules. Realising he was heading for treacherous territory Alexander split his army into three: Craterus headed through Arachosia and Drangiana;[64] Nearchus went by sea along the coast of Gedrosia; and where possible, Alexander marched along the coast so he could secure anchorages, dig wells to supply Nearchus with fresh water, and attack the Oreitae who had yet to render submission. Alexander's command included infantry, his crack Companion Cavalry, a squadron of horse from the other cavalry regiments, and all the mounted archers.

The route through Gedrosia was hazardous. Supplies were unobtainable; many places were devoid of water. The heat was so intense they had to travel by night, at times being forced to march inland. Cavalry sent to the coast to search for anchorages and water found only a little, and that was brackish. On reaching a better-supplied locale, sealed provisions were dispatched to the coast for Nearchus, but were broken into and consumed by the starving men and guards. The second convoy carrying dates, grain, flour, and driving a flock of sheep, was dispatched under the Thracian officer Cretheus.

The toughest section from Oreitae to Pura took sixty days, but it meant that Alexander could be relatively close to Nearchus as he hugged the coast. The animals suffered most, the greater part dying of thirst and burning sand which was sometimes so deep and loose that mules and horses sank as if it were mud. The hazards show Arrian's appreciation of equine susceptibilities, no doubt gained from his own days as a general and cavalry commander. These hazards cause much distress and stress to endurance horses which can become disfunctional when dehydrated. Deep, loose sand puts abnormal strain on the tendons, muscles, and particularly on the heart. I recall a Florida 100-miler, ridden in very high temperatures, approaching 100 degrees at peak times, where the vets took heart rates after a mile climb through fine, deep sand. It was the hardest mile of the whole 100. And these were horses benefiting from superb nutrition, adequate water, and months of careful training.

Irregular marches, dictated by location of waterholes, took an added toll. Many horses and mules were butchered for their meat. Men incapable of going further were left behind; others fell asleep while marching, and on waking, if they could, struggled on to rejoin the army. At one bivouack by a small stream a monsoon cloudburst, away over the hills, turned the trickle to a flash flood. Many soldiers, camp followers and animals drowned. At other good waterholes other fatalities occurred from men and animals gorging on water. Then the guides lost their way in trackless sand. Alexander and a small cavalry detachment set off to reconnoitre, but most of their horses were overcome by heat, so just he and five others on the best horses eventually reached the coast and water. The rest of the army straggled in for a seven-day march along the coast until the guides again found the route. On reaching Carmania where Craterus and Nearchus rejoined him, Alexander offered sacrifices in thanks, and relief, at escaping from the desert wilderness.[65]

THE DIADOCHI

Alexander had less than two years to live. His empire, dearly bought over twelve incredible years, disintegrated after his death under the rule of his generals. By 301, after much warring between all the Macedonian heirs, Seleucus Nicator ruled Syria, much of the Persian Empire's heartland, the Euphrates Valley, and as far as the Punjab in India.[66] Here he met, and came to an arrangement, with Chandragupta, whose minister Kautilya wrote the *Arthasastra* military treatise. From this it was clear that the Indians already had a very good regimen for training both chariotry and cavalry. Many of the cavalry movements were to serve the Indian army very well right into the reign of Akbar, some two thousand years later.[67] To Seleucus fell the best horses of the ancient world. By 285, after much bitter fighting between his generals and satraps, Alexander's empire was ruled by Lysimachus, who held Thrace, and Ptolemy Lagus, who held Egypt; but Seleucus Nicator held by far the most commanding position.[68] His dynasty survived until 56 but its power dwindled under the might of Parthia and then Rome. Syria, a Seleucid stronghold, was made a Roman province in 64.[69]

Glossary

Most unusual terms are explained within the text. The following words are given in case the meanings are unclear.

anoestrus	when a mare is not fertile. i.e. not 'in season'
appanage	similar to a medieval fief; i.e. land granted by the overlord in return for military service
azoturia	a build-up of lactic acid in the horse, causing swelling of the muscle fibres, followed by degenerative changes, locomotor inability, passage of myoglobin into blood plasma and its secretion into the urine
base narrow	when a horse's hooves are placed too close together, which in turn gives a narrow structure in the whole horse. Alternatively the forelimbs may slant to the hooves, a conformation fault
blood horse	a horse with oriental blood, e.g. Arabian, Turcoman, Thoroughbred
bosal	a rawhide noseband, sometimes with a metal core, used to control horses without recourse to a bit. Action is on the nose and the lower underjaw, and sides of the lowerjaw
bred back	when a mare has recently foaled and is then covered by the stallion for a foal in the next year
burro	very small donkey
chamfron	horse's head armour
charger	ridden warhorse
cold blood	horses with draught horse blood, heavy bodied and limbed. Not to be confused with draught horses of the ancient world which differed little, if at all, with the ridden horses
direct rein	instructions to the horse via the rein actio on the bit, pressure being delivered on the bans of the mouth and the corners of the mouth
dish	forefoot action when instead of being in a straight line the front hooves deviate to the outside of true
écorcheurs	so named for their habit of burning their way through territories of enemy and ally alike when, as mercenaries, they were out of work
entire	stallion
falchion	broad curved sword with sharp side on outer edge
farcy	highly contagious disease of lymphatic system showing in nodules, ulcerations, and degeneration in respiratory passages or in the skin
flex	horse's head position when he drops his nose from the poll to a near vertical position making him better balanced and easier to control
founder	term loosely applied to a horse worked beyond its normal capacity and suffering exhaustion. More accurately degenerative changes in the laminae of the hooves due often to overfeeding, too sudden a change in core body heat after excessive work. Usually manifests itself by lameness and hoof degeneration
frog	the soft V shape in a horse's hoof which is designed to absorb

	concussive effects of hoof hitting the ground
glanders	as for farcy
hackamore	loosely for a bitless bridle. Often this is one constructed of metal cheeks with leather noseband and either leather or metal curb strap. This is more correctly a mechanical hackamore. The all leather variety is the bosal noted above. The term hackamore derives from the arabic hakamah, and the Spanish jaquima meaning noseband
hand	English method of measuring horses using a 4 in width to the hand measurement taken from the withers.
hard treed (saddle)	as implied the tree upon which the saddle is built is made of hard material – in the ancient and medieval worlds of wood. Modern trees can be either of wood or metal
hoplite	Greek heavy infantryman
hot Blood	see Blood Horse
hybrid vigour	in the horse when two different breeds are used to produce offspring. The foal frequently is larger than both parents, and often had the better attributes of each
indirect rein	neck reining where instructions to the horse to turn are by laying the rein on the side of neck, on the opposite side to which you ? it to turn, i.e. right rein on right side of neck means turn to the left, and vice versa
kurgans	steppe nomad burial mounds
lead	horse's leg that extends furthest when in canter (to be absolutely correct the horse on the left lead actually strikes off into that stride with the right hind leg, but visually it is easiest to appreciate the leading foreleg)
levade	a dressing movement where the horse gathers his hindquarters under him and elevates his forehand off the ground. Such a move is usally shown in the depiction of a cavalryman of the ancient world trampling his enemy under his horse's hooves
oestrus	the period when a mare is fertile; i.e. 'in season'
palomino	a colour. not a breed. Shades from dark cream to bronze. Mane and tail white (the Registry has nine shadings)
peltast	Greek light infantryman with small shield and short spear or javelin
razzia	raid
rhyton	drinking vessel in shape of (or made from) horn
rollback	movement where horse at gallop, momentarily pauses turns over his hocks and returns at gallop
scalp	when a horse inflicts an injury on the opposite limb by striking it with a hoof, higherup than the hoof. Striking the hoof with the opposite hoof is called brushing, and with the hindhoof striking a forehoof it is called overreach
stargazer	where a horse raises his head to a degree on a level or near level plane with his neck. Often done to avoid bit control. Can also be because of very poor conformation
TDN	total digestible nutrient (usually lower than stated protein content of feedstuffs)
terret	the ring on the harness (modern) or yoke (ancient) through which the rein passes to the bit
warmblood	mix of hot and cold blood, i.e. oriental and draught

Notes

INTRODUCTION

1. M.A. Littauer and J.H. Crouwel, *Wheeled Vehicles and Ridden Animals in the Ancient Near East* (Leiden/Kiln, 1979), p. 65.
2. *Ancient Records of Egypt*, tr. J.H. Breasted (University of Chicago Press, Chicago 1906), vol. III, no. 300.
3. A.L. Bashan, 'Early Imperial India', in *The Encyclopedia of Ancient Civilizations*, ed. Arthur Cotterell (Windward, 1980), p. 185.

CHAPTER 1

1. Crossing two breeds often results in offspring being larger than either parent. My Arabian stallion of about 15 hh, when put to a non-Arabian mare(s) of the same size produced offspring of up to a hand larger. Other breeders report similar size increases.
2. S. Dalley, 'Foreign Chariotry and Cavalry in the Armies of Tiglath-Pileser III and Sargon II', in *IRAQ*, 47 (1985), 31–48, esp. p. 41.
3. *Ancient Records of Assyria and Babylonia*, tr. D.D. Luckenbill (University of Chicago Press, Chicago, vol. I, 1926; vol. II, 1927), vol. I, no. 249.
4. B. Brun and Sherif Baha el Din, *Common Birds of Egypt* (American University in Cairo Press, 1985 (1990)), plates 2: Herons and Egrets; 3: Goose; 5: Lanner Falcon, personal sightings and paintings of real life birds.
5. J. Clutton-Brock, 'The Buhen Horse', in *JAS*, I (1974), 89–100, esp. 89, 97, 99 and illustration on p. 91 of dished skull.
6. P. Bartolini, *I. Fenici* (Bompiani, Milan, 1988), p. 132f.
7. W. Keller, *The Etruscans* (BCA, 1975), p. 164, and on DNA. Personal comment, F. Sivieri, CEM VET, Grosseto, Italy.
8. Y. Yadin, *The Art of Warfare in Biblical Lands* (Weidenfeld and Nicholson, London, 1965), picture on p. 212.
9. Y. Telegin, *Dereivka, A Settlement and Cemetery of Copper Age Horse Keepers in the Middle Dneiper* (Oxford, BAR International Series, no. 287, 1986); V.I. Bibikova, Appendix 3 in Telegin as above; D.W. Anthony and D. Brown, 'The Origins of Horseback Riding', in *Antiquity*, 65 (1991), 22–38; M. Levine, 'The Origins of Horse Husbandry on the Eurasian Steppe', in *Late Prehistoric Exploitation of the Eurasian Steppe* (McDonald Institute Monographs, McDonald Institute for Archaeological Research, 1999).
10. Levine, 'Origins of Horse Husbandry', p. 9.
11. J.N. Postgate, 'The Equids of Sumer, Again', in R.H. Meadow and H.P.

Uerpmann (eds), *Equids in the Ancient World* (Dr Ludwig Reichert Verlag, Wiesbaden, vol. I, 1986, vol. II, 1991), vol. I, p. 194.

12. P.R.S. Moorey, 'Pictorial Evidence for the History of Horse Riding in Iraq before the Kassite Period', in *IRAQ*, 32 (1970), 36–50, esp. 36ff and illustration p. 41.
13. A.R. Schulman, 'Egyptian Representatives of Horsemen and Riding in the New Kingdom', in *JNES*, XVI (1957), 263–71.
14. Yadin, *War Bible*, illustration on p. 192.
15. Ibid., p. 218.
16. Ibid., p. 230.
17. Ibid., p. 220.
18. Ibid., p. 220 and personal sighting.
19. Ibid., p. 229.
20. Levine, 'Origins of Horse Husbandry', pp. 20–2.
21. Ibn Battuta, *The Travels of Ibn Battuta 1325–1354*, tr. H.A.A. Gibb (4 vols, London, Hakluyt Society; 2nd Series CX, Cambridge University Press, Cambridge, vol. II, 1962), pp. 478f.
22. Levine, 'Origins of Horse Husbandry', pp. 27f, 24.
23. Ibid., pp. 34, 36, 41, 43, 37, 45, 10 (order in which points occur).
24. Ibid, pp. 16, 40, 45–53.
25. Which is why first mountings today are by being subsequently led.
26. On the same visit at a village one mile away a marauding lion took a cow and calf, and one night out in the bush we spooked a leopard off his kill only a stone's throw from the same village.
27. H.W.F. Saggs, *The Might that was Assyria* (Sidgwick and Jackson, London, 1984), pp. 42f.
28. Ibid., p. 72.
29. T. Kendall, *Warfare and Military Matters in the Nuzi Tablets* (Brandeis University, Michigan, June 1974), pp. 140f; M.S.F. Hood, 'A Mycenaean Cavalryman', in *ABSA*, XLVIII (1953), 84–93; L.J. Worley, *Hippeis, the Cavalry of Ancient Greece* (Westview Press, Boulder, San Francisco, Oxford, 1994), p. 13.

CHAPTER 2

1. Roger Highfield, The *Daily Telegraph*, 14 August 2002. C.P. Groves, 'The Taxonomy, Distribution and Adaptations of Recent Equids', in *M & U*, I (1986), p. 18.
2. *L & C*, p. 41 (Syria); J. Zarins, 'Equids Associated with Human Burials in Third Millennium BC Mesopotamia. Two Complementary Facets', in *M & U*, I (1986), pp. 164–93, esp. pp. 179f; R.H. Meadow, 'Some Equid Remains from Cayönü, Southeastern Turkey', in *M & U*, I (1986), pp. 266–301, esp. p. 273.
3. Zarins, 'Human Burials', p. 164.
4. Postgate, 'Equids of Sumer', pp. 194–206, esp. pp. 194f.
5. Yadin, *War Bible*, p. 37.
6. Ibid., illustrations of onagers, pp. 127–30; Sir Leonard Woolley, *Ur of the Chaldees* (Herbert Press, 1964 edn), illustration of terret, p. 134. There are

many other representations held in museums in Baghdad, University of Pennsylvania, USA, and in the British Museum.

7. See, for example, the papers in *M & U* as above.
8. Postgate, 'Equids of Sumer', p. 198.
9. J.B. Pritchard (ed.), *Ancient Near Eastern Texts Relating to the Old Testament* (3rd edn with supplement, Princeton University Press, Princeton, New Jersey, 1969), pp. 646ff, esp. p. 647, n. 2.
10. E.I. Gordon, 'Sumerian Animal Proverbs and Fables', in *JCS*, 12 (1958), pp. 1–21, 43–75, esp. pp. 19, 18.
11. J. Zarins, 'The Domesticated Equidae of Third Millennium BC Mesopotamia', in *JCS*, 30/L (1978), 3–17, esp. 4–15, and Zarins, op. cit., 183ff.
12. Postgate, 'Equids of Sumer', p. 194.
13. Ibid., p. 198.
14. Personal comment, Russell Lyon, MRCVS.
15. J. Clutton Brock, 'The Buhen Horse', *JAS*, 90.
16. Zarins, 'Human Burial', p. 185, but taking Postgate's BAR × An – hybrid donkey/onager – not Zarin's mule. Mathematics in the ancient world do not always agree, hence the totals do not always match the figures given.
17. M. Zeder, 'The Equid Remains from Tel-e-Malyan, Southern Iran', in *M & U* op. cit., pp. 366–410, esp. pp. 366, 368.
18. Clutton Brock, 'The Buhen Horse', p. 95.
19. J.E. Quibell and A. Olver, 'An Ancient Egyptian Horse', in *Annales du Service des Antiquities de L'Egypte*, 26 (1926), pp. 172–7, esp. p. 174.
20. Zeder, 'Equid Remains', p. 400.
21. Ibid.
22. Ibid., p. 406.
23. H. Craig Melchert, 'The Use of Iku in Hittite Texts', in *JCS*, 32/1 1980), 50–6, esp. p. 55; and F. Hancar, *Das Pferd in Prähistorischer und Früher Historischer Zeit* (Vienna, 1955), p. 460.
24. There are several modern breeds with a height requirement of at least 14.1 hh, and the bulk of the animals stand around 15 hh, give or take an inch or two; for example, the Quarterhorse, the Appaloosa, the Morgan and the Arabian.
25. Sándor Bökönyi, 'The Equids of Dabaghiyah, Iraq', in *M & U*, op. cit., pp. 302–18, esp. pp. 312, 315.
26. Herodotus, *The Histories*, tr. Aubrey de Selincourt (Penguin, 1974), Book 3, 152f (p. 266).
27. A. Dent, 'Domestication and the Early Horse Peoples', in *Encyclopedia of the Horse*, ed. E. Hartley Edwards (Octopus, 1977), p. 18.
28. R. Miller, DVM, 'Pilgrim the Mule', in *The Western Horseman* (March 1984), p. 12 (short article).

CHAPTER 3

1. T. Save-Soderbergh, 'The Hyksos Rule in Egypt', *JEA*, 37 (1951), 52–71, esp. 53, 55.

2. W. Keller, *The Bible as History* (rev. BCA, by arrangement with Hodder & Stoughton, 1980), p. 99 (as one example).
3. Save-Soderbergh, 'Hyksos Rule', pp. 55f.
4. Ibid., p. 61.
5. Richard Burleigh, Juliet Clutton-Brock, and John Gowlett. 'Early Domestic Equids in Egypt and Western Asia; An Additional Note', in *M & U*, II, pp. 9–11.
6. Clutton-Brock, 'The Buhen Horse', *JAS*, I (1974), 89, 92f.
7. Patrick Houlihan, *The Animal World of the Pharaohs* (Thames & Hudson, London, 1996), p. 33. I have contacted Professor Joris Peters who is head of the dig at the Delta site, but to date no response to my enquiry has been received.
8. The Bible (New International Version, Hodder & Stoughton, London, first published 1979 (2000)), Genesis 47.16f; *The Westminster Historical Atlas to the Bible*, eds G.E. Wright and F.V. Filson (London, 1945), pp. 28f.
9. My own feeling is that I am suspicious of biblical history except where it is corroborated by other historical parallel sources.
10. Save-Soderbergh, 'Hyksos Rule', p. 70.
11. *ANET*, pp. 233, 554.
12. Ibid.
13. Ibid.
14. J. Breasted, *ARE*, II, no. 81.
15. Ibid., nos 396–589, esp. no. 476.
16. G. Roux, *Ancient Iraq* (Penguin, 1976 (1966)), pp. 173f, 180; mileages are my rough reckoning from maps of the area.
17. Jack M. Sasson, *The Military Establishments at Mari* (Studia Pohl, Dissertationes scientificae de rebus orientis antiqui, no. 3, 1969, Rome), pp. 22, 31f.
18. Gordon, 'Sumerian Animal Proverbs and Fables', p. 19.
19. Sasson, *Military Establishments*, pp. 11ff.
20. Ibid., pp. 31f.
21. Roux, *Ancient Iraq*, p. 180.
22. M.S.F. Hood, 'A Mycenaean Cavalryman', in *ABSA*, XVIII (1953), 84–93, esp. 89.
23. Roux, *Ancient Iraq*, pp 181f.
24. C.J. Gadd, 'The Tablets from Chagar Bazar and Tall Brak', *IRAQ*, VIII (1937–8), 22–66, no. 946.
25. Ibid., no. 920.
26. Ibid., nos 922f, 928, 934.
27. Ibid., nos 929, 972.
28. Ibid., nos 972, 981.
29. Ibid., nos 929, 972.
30. Ibid., nos 929, 972.
31. Ibid., no. 972.
32. Ibid., no. 979.
33. Saggs, *Might that was Assyria*, pp. 38ff.

CHAPTER 4

1. Strabo, *Geography* (16 February 1910); E. Schiele, *The Arab Horse in Europe*, tr. A. Dent (G. Harrap, London, 1970), p. 27; Cecil G. Trew, *From 'Dawn' to 'Eclipse'* (Methuen & Co. Ltd, London, 1939), pp. 122, 125; Usāmah ibn Munqidh, *Memoirs of Usāmah ibn Munqidh (Kitab al-Tibār)*, tr. P.L. Hitti, (Columbia University Press, Princeton University, New York, 1929), chapter on hunting, passim.
2. Roux, *Ancient Iraq*, pp. 202–6, passim.
3. A.K. Grayson, 'Mitanni', in *Encyclopedia of Ancient Civilizations (EAC)*, ed. A. Cotterell (Windward, 1980), p. 109.
4. *The Shorter Oxford English Dictionary* (Book Club Associates edn, 1983), p. 111, Aryan; p. 1060, Indo-European from same group.
5. Roux, *Ancient Iraq*, pp. 206, 204.
6. For example, Roucadour, France; Flitcham and Thatcham, England; Co. Antrim, Ireland. Van Wijngaarden-Bakker, 'Animal Remains from the Beaker Settlement at New Grange, Co. Meath', in *Proceedings of the Royal Irish Academy*, 74 (Dublin, 1974), section c, no. 11, 345–8.
7. J. Clutton-Brock and R. Burleigh, 'The Skull of a Neolithic Horse from Grimes Graves, Norfolk, England', in *M & U*, LL, pp. 242–9.
8. S. Piggott, *Prehistoric India to 1,000 BC* (Cassell, London, 1962 (1950)), pp. 250f.
9. Grayson, 'Mitanni', p. 109.
10. Gurney, 'The Hittites', p. 111.
11. Roux, *Ancient Iraq*, p. 202.
12. Piggott, *Prehistoric India*, p. 269.
13. T. Burrow, 'The Aryan Invasion of India', p. 182.
14. Grayson, 'Mitanni', p. 109.
15. *The Sacred Books of the East. The Zend Avesta*, Part II, tr. James Darmesteter (Clarendon Press, Oxford, 1883), respectively: pp. 100, no. 10; p. 204, n. 3; p. 326, no. 4.
16. W. McGovern, *The Early Empires of Central Asia* (Chapel Hill, North Carolina, 1939), pp. 76f.
17. Burrow, 'Mitanni', p. 182; Gurney, 'The Hittites', p. 124, both in *EAC*.
18. Piggott, *Prehistoric India*, p. 253; W.F. Albright, 'Mitannian Maryannu (Chariot Warriors), and the Canaanite and Egyptian Equivalents', in *AFO*, VI (1930–1), 217–21, esp. 217.
19. M. Jankovich, *They Rode into Europe*, tr. A. Dent (G. Harrap, London, 1971), p. 30.
20. A. Hyland, from an unpublished paper given at Durham University Roman Army course *c.* 1995, *The Warhorse 1250–1600* (1998), p. 146, and *The Medieval Warhorse from Byzantium to the Crusades* (1994), p. 19, both published by Sutton Publishing, Stroud.
21. Illustration on p. 37 of Jankovich, op. cit., from Hancar.
22. H.G. Creel, 'The Role of the Horse in Chinese History', in *American Historical Review*, LXX, no. 3 (April, 1965), 647–72; Hancar, *Das Pferd*,

pp. 355–72, passim; Ssu-Ma-Ch'ien, *Records of the Historian, Chapters from the Shih Chi of Ssu-Ma-Ch'ien*, tr. B. Watson (Columbia University Press, New York and London, 1969), Shih Chi no. 123, passim; Hyland, *Medieval Warhorse*, pp. 19, 126ff, 39, and *Warhorse 1250–1600*, pp. 69, 159.

23. X.Anab., tr. Rex Warner (Penguin Classics, 1949 (1986)), Book IV, p. 201.

24. IAES, summer 1997, Editorial pp. 1, 3, no. 4 (Published by Hartwick College, Oneonta, New York, 13820 (periodic newsletters)).

25. Richard Edwards, 'The Cave Reliefs at Ma Hao', in *Artibus Asiae* XVII (1954), part I, 5–28, esp. p. 19.

26. *ZA*, p. 58, no. 21, and repeated throughout, e.g. p. 59, no. 25; p. 60, no. 29; p. 61, no. 33; p. 62, no. 37; p. 63, no. 41; p. 66, no. 49.

27. Hyland, *Warhorse 1250–1600*, pp. 67, 69.

28. Marek Zvelebil, 'The Rise of the Nomads in Central Asia', in *EAC*, ch. 38, pp. 25ff; A. Hyland, *Equus, the Horse in the Roman World* (Batsford, 1990), pp. 78, 183, 185f, 191, 193; Ssu-Ma-Ch'ien, *Records of the Historian*, on Wu Sun and Hsiung Nu. Shih Chi no. 110, from vol. II (1961, edn.), Shih Chi no. 123, pp. 281–5 (1969 edn); Herodotus, *Histories*, on Scythians, Book 4, pp. 1–142, passim; Book 7.7.22f, 452–3, pp. 271–317; W. McGovern, *Early Empires of Central Asia*, on Parthians, pp. 7f; Hyland, *Warhorse 1250–1600*, Sakae, p. 146; D.D. Luckenbill, *ARAB*, II, no. 910, on Cimmerians who had overrun Lydia in the reign of Ashurbanipal.

29. Yadin, *War Bible*, p. 86.

30. Nowadays in Palestine, but in our period borders, areas and countries constantly changed borders.

31. Breasted, *ARE*, II, no. 435.

32. Ibid., no. 398.

33. Ibid., no. 449.

34. Ibid., nos 498–501.

35. Ibid., no. 508.

36. Ibid., no. 511.

37. Ibid., nos 509, 518.

38. Ibid., no. 476.

39. Luckenbill, *ARAB*, I, no. 245.

40. Ibid., no. 236.

41. Ibid., no. 301.

42. Ibid., nos 249, 254.

43. The Bible, Genesis 47.17 and *The Westminster Historical Atlas to the Bible*, pp. 29f.

44. The Bible, I Kings 10.24f.

45. Ibid., I Kings 10.38f.

46. Ibid., II Chronicles I.16 and 17.

47. Hyland, *Warhorse 1250–1600*, pp. 40, 80, 89. Many other instances are recorded.

48. The Bible, I Kings 4.26.

49. Ibid., I Kings 10.26.

50. Ibid., II Chronicles I.14.

51. Ibid., II Chronicles 9.25.

52. Ibid., I Kings 4.28.
53. G.I. Davies, Urwot in I Kings 5.6 and the Assyrian Horse Lists in *JSS*, 34 (1989), 25–37, esp. 26.
54. Ibid., pp. 36f.
55. The Bible, Ezekiel 27.12–25, specifically 27.14 for horses.
56. Saggs, *Might that was Assyria*, pp. 65, 69.
57. Luckenbill, *ARAB*, I, no. 374.
58. Ibid., no. 406.
59. Ibid., no. 505.
60. Ibid., no. 414.
61. Ibid., nos 440f, 443, 446f, 449ff, 466, 470, 476, 479.
62. Ibid., e.g. nos 587f; 605ff.
63. Ibid., nos 611, 663, 672, 691.
64. Ibid., no. 587.
65. Ibid., II, no. 148.
66. Ibid., no. 809.
67. Ibid., no. 540.
68. Ibid., no. 781.
69. Ibid., Sargon, nos 18, 55, 74; Ashurbanipal, no. 778.
70. *ANET*, p. 285(c), from Broken Prisms.
71. Cook, *Persian Empire*, p. 78.
72. J.N. Postgate, *Taxation and Conscription in the Assyrian Empire* (Studia Pohl, Series Maior no. 3, Biblical Institute Press, Rome, 1974), pp. 17f; *RCAE*, tr. L. Waterman (vol. I, University of Michigan Press, Ann Arbor, Parts I and II, 1930; Part III, commentary 1931; Part IV, supplement and indexes, 1936), vol. I, no. 375.
73. Cook, *Persian Empire*, p. 200.
74. Postgate, *Taxation and Conscription*, pp. 7, 18.
75. Ibid., p. 13.
76. Ibid., pp. 11f and table, pp. 8f.
77. Ibid., table nos 2, 3, 12, 23, and p. 12.
78. Ibid., table, pp. 8f, and p. 13.
79. M.A. Littauer, 'V.C. Vitt and the Horses of Pazyryk', *Antiquity*, XLV (1971), 293–4.
80. S.I. Rudenko, *The Frozen Tombs of Siberia* (J.M. Dent, 1970), p. 56.
81. Littauer, 'Horses of Pazyryk', pp. 293f.
82. H.G. Creel, 'The Role of the Horse in Chinese History', *AHR*, LXX, no. 3 (April 1965), 647–72, esp. 661f.
83. *National Geographic Magazine*, map of the Caspian and surrounding area (May 1999); *Cassell's New Atlas* (no date but after 1921, immediately after the Treaties of 1919 and 1920), p. 30; and see above Hancar, n. 22.
84. Herodotus, *Histories*, Book 7.40.2, p. 459.
85. A. Azzaroli, *An Early History of Horsemanship* (Leiden, E.J. Brill/Dr W. Backhuys, 1985), p. 177.
86. Oppian, *Cynegetica*, tr. A.W. Mair (Loeb Classical Library, Heinemann, 1928).

87. ARRIAN.AN., tr. Aubrey de Selincourt (Penguin Classics, 1986), Book VII.4, p. 352.
88. Cook, *Persian Empire*, p. 54.
89. A. Hyland, *Foal to Five Years* (Ward Lock, London, 1980), p. 114.
90. G.M. Trevelyan, *English Social History* (Pelican Books, London, 1972), p. 393.
91. Hyland, *Warhorse 1250–1600*, p. 192.
92. X.Anab., p. 201.
93. Strabo, *Geography*, II.14.9.
94. Cook, *Persian Empire*, pp. 1, 6f.
95. Strabo, *Geography*, II.23.7.
96. ARRIAN.AN., B.7.13, p. 369.
97. Breasted, *ARE*, III, nos 570, 589.
98. Herodotus, *Histories*, Book IV, p. 332.
99. H. Lhote, *The Search for the Tassili Frescoes*, tr. Alan Houghton Brodrick (Hutchinson and Co. Ltd, London, 1973 (1959)), p. 149; H. Lhote, 'Le Cheval et le Chameau dans les Peintures et Gravures Ruprestres du Sahara', *Bulletin de L'Institut Francais D'Afrique Noire*, IV, no. 3 (July 1953), 1138–228, esp. 1138–42, 1158f.
100. Lhote, 'Le Cheval', p. 1140.
101. Breasted, *ARE*, III, nos 570, 589.
102. Lhote, *Search for the Tassili Frescoes*, p. 123.
103. Sylvia Loch, *The Royal Horse of Europe* (J.A. Allen Ltd, London, 1986), pp. 50f.
104. Strabo, *Geography*, 16.4.18 and 20.
105. *Arab Horse Society News* (winter 1987).

CHAPTER 5

1. X.Horse., tr. H. Morgan (J.A. Allen & Co. Ltd, 1962 (1979), from original text published by J.M. Dent & Co., 1894 edn), chapter 1, passim.
2. Rudenko, *Frozen Tombs*, p. 56.
3. Strabo, *Geography*, 7.4.8.
4. Breasted, *ARE*, II, no. 589; *The Amarna Letters*, ed. and tr. W.L. Moran (The John Hopkins University Press, Baltimore and London, 1992), nos 244, 245; *ANET*, supplement, p. 241.
5. *ARAB*, I, no. 813; II, no. 20.
6. Claude F.A. Schaeffer, *The Cuneiform Texts of Ras Shamra-Ugarit* (Oxford University Press, London, for the British Academy, 1939), plate XVIII, fig. 1.
7. *ARAB*, I, nos 248, 375, 392.
8. A. Kammenhuber, *Hippologia Hethetica* (Wiesbaden Harrassowitz, 1961), p. 300.
9. H.G. Guterbock, review of *Hippologia Hethetica* in *JAOS*, 84, no. 3 (1964), 267–73, esp. 270.
10. My own winning time for Great Britain's first 100-miler in twenty-four hours was 8.33 mph in 1975. Prior to the event I had done a training session of 60 miles in one unbroken stretch at competition speeds ten days earlier.
11. Hyland, *Medieval Warhorse*, p. 137.

12. *ARAB*, II, no. 170.
13. Kammenhuber, *Hippologia Hethetica*, whole text, passim; Guterbock, *JAOS*, op. cit., p. 270.
14. Bedřich Hrozný, 'L'Entraînement des Chevaux Chez Les Anciens Indo-Européens d'Après un Texte Mîtannien–Hittite Provenant du 14ᵉ Siècle', in *Archive Orientalni*, 3 (1931), 431–61, passim.
15. A. Hyland, *The Horse in the Middle Ages* (Sutton Publishing, 1999), pp. 28ff for full analysis; J. Warren Evans, A. Borton, H.F. Hintz, and L. Dale van Vleck, *The Horse* (W.H. Freeman & Co., San Francisco, 1977), chapter by Anthony Borton, University of Massachusetts, pp. 229–31, esp. p. 231.
16. Personal sightings on my India trips.
17. This 'donkey seat' or a near approximation can still be seen on occasion in the American showring when some riders of five-gaited and walking horses sit far back on the horse's loins. I recall seeing an exaggerated and comical example on one occasion.
18. Kammenhuber, *Hippologia Hethetica*, pp. 300ff; Hrozný, 'L'Entraînement des Chevaux', n. 14, in op. cit., 436ff; J. Potratz, *Das Pferd in der Fruhzeit* (1938), pp. 180f.
19. In the nineteenth century AD racehorses were often galloped blanketed to sweat off fat, a practice Kikkuli also used – see Kammenhuber, op. cit., pp. 170–225. Also, some riders today try to refine the throatlatch by putting a sweat hood on their horses; all it does is temporarily remove fluids, quickly regained.
20. Kammenhuber, *Hippologia Hethetica*, passim.
21. A. Hyland, *The Endurance Horse* (J.A. Allen Ltd, London, 1988), end of the foreword by Dr Barsaleau, DVM.
22. A. Hyland, *Endurance Riding* (J.B. Lippincott Co., Philadelphia and New York, 1975), illustration opposite p. 97, and text pp. 149f.
23. Melchert H. Craig, 'The Use of the Iku in Hittite Texts', *JCS*, 32/1 (1980), 50–6, esp. 51ff.
24. Ibid., 54f.
25. 'Bruchstücke einer Mittelassyrischen Vorschriftensammlung für die Akklimatisierung und Trainierung von Wagenpferden', tr. Erich Ebeling, in *Deutsche Akademie der Wissenschaften zu Berlin, Institut fur Orientforschung*, no. 6 (1952) (pages used 6–55), passim.
26. Kammenhuber, *Hippologia Hethetica*, passim.
27. 'Bruchstücke einer Mittelassyrischen', tr. Ebeling, in *AFO*, no. 6 (1952), 50.
28. All care is incorporated in the day by day regime.
29. X.Horse., chapter II, passim.
30. Ibid., chapter IV, passim.
31. Ibid., chapter IV, p. 37.
32. Ibid., chapter VII, passim.
33. Feeling the back muscles was an enormous help to me when breaking young horses in as countermeasures could be taken before an eruption occurred.
34. X.Horse., chapter VII, pp. 41ff.
35. A. Hyland, *Training the Roman Cavalry from Arrian's* Ars Tactica (Sutton

Publishing Ltd, 1993), pp. 33, 44, 74. On p. 155 the mechanics of the movement are explained in equestrian terms and pictures of same.

36. X.Horse., chapter VII, p. 44.
37. Ibid., chapter VIII, p. 48.
38. Ibid., chapter VIII, passim.
39. Ibid., chaper IX, pp. 51ff.
40. *Kautilya's Arthasastra*, tr. Mahamahopadhyaya, Arthasastravisahada, Vidyalankara, Panditaraja (4th edn, Dr R. Shamastry, Sri Raghuveer Printing Press, Mysore, 1951; 1st edn, 1909), from the introduction by J.F. Fleet.
41. Ibid., Book II, chapter xxx, p. 148.
42. ARRIAN.AN., Book 3, p. 30.
43. Hyland, *Warhorse 1250–1600*, pp. 170f and personal comment from S.A.H.A.A. Imam, Indian equestrian author and historian.
44. *Kautilya*, Book I, chapter xix, p. 37.
45. Ibid., Book I, chapter xxl, p. 43.
46. Ibid., Book II, chapter xxx, passim.
47. Hyland, *Warhorse 1250–1600*, p. 170, and personal comment from S.A.H.A.A. Imam.
48. *Kautilya*, Book II, chapter xxx, passim.
49. Ibid., Book 10, chapter v, passim.
50. Ibid., Book 10, chapter iv, passim.

CHAPTER 6

1. Patrick Houlihan, *The Animal World of the Pharaohs*, quoted on pp. 34f.
2. Tacitus, *The Agricola and the Germania*, tr. H. Mattingly (Penguin Books, 1985 edn), p. 37.
3. Kammenhuber, *Hippologia Hethetica*, for example on day 36 of training, p. 209, line 11.
4. Richard H. Beale, *The Organization of the Hittite Military* (Heidelberg, 1992, Carl Winter Universitatsverlag (Chicago University Dissertations 1986)), p. 419.
5. Yadin, *War Bible*, illustrations from pp. 220f, 385, 397, 403, 416f, 457, 450, and from the British Museum.
6. Hyland, *Horse in the Middle Ages*, pp. 28ff for full analysis of gaits.
7. Pliny the Elder, *Natural History*, Book VIII (Loeb Classical Library, Heinemann, 1937).
8. X.Horse., chapter 12, p. 67.
9. Rudenko, *Frozen Tombs*, p. 133.
10. Tamara Talbot-Rice, *The Scythians* (Thames & Hudson, London, 1957), p. 139, fig. 46, and p. 141.
11. Cook, *Persian Empire*, pl. 22.
12. A. Hyland, *Equus* (Batsford, 1990), chapter on tack; Georgina Hermann, 'Parthian and Sassanian Saddlery', in *AIO*, II, Miscellanae in Honorem Louis Vanden Berghe (Gent, 1989), 757–809, pl. XI b.

13. Chauncy J. Goodrich, 'Riding Astride and the Saddle in Ancient China', in *HJAS*, 44, no. 2 (December 1984), 279–306, esp. 297.
14. Ssu-Ma-Ch'ien, *Records of the Historian*, Shih Chi no. 109, p. 262.
15. Piggott, *Prehistoric India*, p. 268.
16. Goodrich, 'Riding Astride', p. 304.
17. X.Horse., chapter X, pp. 56f.
18. Littauer and Crouwel, *Wheeled Vehicles*, p. 10.
19. Paul E. Zimansky, *Ecology and Empire: the Structure of the Urartian State* (Oriental Institute of the University of Chicago, Studies in Ancient Oriental Civilizations, no. 41, Oriental Institute, Chicago, Illinois, 1985), p. 126, n. 105.
20. Telegin, *Dereivka*, p. 83; Rudenko, *Frozen Tombs*, illustration 74D; Littauer and Crouwel, *Wheeled Vehicles*, illustration no. 71.
21. Levine, 'Origins of Horse Husbandry', p. 18.
22. Ibid., pp. 37–45.
23. Ibid., pp. 11f, 45.
24. Littauer and Crouwel, *Wheeled Vehicles*, p. 87, n. 59.
25. C.T. Lewis and C. Short, *A Latin Dictionary* (Clarendon Press, Oxford, 1966 (1879)), p. 1085.
26. X.Horse., chapter 10, p. 57.
27. Pelagonius, *Ars Veterinaria*, ed. M. Ihm (Leipzig, 1892), chapter V, no. 66.
28. Haroun, a champion Arabian stallion broke his rider's leg in seven places – personal comment from Paul Atkinson, trainer.
29. J.K. Anderson, *Greek Horsemanship* (University of California, 1961), p. 60.
30. Yadin, *War Bible*, p. 45, and seeing it in the British Museum.
31. W.G. Lambert, 'Sultantepe Tablets VIII. Shalmaneser in Ararat', *Anatolian Studies* IX (1961), 143–58.
32. Yadin, *War Bible*, illustrations on pp. 458, 457, 452, 427 in that order, and British Museum visit.
33. X.Horse., chapter 10, p. 57.

CHAPTER 7

1. G. MacLeod, *Treatment of Horses by Homeopathy* (Health Science Press, Holsworthy, Devon, 1977), pp. 115, 117.
2. Robin E. Walker, *Ars Veterinaria* (Schering-Plough Animal Health, Kenilworth, NJ, 1st edn, 1991, 2nd edn, no date), p. 10.
3. Ibid., p. 10.
4. Pelagonius, *Ars Veterinaria*, chapter VII, no. 118; Hyland, *Equus*, pp. 38f, 58.
5. *The Alalakh Tablets*, tr. J. Wiseman (London, 1953), nos 256, 260.
6. *A Dictionary of Assyrian Botany*, tr. R. Campbell Thomson (London, British Academy, 1949), pp. 72f.
7. Hyland, *Equus*, p. 38.
8. C. Virolleaud, 'Fragments d'un Traité Phénicien de Thérapeutique Hippologique', in *Syria*, 15 (1934), 75–83.
9. Walker, *Ars Veterinaria*, p. 12.

10. The translator had put 'wild or not broken in for riding'. One would hardly ride a foal, nor indeed would yearlings be pulling chariots, but only have been received into the respective equine division for later use. Backing a horse as a two-year-old, then turning it away, is better than waiting until it is a four-year-old, when it is far more inclined to offer resistance. I rather suspect that riding was not done as a general thing at this early date.
11. Xenophon, *The Cavalry Commander*, Book 1, pp. 13–15.
12. Herodotus, *Histories*, Book V, p. 110.
13. X.C.C., II, pp. 10–13.
14. X.Horse, chapter VIII, p. 48.
15. X.C.C., II, pp. 2–6.
16. Personal experience of cattle-cutting, and using volunteer Pony Clubbers for cutting (harrying) for a demonstration.
17. Richard H. Beale, *The Organization of the Hittite Military*, pp. 18f, n. 67, KUB 7.54.i.2–3.
18. Pelagonius, *Ars Veterinaria*, III, no. 34.
19. J. Clabby, *The History of the Royal Army Veterinary Corps, 1919–1961* (J.A. Allen & Co., London, 1963), chapters on various theatres of war in the Middle East, Italy, Sicily, Greece, Syria, North Africa and the Indian base; Horace Hayes, *Veterinary Hints for Horse Owners* (Stanley Paul, London, rev. edn 1968), chapter 15, passim.
20. Virgil, *Georgics*, tr. C. Day-Lewis (Cape, 1943), Book 3, lines 497–520 (on rabies).
21. Pelagonius, *Ars Veterinaria*, chapter V under 'Cures and medicines for head ailments'.
22. I have had two horses contract this from being in a pasture that had, unknown to me, had a horse that was incubating the disease but showed no obvious signs, and was subsequently removed from the pasture leaving the bacillus behind. One was a two-year-old filly, the other an eight-year-old gelding.
23. Personal comment, Russell Lyon, MRCVS.
24. *ANET*, p. 485, from EA 244 and 245.
25. The Bible, Samuel 8.4.
26. M.A. Littauer, 'The Function of the Yoke Harness', *Antiquity*, XLII (1968), 27–31, passim.
27. Personal comment, Russell Lyon, MRCVS.
28. Hyland, *Equus*, p. 224; Sidonius Apollinaris, *Poems and Letters*, tr. W.B. Anderson (Loeb Classical Library, Heinemann, 1968), carm. no. XXIII.
29. Polybius, *The Rise of the Roman Empire*, tr. Ian Scott-Kilvert (Penguin, 1979), II, p. 79.
30. This condition is encountered in wet, claggy soil when horses are exposed to considerable time in such conditions, such as out hunting.
31. Clabby, *RAVC History*, see n. 20, p. 55.
32. Pelagonius, *Ars Veterinaria*, VIII, no. 141.
33. Breasted, *ARE*, IV, no. 846.
34. Ibid., no. 850.

35. Arrian, *Anabasis*, B.III.16, pp. 171f.

CHAPTER 8

1. Margaret A. Murray, *The Splendour that was Egypt* (BCA, London, 1981 (1979)), p. 42.
2. Breasted, *ARE*, III, nos 420f.
3. Grayson, 'Mitanni', pp. 109f.
4. Gurney, 'The Hittites', p. 111.
5. Roux, *Ancient Iraq*, p. 211; Saggs, *Might that was Assyria*, pp. 40f.
6. *Alalakh Tablets*, no. 369.
7. Ibid., nos 128–78.
8. Ibid., nos 329–31.
9. Ibid., no. 227.
10. Ibid., no. 189.
11. Ibid.
12. Ibid., nos 180–4.
13. Ibid., no. 183.
14. Timothy Kendall, *Warfare and Military Matters in the Nuzi Tablets* (Brandeis University, Michigan, June 1974), pp. 172f.
15. Ibid., pp. 194, 288, 226.
16. Abou Bekr ibn Bedr, *Le Naceri*, tr. M. Perron (3 vols, Ministry of Agriculture of France, Paris, 1860), Arabians, passim.
17. Kendall, *Nuzi Tablets*, p. 288.
18. Ibid., p. 304.
19. Ibid., pp. 287f, 306.
20. Ibid., p. 304.
21. Ibid., pp. 300–4.
22. Ibid., pp. 288ff.
23. Ibid., pp. 134, 138.
24. Ibid., pp. 140f.
25. Ibid., p. 223.
26. Ibid., p. 181.
27. Ibid., pp. 189, 193.
28. Ibid., p. 223.
29. Ibid., p. 197.
30. Ibid., p. 290.
31. Ibid., p. 305.
32. R.O. Faulkner, 'Egyptian Military Organization', *JEA*, 39 (1953), 32–47, esp. 41f.
33. Ian Shaw, *Egyptian Warfare and Weapons* (Shire Egyptology, Shire Publications Ltd, Princes Risborough, 1991), pp. 27f.
34. Faulkner, 'Egyptian Military Organization', p. 43.
35. 'Anastasi Papyrus I', in *Egyptian Hieratic Texts*, tr. A.H. Gardiner (Series I, Literary texts of the New Kingdom, Part 1); Papyrus Anastasi I and the Papyrus Koller, Leipzig (J.C. Heinrichs's sohe, Buchhandlung, 1911), pp. 6,

29f. Month was the wargod.

36. Faulkner, 'Egyptian Military Organization', p. 43.
37. Yadin, *War Bible*, pp. 86f, and illustrations pp. 193f, 186f, 214f.
38. *ANET*, 3rd edn with supplement, p. 534.
39. Yadin, *War Bible*, illustration p. 202.
40. Anastasi Papyrus I, pp. 27f.
41. Beale, *Hittite Military*, pp. 523f.
42. Gurney, 'The Hittites', p. 25.
43. The Bible, I Kings 10.26.
44. Herodotus, *Histories*, 3.91.
45. The Bible, Ezekiel 26.14.
46. Luckenbill, *ARAB*, II, no. 781.
47. Hyland, *Equus*, pp. 11, 25 and map pp. 12f.
48. L&C, p. 59.
49. E. Neufeld, *The Hittite Laws* (Luzac and Co. Ltd, London, 1951), p. 118.
50. Beale, *Hittite Military*, p. 521.
51. Ibid., pp. 521, 159, 172.
52. Ibid., p. 178.
53. Ibid., pp. 149–53, passim.
54. Ibid., p. 526.
55. Ibid., p. 34.
56. Ibid., pp. 127, 537f.
57. Ibid., pp. 127f, 537f.
58. Ibid., pp. 136f.
59. Ibid., p. 146.
60. Neufeld, *The Hittite Laws*, e.g., nos 58, 178, 180, 181.
61. Ibid., no. 162.
62. Ibid., no. 75.
63. Beale, *Hittite Military*, p. 190.
64. Sasson, *Military Establishments*, p. 22; Beale, *Hittite Military*, pp. 190–8, passim; Kendall, *Nuzi Tablets*, p. 138; A.R. Schulman, 'Egyptian Chariotry', in *JARCE*, 2 (1963), 84.
65. Shaw, *Egyptian Warfare and Weapons*, p. 47.
66. Yadin, *War Bible*, pp. 100f; Shaw, *Egyptian Warfare and Weapons*, p. 47; *National Geographic Magazine* (December 1989), map of the Holy Land.
67. Breasted, *ARE*, III, nos 420f, 424, 430f, 435ff; Yadin, *War Bible*, pp. 102f.
68. M.L. Bierbrier, 'Tuthmose III', in *100 Great Lives of Antiquity*, ed. John Canning (Guild Publishing, London, 1985), p. 9.
69. Breasted, *ARE*, III, Horemheb, no. 7; Ramses II, no. 428, herds of horses from Hattusas; Merneptah, no. 571 from Libya. IV, Ramses III, no. 111, Libya; Piankhi, various, including nos 796, 807, 850, 852, 875, 877.
70. A. Azzaroli, *An Early History of Horsemanship*, (E.J. Brill/Dr W. Backhuys, Leiden, 1985), p. 50.
71. The Bible, I Kings 18.24.
72. Ibid., Ezekiel 17.15.
73. Dalley, 'Foreign Chariotry', pp. 31–48, esp. pp. 44f.

74. *ANET*, 3rd edn, with supplement, p. 286 (c) from Broken Prisms.
75. Dalley, 'Foreign Chariotry', p. 44.
76. M. Rostovtzeff, 'Foreign Commerce of Ptolemaic Egypt', in *Journal of Economic and Business History*, II (1931–2), 728–69.
77. Robin Law, *The Horse in West African History* (published for the International African Institute by Oxford University Press, 1980), pp. 24f, 39 n. 209, 45, 51, 178.
78. Ibn Battuta, *Travels*, vol. IV, p. 879.
79. Hyland, *Equus*, on Oppian, p. 25; Hyland, *Medieval Warhorse*, pp. 40–4, passim; Hyland, *Horse in Middle Ages*, pp. 87–90, passim on Usamãh; Hyland, *Warhorse 1250–1600*, pp. 151, 161 on Mughals.
80. *The Amarna Letters*, ed. and tr. William L. Moran (John Hopkins University Press, Baltimore and London, 1992), EA nos 2, 7, 14ff.
81. Ibid., EA nos 17, 19, 22; Roux, *Ancient Iraq*, p. 231.
82. Ibid., p. 231; Murray, *Splendour that was Egypt*, p. 85.
83. Roux, *Ancient Iraq*, p. 233.
84. *Amarna Letters*, p. xxxiii.
85. Ibid., EA nos 53, 55, 59f, 62.
86. Ibid., EA nos 68f, 71, 73, 75ff.
87. Ibid., EA nos 84–7.
88. Ibid., EA no. 92.
89. Ibid., EA no. 89.
90. Ibid., EA nos 101, 103, 105.
91. Ibid., EA no. 108.
92. Ibid., EA no. 112.
93. Ibid., EA nos 112, 124.
94. Ibid., EA no. 121.
95. Ibid., EA nos 139, 144–9.
96. Ibid., EA nos 156–68, passim.
97. Breasted, *ARE*, III, nos 81–4.
98. Ibid., nos 337, 347, 361.
99. Shaw, *Egyptian Warfare and Weapons*, p. 52.
100. *The Kadesh Inscriptions of Rameses II*, tr. Sir Alan Gardiner (Griffith Institute, Oxford, 1960), p. 5; Breasted, *ARE*, III, no. 298.
101. The Koller Papyrus in *Egyptian Hieratic Texts*, pp. 37f.
102. Breasted, *ARE*, III, nos 298–303; Yadin, *War Bible*, pp. 103–8, passim; Gardiner, *Kadesh Inscriptions*, p. 5 and pp. 25–50, passim on the poem.

CHAPTER 9

1. Saggs, *Might that was Assyria*, p. 246.
2. *ARAB*, I, nos 220ff.
3. Ibid., nos 249, 254; Saggs, *Might that was Assyria*, p. 60.
4. Ibid., p. 72.
5. *ARAB*, I, nos 405, 414, 440.
6. M. Chahin, *The Kingdom of Armenia* (Dorset Press, New York, 1991, originally

published by Routledge, 1987), p. 66.

7. Ibid., pp. 42ff.
8. *ARAB*, II, nos 15f.
9. X.Anab., on Armenia and Persia, chapter 5, IV, p. 201; Strabo, *Geography*, on Media II.13.7, on Armenia II.14.9.
10. Chahin, *Kingdom of Armenia*, pp. 65f; Saggs, *Might that was Assyria*, p. 97; E.D. Phillips, 'New Light on the Ancient History of the Eurasian Steppe', in *AJA*, 61 (1957), 269–80.
11. *Royal Correspondence of the Assyrian Empire*, tr. Leroy Waterman (University of Michigan Press, Ann Arbor, Parts I and II, 1930, Part III commentary, 1931, Part IV supplement and indexes, 1936), II, no. 1237.C.III, pp. 325f.
12. Ibid., C.III, p. 325.
13. J. Sandalgian, *Les Inscriptions Cuneiformes Urartiques* (L'Académie des Inscriptions de France, Veneze, 1900), no. 19, pp. 58–114, passim.
14. Ibid., p. 80, col. iv, line 16.
15. Postgate, *Taxation and Conscription*, pp. 7–18, passim.
16. Ibid., Tel Billa text no. 72, and pp. 11–18, passim.
17. Ibid., p. 61.
18. Ibid., p. 62.
19. Ibid., pp. 144f, 2.3.1, 2.3.2, 2.4, and p. 373.
20. Ibid., pp. 119f.
21. Ibid., pp. 148 1.10; 149 1.13.2.1; and 1.13.2; 154, 2.1.
22. Ibid., pp. 209ff.
23. Ibid., p. 208 2.2.2.
24. *ARAB*, I, no. 812.
25. Ibid., II, no. 64.
26. Ibid., II, no. 58.
27. Postgate, *Taxation and Conscription*, table of acquisitions, pp. 8f.
28. *RCAE*, I, e.g. nos 71, 372 and many others.
29. Postgate, *Taxation and Conscription*, p. 16.
30. Strabo, *Geography*, 16.2.10.
31. Hyland, *Warhorse 1250–1600*, chapter 6, passim.
32. *ARAB*, II, no. 781.
33. The Bible, I Kings 10.28; Herodotus, *Histories*, III.91.
34. Chahin, *Kingdom of Armenia*, pp. 78f.
35. Dalley, 'Foreign Chariotry and Cavalry', pp. 31–48, esp. pp. 46f.
36. Ibid., pp. 45ff.
37. *RCAE*, I, no. 329.
38. Ibid., I, no. 336.
39. *ARAB*, I, nos 769, 772, 775 Urartu; 809 Tabal, 2000 head; 812 Media, 5,000 head.
40. Chahin, *Kingdom of Armenia*, p. 80.
41. Ibid., p. 73.
42. Postgate, *Taxation and Conscription*, p. 13.
43. *ARAB*, II, nos 74, 778.
44. Dalley, 'Foreign Chariotry and Cavalry', pp. 43, 48.

45. George G. Cameron, *History of Early Iran* (University of Chicago Press, Chicago (no date)), p. 145.
46. *ARAB*, II, nos 148, 519.
47. Ibid., II, nos 809, 781.
48. Clutton-Brock, 'The Buhen Horse', pp. 89–100, esp. p. 95; Zeder, 'Equid Remains', pp. 366, 368.
49. I bred two full brothers. Both had excellent feeding as youngsters, but one did not have access to superb grazing. The difference in height was 2 in, and in mature body mass about 150/200 lb. One only has to see the weedy stock raised in Egypt, and worked too young on the streets, to realise that such horses well fed earlier on would have a much improved physique.
50. Saggs, *Might that was Assyria*, pp. 243ff.
51. Postgate, *Taxation and Conscription*, pp. 93 *ilku* 3.5; 224 3.1.5 and 210.
52. Dalley, 'Foreign Chariotry and Cavalry', p. 37.
53. Ibid., pp. 37ff, 33.
54. Ibid., p. 39.
55. The Bible, Ezekiel 23.5–6 and 11–12.
56. In this instance in a playful not an aggressive manner.
57. Hyland, *Warhorse 1250–1600*, the striking of an Indian warhorse's hooves against the head of an elephant executed in the Oran (variously known as the Uran or Udaan), from the Hindi verb 'to fly', pp. 170f.
58. *Westminster Historical Atlas to the Bible*, map 9; Yadin, *War Bible*, pp. 271, 306–9. Yadin quotes from Field Marshal Lord Wavell's account of the Turkish defeat by the British in exactly the same spot, where the Turks were caught as they descended the tortuous Wadi Fara; The Bible, I Kings 20.
59. Dalley, 'Foreign Chariotry and Cavalry', p. 37.
60. Postgate, *Taxation and Conscription*, ND 2451, pp. 476–9.
61. *ARAB*, II, no. 155.
62. Ibid., no. 39.
63. *RCAE*, I, 61.C.311.32.
64. Ibid., no. 372.
65. Ibid.
66. Postgate, *Taxation and Conscription*, p. 188, 2.3.1.
67. Robert O. Fink, *Roman Military Records on Papyrus* (American Philological Association, 1971), passim.
68. Ammianus Marcellinus, *The Later Roman Empire AD 354–378*, tr. Walter Hamilton (Penguin, 1986), p. 232.
69. Postgate, *Taxation and Conscription*, p. 202, 2.1.
70. Personal comment, Professor Peter Edwards.
71. Postgate, *Taxation and Conscription*, pp. 171f, 2.2.1.
72. Yadin, *War Bible*, p. 302.
73. Ibid., assessment from illustrations p. 442 from the depiction in situ at Nineveh.
74. Ibid., assessment from illustration on pp. 450f.
75. *ARAB*, II, no. 22.

76. Ibid., I, no. 613.
77. H. Tadmor, 'The Campaigns of Sargon II of Assur', in *JCS*, 12 (1958–60), 22–40, 77–100, esp. 22, 95ff.
78. Ibid., p. 95.
79. Ibid., p. 95; The Bible, I Kings 10.26 and Ezekiel 27.14; Chahin, *Kingdom of Armenia*, p. 21.
80. *RCAE*, I, no. 375.
81. Edwin M. Wright, 'The Eighth Campaign of Sargon II of Assyria (714 BC)', *JNES*, II, no. 3 (1943), 173–86, passim and map on page 176. The author had personal knowledge of the area from hiking and riding over it for several years. This enabled him to give a graphic account of the variables encountered.
82. Saggs, *Might that was Assyria*, p. 253.
83. *ARAB*, I, no. 611.
84. Ibid., II, no. 142.
85. Ibid., no. 24.
86. Ibid., nos 154 and 20.
87. Ibid., no. 158.
88. Ibid., nos 158–61; Wright, 'Eighth Campaign of Sargon', pp. 173–86, passim, esp. map on p. 176 with names of districts and cities in the Assyrian era and many of the modern equivalents.
89. Chahin, *Kingdom of Armenia*, pp. 87f.
90. *ARAB*, II, nos 169–71.
91. Ibid., no. 177.
92. Saggs, *Might that was Assyria*, p. 75.
93. Chahin, *Kingdom of Armenia*, p. 90.
94. Ibid., pp. 93f.

CHAPTER 10

1. Roux, *Ancient Iraq*, p. 206; Marek Zvelebil, 'The Rise of the Nomads in Central Asia', in *CEA*, chapter 38, pp. 252–4.
2. Roux, *Ancient Iraq*, p. 206.
3. H.G. Creel, 'The Role of the Horse in Chinese History', *AHR* LXX, no. 3 (April 1965), 647–72, esp. 653; Hancar, *Das Pferd*, pp. 365–72; Roux, *Ancient Iraq*, map of invasion routes, p. 466; *National Geographic*, map of Caspian and surrounding area (May 1999).
4. David Stronach, 'Iran under the Achaemenians and Seleucids', in *CEA*, chapter 23, p. 206.
5. *ARAB*, II, no. 24.
6. Cameron, *History of Early Iran*, pp. 148f.
7. *ARAB*, I, no. 812 and II, nos 24, 58.
8. Cook, *Persian Empire*, pp. 3, 7, 11.
9. Bryce, 'Phrygia and Lydia' in *EAC*, p. 146.
10. Herodotus, *Histories*, I, p. 72.
11. Cook, *Persian Empire*, p. 27.

12. Roux, *Ancient Iraq*, pp. 350, 352.
13. Cook, *Persian Empire*, fig. I, map; *National Geographic*, Caspian map.
14. Herodotus, *Histories*, III, pp. 206f, 211.
15. Ibid., III, pp. 215, 229; *The Behistun Inscriptions*, tr. L.W. King and R.C. Thompson, in *The Sculptures and Inscription of Darius the Great on the Rock of Behistun in Persia* (London, 1907), tr. taken from the Internet at http//www.livius.org/be-bm/behistun/Behistun03.html, nos 1, 11, 11.
16. Herodotus, *Histories*, III, pp. 230–2.
17. *Behistun*, no. 13.
18. Cook, *Persian Empire*, p. 41.
19. *Behistun*, no. 52.
20. Ibid., passim in various accounts, nos 13–50.
21. Ibid., nos 68f.
22. Herodotus, *Histories*, III, pp. 240f.
23. Cook, *Persian Empire*, p. 55.
24. Herodotus, *Histories*, III, pp. 241f.
25. *Behistun*, e.g. no. 18.
26. Ibid., nos 13–50, passim.
27. Ibid., no. 71.
28. Ibid., no. 74.
29. Ibid., no. 6.
30. Herodotus, *Histories*, III, pp. 242f.
31. Cook, *Persian Empire*, pp. 77–81, passim for full discussion of territorial discrepancies.
32. T. Cuyler Young Jr, 'Persia', in *EAC*, p. 151.
33. Herodotus, *Histories*, IV, p. 310.
34. Ibid., IV, pp. 310–15, passim.
35. Cook, *Persian Empire*, p. 96.
36. Herodotus, *Histories*, VI, p. 403.
37. Ibid., V, pp. 380f.
38. Ibid., VI, p. 404.
39. Ibid., VI, pp. 421–6, passim.
40. A.R. Burn, *Alexander the Great and the Hellenistic Empire* (Hodder & Stoughton, 1947). Burn reckoned eight to nine hours for the Athenian march; solo, he did it in six hours.
41. Ibid., p. 245.
42. Herodotus, *Histories*, VI, p. 249; Cook, *Persian Empire*, p. 98.
43. Ibid.
44. Herodotus, *Histories*, VI, pp. 428ff.
45. Ibid., VII, pp. 441f.
46. Cook, *Persian Empire*, p. 113.
47. Herodotus, *Histories*, IX, pp. 535, 583, 593, 611 and VII, p. 443.
48. Ibid., IX, pp. 579ff.
49. Burn, *Alexander the Great*, p. 321.
50. Herodotus, *Histories*, pp. 452f.
51. Ibid., VII, pp. 459f.

52. Ibid., VII, pp. 506f.
53. Cook, *Persian Empire*, p. 116.
54. Herodotus, *Histories*, VII, pp. 466–71, passim, 472–5, passim.
55. Cook, *Persian Empire*, p. 119; Herodotus, *Histories*, VII, pp. 503f, 507–10, passim.
56. Ibid., VII, pp. 503f, 513.
57. Ibid., VII, pp. 480, 513–19, passim.
58. Ibid., VIII, pp. 540f.
59. Ibid., VIII, pp. 551–4, passim, 557f, 562.
60. Cook, *Persian Empire*, p. 123.
61. Herodotus, *Histories*, VIII, pp. 566f, 572ff.
62. Ibid., IX, pp. 577–82, passim.
63. Ibid., IX, pp. 584ff.
64. Ibid., IX, pp. 593f, 597f, 600–4, passim.
65. Ibid., IX, p, 609.
66. N. Sekunda, 'The Persians', in *Warfare in the Ancient World*, ed. Gen Sir John Hackett (Sidgwick & Jackson Ltd, London, 1989), pp. 82–5, passim.
67. Herodotus, *Histories*, I, pp. 72f.
68. Sekunda, 'The Persians', pp. 84f.
69. X.Cyr., Books I and II, passim.
70. Cook, *Persian Empire*, p. 8.
71. X.Cyr., Book III.3.
72. Ibid., Book I.iv.20, and VI.10.
73. Ibid., Book IV, chapter iii, passim.
74. Ibid., Book VIII, chapter i.2.
75. X.Horse, chapter XII, pp. 8–9.
76. Paul Bernard, 'Une Pièce d'Armure Perse sur un Monument Lycien', *Syria*, 41 (1964), 195–212, esp. 195, 197.
77. Ibid., p. 198.
78. Piero Bartolini, *I Fenici* (Bompiani, Milan, 1988), pp. 132f.
79. X.Cyr., VI.i.27–50.
80. Sekunda, 'The Persians', pp. 98f.
81. X.Anab., Book VII, p. 84; Book VIII, pp. 86f.
82. X.Cyr., B.VII.1.27 camels, and battle VII, passim; Herodotus, *Histories*, I, pp. 72f.
83. X.Cyr., e.g. VII. i.46, 47.
84. Ibid., VII.v.62.
85. Ibid., VIII.34.
86. Ibid., VIII.ii.16.
87. Ibid., 18.
88. Ibid., VIII.vi.10.
89. Ibid., VIII.vi.17.
90. Herodotus, *Histories*, I, pp. 94f; VII, p. 471.
91. *ARAB*, II, no. 158.
92. Using Edwin Wright's map of Sargon II's eighth campaign and a modern map of Iran.

93. X.Anab., Book IV, chapter 5, p. 201.
94. Strabo, *Geography*, II.13.7.
95. Ibid., II.14.9.
96. Ibid., II.14.12, II.13.9.
97. Herodotus, *Histories*, VIII, pp. 562, 567.
98. Ibid.
99. Strabo, *Geography*, 12.2.10.
100. Herodotus, *Histories*, III, p. 243.
101. Ibid.
102. Cook, *Persian Empire*, p. 80.
103. Herodotus, *Histories*, I, p. 119.
104. Cook, *Persian Empire*, p. 102.
105. Herodotus, *Histories*, V, pp. 359f.
106. Ibid., VIII, p. 556.
107. Cook, *Persian Empire*, p. 108.
108. Hyland, *Endurance Horse*, pp. 56–9, and personal experience of riding in 100-milers.
109. *Persepolis Fortification Tablets*, tr. R.T. Hallock (University of Chicago Oriental Institute Publications, vol. XCII, 1969), numbers as quoted, passim.
110. *Persepolis*, p. 72.
111. Ibid., no. 1672.
112. Ibid., no. 1667.
113. Ibid., nos 1661–6.
114. Ibid., no. 1648.
115. Ibid., no. 1635.
116. Ibid., e.g. nos 1636, 1637.
117. Cook, *Persian Empire*, pp. 46, 89.
118. *Persepolis*, e.g. nos 1782, 1783.
119. Ibid., no. 1781.
120. Ibid., no. 1784.
121. Personal experience of 100-milers. For this type of event the horse was fed 15 lb hard feed (grain) per day. Training was over a period of six months.
122. *Persepolis*, no. 1764.
123. The Bible, Book of Esther 8.10.
124. *Persepolis*, no. 1672.
125. Ibid., no. 1766.
126. Ibid., no. 1670.
127. Ibid., no. 1673.
128. Ibid., no. 1781.
129. Ibid., no. 1670.
130. Ibid., nos 1671, 1672, 1673.
131. Ibid., no. 1670.
132. Ibid., nos 1946, 1947.
133. Ibid., no. 1793.
134. Ibid., no. 2056; Cook, *Persian Empire*, p. 190.

CHAPTER 11

1. Leslie J. Worley, *Hippeis. The Cavalry of Ancient Greece* (Westview Press, Boulder, San Francisco, Oxford, 1994), pp. 28f.
2. Zvelebil, 'Rise of the Nomads', chapter 38, p. 255.
3. *Pausanias' Guide to Greece*, tr. Peter Levi (2 vols, Penguin, 1979), Books V and VI, passim.
4. Anderson, *Greek Horsemanship*, p. 37; Azzaroli, *History of Horsemanship*, p. 136.
5. E. Delebecque, *Le Cheval dans L'Iliade* (Paris, 1951), pp. 71–109, passim.
6. J.K. Anderson, 'Greek Chariot-borne and Mounted Infantry', *AJA*, 79 (1975), 175–87, esp. 179.
7. M.S.F. Hood, 'A Mycenaean Cavalryman', in *ABSA*, XIV, no. III (1953), pp. 84–93, esp. pp. 86ff; Worley, *Hippeis*, pp. 9f. I do not agree that the length of the lance at 10 ft is too long to wield from horseback. Illustration of the frieze.
8. Ibid., pp. 23f; *Pausanias' Guide to Greece*, Book 4, p. 11.
9. Xenophon, *The Lacedaemonians*, XI.4, in *Scripta Minora*, tr. E.G. Marchant (Loeb Classical Library, Heinemann, London, and J.P. Putnam Sons, New York, 1925).
10. Worley, *Hippeis*, p. 25.
11. THUC., 4.55.2.
12. Worley, *Hippeis*, p. 26.
13. P.A. Greenhalgh, *Early Greek Warfare* (Cambridge University Press, Cambridge, 1973), pp. 146f.
14. John Lazenby, 'Hoplite Warfare', in *WAW*, 54–81, esp. 54–58, passim.
15. Greenhalgh, *Early Greek Warfare*, pp. 122, 130f.
16. Tomlinson, 'Solon', in *100 Great Lives of Antiquity* (Guild Publishing, London, 1985), pp. 354–9, esp. pp. 357f.
17. Anderson, *Greek Horsemanship*, p. 129.
18. J.T. Hooker, 'Archaic Greece', in *EAC*, p. 219.
19. Anderson, *Greek Horsemanship*, pp. 129f; Worley, *Hippeis*, pp. 65f.
20. Herodotus, *Histories*, IX, p. 599.
21. Ibid., p. 604.
22. Worley, *Hippeis*, p. 68.
23. Ibid., p. 68.
24. THUC., Book I, p. 73.
25. Ibid., Book II, p. 106.
26. Ibid., Book IV, pp. 250f, 254, 259f; Book V, p 309; Book VI, pp. 371, 394, 426.
27. Ibid., Book II, p. 144.
28. Ibid., Book II, chapter 10, passim.
29. Ibid., Book II, p. 114.
30. Ibid., Book IV, chapter 5, passim.
31. Ibid., Book IV, p. 260.
32. Ibid., Book IV, chapter 6, passim.
33. Ibid., Book IV, pp. 283ff.

34. Ibid., Book IV, pp. 288–91.
35. Ibid., Book IV, chapter 9, passim.
36. Ibid., Book IV, p. 301.
37. Ibid., Book V, chapter 1, passim.
38. Ibid., Book V, chapter 5, passim, chapter 4, pp. 337–9; Book V, p. 353; Worley, *Hippeis*, p. 83.
39. THUC., Book VI, chapter 2, p. 380.
40. Ibid., Book VI, chapter 4, p. 394.
41. Ibid., Book VI, chapter 2, p. 370, chapter 3, p. 391.
42. Ibid., Book VI, chapter 6, passim.
43. Ibid., Book VI, chapter 9, passim.
44. Ibid., Book VII, passim.
45. X.Hell and X.Cyr., Book I.1.9, chapters 3 and 4, passim; Book II, chapter 2, passim.
46. X.Anab., introduction pp. 11–16, passim.
47. Ibid., V.3, p. 232.
48. Ibid., II, chapter 1, p. 106.
49. Ibid., chapter 2, passim.
50. Ibid., I, chapter 10, p. 98.
51. Ibid., II.4, p. 117; II.5, pp. 123f.
52. Ibid., II, chapter 6, passim.
53. Ibid., III, chapter 1, pp. 139, 147.
54. Ibid., III, chapter 3, pp. 151f, 158.
55. Ibid., IV, pp. 161f.
56. Ibid., III, chapter 4, pp. 172f.
57. Ibid., IV, chapter 1, p. 177; chapters 3 and 4, passim.
58. Ibid., IV, chapter 5, passim.
59. Ibid., IV, chapter 7, p. 211.
60. Ibid., IV, chapter 8, pp. 215ff.
61. Ibid., V, chapter 3, p. 230; VI, chapter 1, p. 263.
62. Ibid., VI, chapter 2, p. 273.
63. Ibid., VI, chapter 4, passim.
64. Ibid., VII, chapter 6, pp. 333f.
65. Xenophon, *Hellenica*, Book III. I.3–7.
66. Ibid., Book III, chapter II.1–2.
67. Ibid., Book III, chapter II.8–10.
68. Ibid., Book III, chapter II.11–20.
69. Ibid., Book III, chapter IV.5–6.
70. Ibid., Book III, chapter IV.5–6, 11–14.
71. Ibid., Book III, chapter IV.20–8.
72. Ibid., Book III, chapter VI, passim.
73. Ibid., Book IV, chapter I.1–3.
74. X.Anab., Book V, chapter 5, p. 241; Book I, chapter 8, p. 86.
75. X.Age., I.35.
76. X.Hell., Book IV, chapter I, 15–20.
77. Ibid., 20–7.

Notes

78. Ibid., 29–40.
79. Ibid., Book IV, chapter II, passim.
80. Ibid., Book IV, chapter II, 5, 7; chapter III, 3–9.
81. Ibid., Book IV, chapter III, 15–22.
82. Ibid., Book IV, chapter VIII, 17–19.
83. Ibid., Book VI, chapter IV, 10–15.
84. Ibid., Book VI, chapter I, 1, 18f.
85. X.C.C., I.3–4.
86. Ibid., I.1.
87. Ibid., I.8–12.
88. Aristophanes, *The Clouds* (Greek text published for Greek Play Committee, W. Heffer and Sons Ltd, Cambridge, 1962), lines 15, 24–40, 60, 73, 84f, 109, 121–4, 243, 437, 1227–9.
89. Aristotle, *The Athenian Constitution*, tr. H. Rackham (W. Heinemann Ltd, London, and Harvard University Press, Cambridge, Mass, 1935 (Loeb)), XLIX.2.
90. X.C.C., I.11.
91. Ibid., I.5.
92. Hyland, *Horse in Middle Ages*, p. 108 on Boucicault.
93. X.C.C., I.6.
94. X.Horse., chapter XII, pp. 8f; X.C.C., I.8.
95. Aristotle, *Athenian Constitution*, B.VII.3, 6; XXIV.3; IV.2; XXX.2; VII 3, 4; XXIV.3.
96. Ibid., B.LXI.5.
97. X.C.C., II.2.
98. Aristotle, *Athenian Constitution*, B.LXI.4, 6.
99. X.C.C., I, n. 1.
100. J.H. Kroll, 'An Archive of the Athenian Cavalry', *Hesperia* 46, no. 2 (1977), 83–140, esp. 97f, n. 36.
101. Ibid., pp. 95ff.
102. X.C.C., I.13–17.
103. Ibid., I.18–31, 25.
104. Ibid., I.26.
105. Ibid., III.1.
106. Ibid., II.1.
107. Ibid., III.2–4, 6–8.
108. Ibid., III.10–14.
109. Eugene Vanderpool, 'Victories in the Anthippasia', *Hesperia* 43 (1974), 311–13.
110. X.C.C., Books IV and V, passim.
111. Ibid., V.1.
112. Ibid., V.1, 4.
113. Ibid., IV.1–8.
114. Ibid., V.13.
115. Ibid., VI, passim.
116. Ibid., VII.1–3.
117. Ibid., VIII.1–4.

118. Ibid., VIII, passim.
119. Ibid., IX.3–6.
120. Ibid., VII.9–10.
121. Ibid., IV.5.
122. Kroll, 'Archive of Athenian Cavalry', pp. 84f.
123. X.Anab., Book VII, chapter 8, p. 349.
124. Aristophanes, *The Clouds*, lines 21–3.
125. Kroll, 'Archive of Athenian Cavalry', p. 89.
126. Ibid., p. 89.
127. Ibid., p. 88.
128. Ibid., p. 86.
129. Ibid., pp. 97ff.
130. Ibid., p. 103.
131. Ibid., p. 97, n. 36.
132. Aristotle, *Athenian Constitution*, Book XLIX.1.
133. Kroll, 'Archive of Athenian Cavalry', p. 94.
134. Ibid., p. 93.
135. National endurance ride records show names of individual horses appearing in the annual top six rankings. My own Nizzolan did so for seven years until an accident finished his career. Others, such as Margaret Montgomerie's Tarquin had similar longevity at the top.
136. Kroll, 'Archive of Athenian Cavalry', p. 94.

CHAPTER 12

1. N.G.L. Hammond, 'Macedon', *EAC*, 228–33, esp. 229; J.R. Ellis, *Philip II and Macedonian Imperialism* (Thames & Hudson, 1976), pp. 197f, 203ff, 208f.
2. Ibid., pp. 219ff; Amélie Kuhrt, *The Ancient Near East* (vol. II, Routledge, London, 1995), p. 675; E.W. Marsden, *The Campaigns of Gaugamela* (Liverpool University Press, 1964), p. 26; Arrian, *Anabasis*, Book I.If, pp. 42–6, passim.
3. Ibid., Book 4, 6–9, pp. 211–16, passim.
4. A. Devine, *Alexander the Great*, in *WAW*, p. 106.
5. Worley, *Hippeis*, p. 155.
6. Devine, *Alexander the Great*, pp. 104–7, passim.
7. Arrian, *Anabasis*, Book III.14, p. 169.
8. Arrian, *Ars Tactica*, 16.3, 6–9, tr. F.W. Walbank for Hyland's *Training the Roman Cavalry*, pp. 70f.
9. Ellis, *Philip II*, p. 56.
10. Diodorus Siculus, *Library of History*, Book XVII.17, in vol. VIII, tr. B. Welles (Loeb Classical Library, Heinemann, 1963); P.A. Brunt, 'Alexander's Macedonian Cavalry', *JHS*, 83–4 (1963–4), 27–46, esp. 46 and passim.
11. Herodotus, *Histories*, B.7.41, p. 459.
12. Ibid., B.8.116, p. 563.
13. Ibid., B.8.129, p. 568; B.9.18, p. 583.
14. Ibid., B.7.41, p. 459.

15. Ibid., B.9.23, p. 584.
16. Ibid., B.9.62, p. 602.
17. Ibid., B.7.115, p. 479.
18. A. Fol and I. Marazov, *Thrace and the Thracians* (Cassell, London, 1977), pp. 118, 25; Hyland, *Equus*, p. 16.
19. Fol and Marazov, *Thrace*, pp. 18, 118.
20. Ibid., p. 118.
21. Ibid., p. 56.
22. X.Anab., Book 7, chapter 3, p. 317.
23. Grattius Faliscus in *Minor Latin Poets*, tr. J. Wight Duff and A.M. Duff (Loeb Classical Library, Heinemann, 1968), lines 150–541.
24. A.J. Butler, *Sport in Classic Times* (Ernest Benn, London, 1930), p. 69.
25. *Justinus*, tr. R. Ruehl (Teubner, Leipzig, 1885), B.9.2.16.
26. Rudenko, *Frozen Tombs*, p. 56; Talbot Rice, *The Scythians*, pl. 30.
27. Kroll, 'Archive of the Athenian Cavalry', pp. 83–140, esp. p. 88; and illustration of coin of Pausanias, p. 184 of Xenophon's *Art of Horsemanship*.
28. Ellis, *Philip II*, p. 54; Arrian, *Anabasis*, B.I.12, 14f, pp. 68, 71f.
29. Kroll, 'Archive of the Athenian Cavalry', p. 88.
30. ARRIAN.AN., B.5.19, p. 282; M.M. Morgan in X.Horse., pp. 101ff; Plutarch, 'Alexander', in *The Age of Alexander. Nine Greek Lives*, tr. Ian Scott Kilvert (Penguin 1973 (1982)), p. 257.6.
31. P.A. Brunt, 'Alexander's Macedonian Cavalry', and G.T. Griffith, 'A Note on the Hipparchies of Alexander', pp. 68–74, both in *JHS*, 183–4 (1963–4).
32. Herodotus, *Histories*, B.I.78ff, pp. 72f; *ARAB*, II, no. 781; Arrian, *Anabasis*, B.I.16, pp. 74f.
33. Ibid., B.II.8–12, pp. 114–21, passim; Devine, 'Alexander the Great', map p. 112, pp. 113–16, passim.
34. ARRIAN.AN., B.III.7–9, 11–12, 14, pp. 158–69, passim; Strabo, *Geography*, B.11.14.9, II.5.1; Hancar, *Das Pferd*, pp. 355–72; Creel, 'The Role of the Horse', pp. 647–72, esp. p. 661; Marsden, *Campaigns of Gaugamela*, pp. 31–7, passim; and maps used. M. Jankovich, *They Rode into Europe*, tr. A. Dent (George G. Harrap & Co., Ltd, London, 1971), p. 41, map of Turanian swathe, and p. 37, illustration of Aravan rock carvings; Cook, *Persian Empire*, map, fig. I; *National Geographic* (May 1999), the Caspian region; Donald W. Engels, *Alexander the Great and the Logistics of the Macedonian Army* (University of California Press, Berkeley and Los Angeles, 1978), maps of Alexander's route. These maps helped fix the horses in the relative areas corresponding to modern and ancient names.
35. Devine, 'Alexander the Great', pp. 122f and map; ARRIAN.AN., B.III.12–13, pp. 166f.
36. Ibid., B.111.9–15, passim, pp. 161–71; Marsden, *Campaigns of Gaugamela*, pp. 61f; Diodorus Siculus, Book XVII.61.3; A. Savill, *Alexander the Great and his Time* (Rockcliff, London, 1955), p. 51.
37. ARRIAN.AN., Book I.26f, pp. 94–6.
38. Engels, *Logistics*, p. 54 and Quintus Curtius, see n. 41, Book 3.16.
39. Herodotus, *Histories*, B.I.191f, pp. 118f.

40. ARRIAN.AN., B.3.15, p. 171.
41. Quintus Curtius, *History of Alexander*, tr. John C. Rolfe (2 vols, Loeb Classical Library, Heinemann, 1946), Book V.i.21.
42. ARRIAN.AN., B.7.13, p. 369.
43. Ibid., B.3.30, pp. 198f.
44. Ibid., B.3.18, p. 176.
45. Ibid., B.2.14.7, p. 127.
46. Ibid., B.5.13, p. 271.
47. Griffith, 'Hipparchies of Alexander', p. 69.
48. ARRIAN.AN., B.I.24, 29, pp. 91, 99; B.III.17, pp. 174f.
49. Ibid., B.III.19f, pp. 180f.
50. Quintus Curtius, *History of Alexander*, Book V.II.ii.10.
51. ARRIAN.AN., B. 4.22, p. 239; W.W. Tarn, *Alexander the Great* (vol. I, Cambridge University Press, Cambridge, 1948), p. 92.
52. Engels, *Logistics*, pp. 15, 26–9, passim.
53. Ibid., pp. 22, 29; Appendix 5, pp. 145, 154f.
54. Ibid., p. 9.
55. Ibid., pp. 93, 64, 27, 55f, 67, 73, 77, 37, 107, 93f.
56. Ibid., p. 153; B.III.1, p. 148.
57. Ibid., B.III.15, p. 171; Engels, *Logistics*, p. 153.
58. ARRIAN.AN., B.III.20ff, pp. 181–4, passim.
59. Engels, *Logistics*, p. 153.
60. Such rides today are ridden at over twice the speed over a full 100 miles, and routes are often over very difficult terrain and in extremely hot conditions.
61. ARRIAN.AN., B.III.30, pp. 197f.
62. Ibid., B.V.8–20, pp. 266–83, passim.
63. Ibid., B.V.20–7, pp. 283–95, passim. The Cathaei (the Katti) were the ancestors of the Kathiawars who migrated from the Punjab to Kathiawar, Gujarat, in the twelfth century AD.
64. ARRIAN.AN., B.VI.17, p. 325.
65. Ibid., B.VI.21–8, pp. 330–43, passim.
66. E.R. Bevan, *The House of Seleucus* (2 vols, Edward Arnold, London, 1902), pp. 57–61, passim.
67. Hyland, *Warhorse 1250–1600*, Indian chapter 9, passim.
68. Bevan, *House of Seleucus*, p. 69.
69. Ibid., vol. II, chapter 31, passim.

Bibliography

PRIMARY SOURCES

Abou Bekr Ibn Bekr, *Le Naceri*, tr. M. Perron, 3 vols, Ministry of Agriculture of France, Paris, 1860.
Alalakh Tablets, The, tr. J. Wiseman, London, 1953.
Amarna Letters, The, ed. and tr. William L. Moran, John Hopkins University Press, Baltimore and London, 1992.
Ammianus Macellinus. *The Later Roman Empire*, tr. W. Hamilton, Penguin, 1986.
'Anastasi Papryus I', in *Egyptian Hieratic Texts*, tr. A.H. Gardiner, Series I, Literary Texts of the New Kingdom, Part I, Papyrus Anastasi I and the Papyrus Koller, Leipzig, J.C. Heinrichs's sohe, Buchhandlung, 1911.
Ancient Near Eastern Texts Relating to the Old Testament, ed. J. Pritchard, Princeton University Press, Princeton, NJ, 1950. The above 3rd edn with supplement, 1969.
Ancient Records of Assyria and Babylonia, tr. D.D. Luckenbill, University of Chicago Press, Chicago, vol. I, 1926; vol. II, 1927.
Ancient Records of Egypt, tr. J.H. Breasted, University of Chicago Press, Chicago, 1906, vols I–IV.
Aristophanes, *The Clouds*, Greek text published for Greek Play Committee, W. Heffer and Sons Ltd, Cambridge, 1962.
Aristotle, *The Athenian Constitution*, tr. H. Rackham, W. Heinemann Ltd, London, and Harvard University Press, Cambridge, Mass, MCMXXXV (Loeb).
Arrian, *Anabasis of Alexander – the Campaigns of Alexander*, tr. Aubrey de Selincourt, Penguin Classics, 1986.
——, *Ars Tactica* (cavalry section, tr. F. Walbank from Flavianus II, rev. edn G. Wirth, Scriptores et Fragmenta Edititi, A.G. Roos, Leipzig, 1967), in A. Hyland, *Training the Roman Cavalry from Arrian's Ars Tactica*, Sutton Publishing, 1993.
——, *Cynegetica*, in *Hounds and Hunting in Ancient Greece*, tr. D.B. Hull, University of Chicago Press, Chicago, 1964.
A Dictionary of Assyrian Botany, tr. H. Campbell Thomson, British Academy, London, 1949.
Babur Nama, tr. A.S. Beveridge, Luzac, London, 1969 (1922).
Behistun Inscription, The, tr. L.W. King and R.C. Thompson in *The Sculptures and Inscription of Darius the Great on the Rock of Behistun in Persia*, London, 1907, tr. taken from the Internet at http//www.livius.org/be-bm/behistun/Behistun03.html.
Bible, The New International Version, Hodder & Stoughton, 1979 (2000).
'Bruchstucke Einer Mittelassyrischen Vorschriftensammlung fur die

Akklimatiesierung und Trainierung von Wagenpferden', tr. Erich Ebeling, in *Deutsche Akademie der Wissenschaften zu Berlin Institut fur Orientforschung*, nr. 6, 1952 (pages used, 6–55).

Diodorus Siculus, *Library of History*, Book XVII in vol. VIII, tr. B. Velles, Loeb Classical Library, Heinemann, 1963.

Evans, J. Warren, Borton A., Hintz H.F., van Vleck, L. Dale, *The Horse*, W.H. Freeman and Co., San Francisco, 1977. Chapter by Anthony Borton, University of Massachusetts, pp. 229–31.

Fink, Robert O., *Roman Military Records on Papyrus*, American Philological Association, 1971.

Gadd, C.J., tr. 'The Tablets from Chagar Bazar and Tall Brak', in *British School of Archaeology in Iraq* (henceforth *IRAQ*), vol. VIII (1937–8), pp. 22–66.

Grattius Faliscus, in *Minor Latin Poets*, lines 150–541, tr. J. Wight Duff and A.M. Duff, Loeb Classical Library, Heinemann, 1968.

Herodotus, *The Histories*, tr. Aubrey de Selincourt, Penguin, 1954 (1974).

Homer, *The Iliad*, Penguin Classics, 1986.

Hrozný – see Kikkuli.

Ibn Battuta, *The Travels of Ibn Battuta 1325–1354*, tr. H.A.A. Gibb, 4 vols, London, Hakluyt Society (2nd Series CX), Cambridge University Press, Cambridge, 1956, vol. II, 1962; vol. III, 1971; vol. IV, 1994.

Justinus, tr. R. Ruehl, Teubner, Leipzig, 1886.

Kadesh Inscriptions of Rameses II, The, tr. Sir Alan Gardiner, Griffith Institute, Oxford, 1960.

Kammenhuber – see Kikkuli.

Kautilya's Arthasastra, tr. Mahamahopadhyaya, Arthasastravisahada, Vidyalankara, Panditaraja, 4th edn, Dr R. Shamastry, Sri Raghuveer Printing Press, Mysore, 1951 (1st edn, 1909).

Kikkuli (translations of):

Kammenhuber, A., *Hippologia Hethetica*, Wiesbaden Harrassowitz, 1961; Hrozný Bedřich, L'Entraînement des Chevaux Chez Les Anciens Indo-Européens d'Après un Texte Mîtannien-Hittite Provenant du 14ᵉ Siècle av. J.C., in *Archiv Orientalni*, 3 (1931), pp. 431–61; Potratz J., *Das Pferd in der Fruhzeit*, 1938; Probst, Gerhard F., *The Kikkuli Text on the Training of Horses*, (c. *1350 BC*), translated from the German of Potratz, King Library Press, University of Kentucky Libraries, Lexington, KY, 1977.

Koller Papyrus, see above under *Anastasi Papyrus I*.

MacLeod, G., *Treatment of Horses by Homeopathy*, Health Science Press, 1977.

Nemesian, *Cynegetica*, in *Minor Latin Poets*, tr. J. Wight Duff and A.M. Duff, Loeb Classical Library, Heinemann, 1968.

Neufeld, E. (tr.), *The Hittite Laws*, London, Luzac and Co. Ltd, 1951.

Nimrud Letters, The, tr. H.W.F. Saggs in *IRAQ*, 17–18 (1955–6), Part I, pp. 21–50; Part II, pp. 126–60; 20 (1958), Part IV, pp. 182–212; 21–2 (1959–60), Part V, pp. 158–79; 25 (1963), pp. 70–80.

Nimrud Tablets, The, D.J. Wiseman and J.V. Kinnear Wilson, *IRAQ*, 13 (1951–2), pp. 102–19.

Nimrud Tablets, administrative tablets from N.W. Palace, Nimrud, Barbara Parker,

Bibliography

IRAQ, 23 (1961), pp. 15–67.

Oppian, *Cynegetica*, tr. A.W. Mair, Loeb Classical Library, Heinemann, 1928.

Pausanias's Guide to Greece, 2 vols, tr. Peter Levi, Penguin, 1979.

Pelagonius, *Ars Veterinaria*, ed. M. Ihm, Leipzig, 1892.

Persepolis Fortification Tablets, tr. R.T. Hallock, University of Chicago Oriental Institute Publications, vol. XCII, 1969.

Pliny, *Natural History*, Book VIII, tr. H. Rackham, in vol. III, Loeb Classical Library, Heinemann, 1940.

Plutarch, *Alexander in the Age of Alexander. Nine Greek Lives*, tr. Ian Scott Kilvert, Penguin, 1973 (1982).

Polybius, *The Rise of the Roman Empire*, tr. Ian Scott-Kilvert, Penguin, 1979.

Potratz, J., 'Die Pferdetrensen des Alten Orients', *Analecta Orientalia* 41, Rome, 1966. See also Kikkuli.

Probst, G. – see Kikkuli.

Quintus Curtius, *History of Alexander*, 2 vols, tr. John C. Rolfe, Loeb Classical Library, Heinemann, 1946.

Royal Correspondence of the Assyrian Empire, tr. Leroy Waterman, University of Michigan Press, Ann Arbor, Parts I and II, 1930; Part III commentary, 1931; Part IV supplement and indexes, 1936.

Sacred Books of the East, the Zend Avesta, Part II, tr. James Darmesteter, Clarendon Press, Oxford, 1883.

Salonen, Armas, *Hippologica Accadica*, Helsinki, 1955.

Sandalgian, J., *Les Inscriptions Cuneiformes Urartiques*, L'Académie des Inscriptions de France, Venice, 1900.

Schaeffer, Claude, F.A., *The Cuneiform Texts of Ras Shamra-Ugarit*, for the British Academy, Oxford University Press, London, 1939.

Sidonius Apollinaris, *Poems and Letters*, tr. W.B. Anderson, Loeb Classical Library, Heinemann, 1968.

Ssu-Ma-Ch'ien, *Records of the Historian, Chapters from the Shih Chi of Ssu-Ma-Ch'ien*, tr. B. Watson, Columbia University Press, New York and London, 1969. Also edn of vol. II, 1961.

Strabo, *Geography*, 8 vols, tr. H.L. Jones, Loeb Classical Library, Heinemann, 1917–32.

'Sumerian Animal Proverbs and Fables', tr. E.I. Gordon, *JCS*, 12 (1958), 1–21, 43–75.

Tacitus, *The Agricola and Germania*, tr. H. Mattingly, Penguin, 1970.

Tadmor, H., 'The Campaigns of Sargon II of Assur', *JCS*, 12 (1958 60), pp. 22–40, 77–100.

Thucydides, *The Peloponnesian War*, tr. Rex Warner, Penguin Classics, 1954 (1956).

Usāmah ibn Munqidh, *Memoirs of Usāmah ibn Munqidh (Kitab al-'Tibār)*, tr. from original manuscript by P.L. Hitti, Princeton University/Columbia University Press, New York, 1929.

Vanderpool, Eugene, 'Victories in the Anthippasia', *Hesperia*, 43 (1974), 311–13.

Varro, *On Farming*, tr. L. Storr-Best, Bell, 1912.

Virgil, *Georgics*, tr. C. Day-Lewis, Cape, 1943.

Virolleaud, C., 'Fragments d'un Traite Phenicien de Therapeutique

Hippoligique', *Syria*, 15 (1934), 75–83.

Xenophon, *Agesilaus*, in *Scripta Minora*, tr. E.C. Marchant, Loeb Classical Library, Heinemann, London, and G.P. Putnam & Sons, New York, 1925.

——, *Anabasis – The Persian Expedition*, tr. Rex Warner, Penguin Classics, 1949 (1986).

——, *The Cavalry Commander*, in *Scripta Minora*, tr. E.C. Marchant (Loeb Classical Library, Heinemann, London, 1925).

——, *The Cyropaedia*, tr. Revd J.S. Watson and Revd Henry Dale, London, George Bell & Sons, 1898.

——, *The Hellenica*, as above.

——, *The Art of Horsemanship*, tr. M.H. Morgan, J.A. Allen & Co. Ltd, 1962 (1979), from original text published by J.M. Dent & Co., 1894 edn.

——, *The Lacedaemonians*, in *Scripta Minora* as above.

SECONDARY SOURCES

Albright, W.F., 'Mitannian Maryannu (Chariot Warriors), and the Canaanite and Egyptian Equivalents', *Archiv fur Orientforschung Int. Zeitschrift* (henceforth *AFO*), VI (1930–1), pp. 217–21.

Anderson, J.K., *Greek Horsemanship*, University of California, 1961.

——, 'Greek Chariot-borne and Mounted Infantry', *American Journal of Archaeology*, 79 (1975), 175–87.

Anthony, David W. and Brown, Dorcas R., 'The Origins of Horseback Riding', *Antiquity* 65 (1991), 22–38.

Azzaroli, A., *An Early History of Horsemanship*, Leiden, E.J. Brill/Dr W. Backhuys, 1985.

Bartolini, Piero, *I Fenici*, Bompiani, Milan, 1988.

Basham, A.L., 'Early Imperial India', in *EAC*, ed. Arthur Cotterell, Windward, 1980, pp. 184–91.

Beale, Richard H., *The Organization of the Hittite Military*, Heidelberg, 1992.

——, 'Carl Winter Universitatsverlag', Chicago University Dissertation, 1986.

Bernard, Paul, 'Une Pièce d'Armure Perse sur un Monument Lycien', *Syria*, 41 (1964), pp. 195–212.

Bevan, E.R., *The House of Seleucus*, 2 vols, Edward Arnold, London, 1902.

Bibikova, V.I., 'On The History of Horse Domestication in South East Europe', (translated from *Archaeologia* 22 (1969), 55–66), Oxford BAR International Series *287*, 1986, as Appendix 3 (see Telegin below).

Bierbrier, M.L., 'Thutmose III', in *100 Great Lives of Antiquity*, ed. John Canning, Guild Publishing, London, 1985.

Bökönyi, Sándor, 'The Equids of Dabaghiyah, Iraq', in Richard H. Meadow and Hans-Peter Uerpmann (eds), *Equids in the Ancient World*, 2 vols: I, 1986; II, 1991, Dr Ludwig Reichert Verlag, Wiesbaden, pp. 302–318 (henceforth *M & U*).

Brown, Dorcas, 'Kazak Conference, A Tremendous Success', *Institute for Ancient Equestrian Studies Newsletter*, 2 (spring 1996), 1 and 4 (henceforth *IAES*).

——, 'Let Them Eat Horses', *IAES* 4 (summer 1997), 1, 3. (The no. 2 and no. 4 issues do not carry author, but Dorcas Brown is the editor of *IAES* and responsible for text.)

——, and Anthony, David, 'Excavations in Russia', *IAES*, 3 (autumn 1996), 1, 3.

Bryce, T.R., 'Phrygia and Lydia', in *EAC*, pp. 144–6.

Brun, Bertel and Sherif Baha el Din, *Common Birds of Egypt*, American University in Cairo Press, 1985 (1990).

Brunt, P.A., 'Alexander's Macedonian Cavalry', *JHS*, 83–4 (1963–4), 27–46.

Burn, A.R., *Alexander the Great and the Hellenistic Empire*, Hodder & Stoughton, 1947.

Burrow, T., 'The Aryan Invasion of India', in *EAC*, pp. 182–4.

Butler, A.J., *Sport in Classic Times*, Ernest Benn, London, 1930.

Cambridge Encyclopedia of Archaeology, The (hereafter *CEA*), ed. Andrew Sherratt, 1980.

Cameron, George G., *History of Early Iran*, University of Chicago Press, Chicago, (no date).

Chahin, M., *The Kingdom of Armenia*, Dorset Press, New York, 1991 (originally Routledge, 1987).

Clutton-Brock, J., *Horse Power*, Natural History Museum Publication, 1992.

——, 'The Buhen Horse', *JAS*, I (1974), 89–100.

——, Burleigh R. and Gowlett J., 'Early Domestic Equids in Egypt and Western Asia; an additional note', *M & E*, II, pp. 9–11.

Cook, J.M., *The Persian Empire*, Book Club Associates, 1983.

Creel, E.G., 'The Role of the Horse in Chinese History', *American Historical Review*, LXX, no. 3 (April 1965), 647–72.

Dalley, S., 'Foreign Chariotry and Cavalry in the Armies of Tiglath-Pileser III and Sargon II', *IRAQ*, 47 (1985), pp. 31–48.

Davies, G.I., 'Urwot in I Kings 5.6 and the Assyrian Horse Lists', *JSS*, 34 (1989), 25–37.

Delebecque, E., *Le Cheval dans L'Iliade*, Paris, 1951.

Dent, A., 'Domestication and the Early Horse People', in *Encyclopedia of the Horse*, ed. E. Hartley-Edwards, Octopus, 1977.

Devine, Albert, 'Alexander the Great', in *Warfare in the Ancient World* (henceforth *WAW*), ed. Sir John Hackett, Sidgwick & Jackson Ltd, 1989, pp. 104–29.

Edwards, Richard, 'The Cave Reliefs at Ma Hao', *Artibus Asiae*, XVII (1954), Part I, pp. 5–28.

Elliot, R. and de Paoli C., *Kitchen Pharmacy*, Chapmans Ltd, 1991.

Ellis, J.R., *Philip II and Macedonian Imperialism*, Thames & Hudson, 1976.

Encyclopedia of Ancient Civilizations (EAC), ed. A. Cotterell, Windward, 1980.

Engels, Donald W., *Alexander the Great and the Logistics of the Macedonian Army*, University of California Press, Berkeley and Los Angeles, 1978.

Faulkner, R.O., 'Egyptian Military Organization', *JEA*, 39 (1953), 32–47.

Fleet, J.F., the introduction to *Kautilya's Arthasastra* (see above, Primary Sources).

Fol, Alexander and Marazov, Ivan, *Thrace and the Thracians*, Cassell, London, 1977.

Goodrich, Chauncy S., 'Riding Astride and the Saddle in Ancient China', *HJAS*,

44, no. 2 (December 1984), 279–306.

Grayson, A.K., 'Mittani', in *EAC*, pp. 109–11.

Greenhalgh, P.A., *Early Greek Warfare*, Cambridge University Press, Cambridge, 1973.

Griffith, G.T., a note on the Hipparchies of Alexander in *JHS*, 83–4 (1963–4), 68–74.

Groves, Colin B., 'The Taxonomy, Distribution, and Adaptations of Recent Equids', in *M & U*, I, pp. 11–66.

Gurney, O.R., 'The Hittites', in *EAC*, pp. 111–17.

——, *The Hittites*, Book Club Associates (henceforth BCA), 1952, 1954.

Guterbock, H.G., review of *Hippologia Hethetica*, in *JAOS*, 84, no. 3 (1964), 267–73.

Hammond, H.G.L., 'Macedon', in *EAC*, pp. 228–33.

Hancar, Franz, *Das Pferd in prahistorischer und fruher historischer Zeit*, Vienna, 1956.

Hayes, Horace M., *Veterinary Notes for Horse Owners*, Stanley Paul & Co., London, rev. edn, 1968.

Herrmann, Georgina, 'Parthian and Sasanian Saddlery', in *Archaeologia Iranica et Orientalis*, II, Miscellanea in Honorem Louis Vanden Berghe, Gent, 1989, pp. 757–809.

Hood, M.S.F., 'A Mycenaean Cavalryman', in *ABSA*, XIVIII (1953), pp. 84–93.

Hooker, J.T., 'Archaic Greece', in *EAC*, pp. 215–23.

Houlihan, Patrick F., *The Animal World of the Pharaohs*, Thames & Hudson, 1996.

Hull, Denison Bingham, *Hounds and Hunting in Ancient Greece*, University of Chicago Press, 1964.

Hyland, Ann, *The Endurance Horse*, J.A. Allen, London, 1988.

——, *Foal to Five Years*, Ward Lock Ltd, London, 1980.

——, *Equus*, Batsford, London, 1990.

——, *Training the Roman Cavalry from Arrian's Ars Tactica*, Alan Sutton Publishing Ltd, Stroud, 1993.

——, *Medieval Warhorse from Byzantium to the Crusades*, Sutton Publishing, Stroud, 1994.

——, *The Warhorse 1250–1600*, Sutton Publishing, Stroud, 1998.

——, *The Horse in the Middle Ages*, Sutton Publishing, Stroud, 1999.

——, *Endurance Riding*, J.B. Lippincott Co., Philadelphia and New York, 1975.

Jankovich, Miklós, *They Rode into Europe*, tr. Anthony Dent, George G. Harrap & Co. Ltd, London, 1971.

Keller, Werner, *The Etruscans*, BCA, 1975.

——, *The Bible as History* (rev.), BCA (by arrangement with Hodder & Stoughton), 1980.

Kendall, Timothy, *Warfare and Military Matters in the Nuzi Tablets*, Brandeis University, Michigan, June 1974.

Kroll, J.H., 'An Archive of the Athenian Cavalry', *Hesperia*, 46, no. 2 (1977), 83–140.

Kuhrt, Amelie, *The Ancient Near East*, vol. I, Routledge, London, 1995.

Lambert, W.G., 'Sultantepe Tablets VIII. Shalmaneser in Ararat', *Anatolia Studies*, IX (1961), 143–58.

Law, Robin, *The Horse in West African History*, published for the International

Bibliography

African Institute by Oxford University Press, 1980.

Lazenby, John, 'Hoplite Warfare', in *WAW*, pp. 54–81.

Levine, Marsha, 'The Origins of Horse Husbandry on the Eurasian Steppe', in *Late Prehistoric Exploitation of the Eurasian Steppe*, McDonald Institute Monographs, McDonald Institute for Archaeological Research, 1999.

Lewis, C.T. and Short, C., *A Latin Dictionary*, Clarendon Press, Oxford, 1966 (1879).

Lhote, H., 'Le Cheval et le Chameau dans les Peintures et Gravures Rupestres du Sahara', *Bulletin de L'Institut Francais D'Afrique Noire*, XV, no. 3 (July 1953), 1138–1228.

——, *The Search for the Tassili Frescoes*, translated from the French by Alan Houghton Brodrick, Hutchinson & Co. Ltd, 1973 (1959).

Littauer, Mary Aiken, 'The Function of the Yoke Saddle in Ancient Harnessing', *Antiquity*, XLII (1968), 27–31.

——, 'V.O. Vitt and the Horses of Pazyryk', *Antiquity*, XLV (1971), 293–4.

—— and Crouwel, J.H., *Wheeled Vehicles and Ridden Animals in the Ancient Near East*, Leiden/Kiln, 1979.

Loch, Sylvia, *The Royal Horse of Europe*, J.A. Allen Ltd, 1986.

Marsden, E.W., *The Campaigns of Gaugamela*, Liverpool University Press, 1964.

McGovern, William M., *The Early Empires of Central Asia*, Chapel Hill, NC, 1939.

Meadow, Richard H. and Uerpmann, Hans-Peter (eds), *Equids in the Ancient World*, Dr Ludwig Reichert Verlag, Wiesbaden, vol. I, 1986; vol. II, 1991.

——, 'Some Equid Remains from Cayonu, Southeastern Turkey', in *M & U*, vol. I, pp. 266–301.

Melchert, H. Craig, 'The Use of the Iku in Hittite Texts', *JCS*, 32, no. 1 (1980), 50–6.

Miller, Richard D.V.M., 'Pilgrim the Mule', *The Western Horseman*, March 1984, p. 12.

Moorey, P.R.S., 'Pictorial Evidence for the History of Horseriding in Iraq before the Kassite Period', *IRAQ*, 32 (1970), pp. 36–50.

Murray, Margaret A., *The Splendour that was Egypt*, BCA, London, 1981 (1979).

Narain, A.K., *The Indo-Greeks*, Clarendon Press, Oxford, 1957.

Phillips, E.D., 'New Light on the Ancient History of the Eurasian Steppe', *AJA*, 61 (1957), 269–80.

Piggott, Stuart, *Prehistoric India to 1,000 BC*, Cassell, London, 1962 (1950).

Postgate, J. Nicholas, *Taxation and Conscription in the Assyrian Empire*, Studia Pohl, Series Maior, no. 3, Biblical Institute Press, Rome, 1974.

——, 'The Equids of Sumer, Again', in *M & U*, I, pp. 194–206.

Qiubell, J.E. and Olver, A., 'An Ancient Egyptian Horse', *Annales du Service des Antiquités de L'Egypte*, 26 (1926), 172–7.

Rostovtzeff, M., 'Foreign Commerce in Ptolemaic Egypt', *Journal of Economic and Business History*, II (1931–2), 728–69.

Roux, Georges, *Ancient Iraq*, Penguin, 1976 (1966).

Rudenko, S.I., *The Frozen Tombs of Siberia*, J.M. Dent, 1970.

Saggs, H.W.F., *The Might that was Assyria*, Sidgwick & Jackson, London, 1984.

Sasson, Jack M., *The Military Establishments at Mari*, Studia Pohl, Dissertations scientificae de rebus orientis antiqui no. 3, Rome, 1969.

Save-Soderbergh, T., 'The Hyksos Rule in Egypt', *JEA*, 37 (1951), 52–71.

Savill, Agnes, *Alexander the Great and his Time*, Rockcliff, London, 1955.

Schiele, Erika, *The Arab Horse in Europe*, tr. A. Dent, George G. Harrap, London, 1970.

Schulman, A.R., 'Some Observations of the Military Background of the Amarna Period', *JARCE*, 3 (1964), pp. 51–69.

——, 'Egyptian Representatives of Horsemen and Riding in the New Kingdom', *JNES*, XVI (1957), pp. 263–71.

——, 'Chariots, Chariotry, and the Hyksos', *JSSEA*, X (1979–80), 105–53.

——, 'Egyptian Chariotry', *JARCE*, 2 (1963), 75–98.

Sekunda, N., 'The Persians', in *WAW*, pp. 82–103.

Shaw, Ian, *Egyptian Warfare and Weapons*, Shire Egyptology, Shire Publications Ltd, Princes Risborough, 1991.

Stronach, David, 'Iran under the Achaemenians and Seleucids', chapter 30 in *CEA*, pp. 206–11.

Talbot-Rice, Tamara, *The Scythians*, Thames & Hudson, London, 1957.

Tarn, W.W., *Alexander the Great*, vol. I, Cambridge University Press, 1948.

Telegin, D.Y. (tr. V.K. Pyalkooskig), *Dereivka. A Settlement and Cemetery of Copper Age Horse Keepers in the Middle Dneiper*, Oxford, BAR International Series, no. 287, 1986.

Tomlinson, R.A., 'Solon', in *100 Great Lives of Antiquity*, Guild Publishing, London, 1985, pp. 354–9.

Trevelyan, G.M., *English Social History*, Pelican Books, London, 1972.

Trew, Cecil G., *From 'Dawn' to 'Eclipse'*, Methuen & Co. Ltd, London, 1939.

Van Wijngaarden-Bakker, 'Animal Remains from the Beaker Settlement at New Grange, Co. Meath', in *Proceedings of the Royal Irish Academy*, vol. 74, section C, no. 11, Dublin, 1974.

Walker, Robin E., *Ars Veterinaria*, Schering-Plough Animal Health, Kenilworth, NJ (1st edn, 1991, 2nd edn, no date).

Warfare in the Ancient World, ed. Gen Sir John Hackett, Sidgwick & Jackson Ltd, London, 1989.

Woolley, Sir Leonard, *Ur of the Chaldees*, Herbert Press, London, 1982 (1929).

Worley, Leslie J., *Hippeis. The Cavalry of Ancient Greece*, Westview Press, Boulder, San Francisco, Oxford, 1994.

Wright, Edwin M., 'The Eighth Campaign of Sargon II of Assyria (714 BC)', *JNES*, II, no. 3 (1943), 73–186.

Wright, G.E. and Filson, F.V., *The Westminster Historical Atlas to the Bible*, London, 1945.

Yadin, Yigael, *The Art of Warfare in Biblical Lands*, Weidenfeld & Nicholson, London, 1963.

Young, T., 'Cuyler, Persia', in *EAC*, pp. 147–54.

Zarins, J., 'The Domesticated Equidae of the Third Millennium BC Mesopotamia', *JCS*, 30/1 (January 1978), 3–17.

——, 'Equids Associated with Human Burials in the Third Millennium BC Mesopotamia', in *M & U*, vol. I.

Zeder, Melinda A., 'The Equid Remains from Tal-e-Malyan, Southern Iran', in *M & U*, vol. I, pp. 366–410.

Zimansky, Paul E., *Ecology and Empire: the Structure of the Urartian State*, Oriental Institute of the University of Chicago, Studies in Ancient Oriental Civilization, no. 41, Oriental Institute, Chicago, 1985.

Zvelebil, Marek, 'The Rise of the Nomads in Central Asia', in *CEA*, chapter 38, pp. 252–6.

General Index

Abdi Asirta 83 f.
Abu Bekr ibn Bedr 82
Abu Simbel 3, 79
Abydos 114
Academy, the 140
Acanthus 130
Achaean mercenaries 153
Achaeans 31
Acropolis 115
Adadittia 96
Adad Nirari II 27, 36
Aegean 112, 145
Afghanistan 109
Africa 26
Agesilaus 132, 135 f.
Agora tablets 141 f.
Agrianians 153, 159
Ahab of Samaria 100
Ahesha 96
Ahmose I 14
Ahmose, son of Eben 14
Aiaukama of Kadesh 84
Aka 84
Akbar 82, 163
Akhenaton 35, 71, 83 ff.
Akizzi of Qatna 84
Alalakh tablets 63, m 72 ff.,
    78
Alborz (Elburz) Mts 23
Aleppo (Halab) 20, 85 f.
Alexander I 149
Alexander III (the Great)
    xvi, 31, 43, 47, 69 f., 82,
    chapter 12 passim
Alexandrian Empire 108
Algeria 32
Altai 23, 52
Amanappa 84
Amarna Letters, The 83 ff.
Ami-'Ba'li of Nairi 27, 90
Amenhotep III 35
Amenhotep, Crown Prince
    49
Amenope 86
Amenophis III 83
American Pony Express 136

Ammianus Marcellinus 29
Ampihipolis 130 f.
Amqu (Beka) 84
Amritsar 161
Amurru (Levant) 4, 27, 83 ff.
Amyntas 145
Anabasis, Arrian's 146
Anabasis, Xenophon's 133 ff.
Anastasi Papyrus I 77
Anatolia xvi, 8 f., 17, 20,
    26 f., 77, 89, 95, 145
Andia 105
Andijan, Ferghana 22, 29
d'Andrade Dr 32
Angarium 121–125 passim
Aniashtania 106, 120
Anittas, King xv
Antihippasia 140
Antonius, Dr O. 8
Apadana Frieze, Persepolis
    28 ff., 53
Apamea 26
Aphek 100
Apiru 84
Aplahanda of Carcemish 16
Appolonia 149
Arabia 26, 32
Arabs 103
Arabian Camel Corps 114
Arachosia 111, 152, 161
Arad, Palestine 8
Arameans 25
Ararat (Urartu) 60
Aravan 22
Arbela 152
Ardumanis 110
Areia 109, 124
Aretas 153
Argishti I 91 f., 96
Argishti II 107
Argos 131, 137
Arieus 136
Aristobulus 146
Ariston 153
Aristophanes 138, 141
Aristotle 127, 139

Armana Period 35
Armenia(ns) xvi, 6, 20 f.,
    111, 120, 133, ch. 9
    passim
Arpad 95, 101
Arrhabaeus 136
Arrian 29, 31, 146, 149
Arses 145
Artabazos 116 f.
Artaphernes 112
Artaxerxes II 108, 118, 133,
    135
Artaxerxes III 145
Artemision 115
Arthasastra of Kautilya xvi,
    19, 43–48 passim
Artybius 64
Aryans 21
Ashmolean Museum 3
Ashur (Assur) 24, 101
Ashurbanipal 27 f., 51, 59,
    82, 91 f., 98, 103
Ashur Dan II 27
Ashurnasirpal II 51, 92
Ashur-Uballit I 6, 83
Asia 20, 112, 145
Asia Minor 6, 109, 126
Assyria(ns) xvi, 1 f., 7, 17,
    20, 27 f, 83, 126, ch. 9
    passim
Assyrian Army 98 f.
Assyrian provisioning 102
Assyrian Empire 7, 109
Asur-Daninanni 94
Assuwa 78
Astyages 109
Asva Medha 23
Asvins 22
Athens 112 f., 115, 129 ff.,
    137, 141, 145
Athenians 113, 128, 130 ff.
Athenian Constitution 139
Athenian forces 129
Athos 112
Attalos 145
Attica 115

202

Index of Horse Related Subjects